POLITICAL CHANGE IN SOUTH KOREA

POLITICAL CHANGE IN SOUTH KOREA

Edited by

Ilpyong J. Kim

and

Young Whan Kihl

A PWPA Book

Paragon House
New York

Published in the United States by
Korean PWPA, Inc.
122 West 27th Street New York, NY 10001

Distributed by
Paragon House Publishers
90 Fifth Avenue
New York, NY 10011

A Professors World Peace Academy Book

Korean PWPA was organized with the specific purpose of promoting research and the exchange of academic information between the United Stated and the nations of Asia. Among its proposed activities are series of forums and seminars which address issues regarding Asia. These include such topics as Korean minorities abroad, American impact on recent socio-cultural change in Korea, an analysis of current political change in the Korean peninsula, and economic and military projections for the Pacific region.

Library of Congress-in-Publication Data

Political Change in South Korea

"A PWPA Book"
Bibliography: p.
Includes Index.
1. Korea (South)—Politics and government I. Kim, Ilpyong J., 1931- . II. Kihl, Young W., 1932-
DS917.8P65 1988 320.9519'5 88-11069
ISBN 0-943852-59-5
ISBN 0-943852-60-9 (pbk.)

Printed in the United States of America

Table of Contents

Acknowledgments

This volume is the first in a series and contains a scholarly analysis of the political changes in South Korea. An initial conference on the theme "Political Change in South Korea," convened in Washington, D.C. in September 1986 and was cosponsored by *The World and I* magazine and Korean PWPA, Inc. The origin and purpose of this book series was conceived by Dong Moon Joo, Executive Director of Korean PWPA. Conference participants were invited to present their research papers, and these papers were then commented on by several discussants. John Merrill, Hong Nack Kim, Jim Young Kim, Thomas Robinson and Yong S. Yim served as the discussants of the papers.

In order to broaden and update this book, several additional papers were commissioned. Those include, "Constitutional Changes from the First to the Sixth Republics: 1948 to 1987" by Gregory Henderson, "Urbanization and Changing Voting Patterns in South Korea" by Hong Nack Kim and Sunki Choe, "Student Activism and the Presidential Politics of 1987 in South Korea" by Wonmo Dong and "The 1987 Political Crisis and Implications for U.S.-Korean Relations" by Hong Nack Kim.

At the recommendation of the reviewer, Ramon Meyer of the Hoover Institution on War, Revolution and Peace at Stanford University, a new introduction chapter and Chapter One were added. Also newly added was Chapter 11 which makes the story of South Korea's political change up-to-date until July, 1988. We are grateful to Professor Meyer for his constructive criticisms and the positive suggestions for improvement. However, any omissions or errors that might have occurred in the process of editing this volume are solely the editor's responsibility.

Financial support for this project was provided by Korean PWPA, Inc. Korean PWPA was founded with the purpose of promoting joint research and the exchange of academic information between the United States and the nations of Asia. The conference was the first in series which Korean PWPA plans to sponsor dealing with the Korean peninsula.

The editors acknowledge the contribution of Dr. James Simmons of Iowa State University for computing the results of the 1987 presidential election for Chapter One. Other valuable support was provided by

Morton A. Kaplan, publisher of *The World and I* magazine. Gordon Anderson, Secretary General of PWPA-U.S.A., and Barbara Kubo, his administrative assistant, rendered their services and support for the project from its inception. The editors are also grateful for the editorial guidance of Robert Brooks, whose support as Publications Director of PWPA was invaluable. *The World and I* staff members, especially Collette Caprara and Mel Haft, also helped make this project a success.

The editors are hopeful that the publication of this book will enhance the understanding of the importance of the most recent episode in Korea's political history. The dramatic turn of events which this political change represents may pave the way toward establishing a better future for the "Land of the Morning Calm."

The Editors

Introduction

ILPYONG J. KIM AND YOUNG WHAN KIHL

South Korea's political change and search for democracy in the late 1980s represents one of the most significant and dramatic political events in Korea's modern history. To understand this process in its proper perspective, we need to start with a brief historical background of South Korea as a new emerging nation in the post-WWII era.

The Koreans are an ancient people with a long recorded history and traditional culture. Nicknamed by the Westerners as the Hermit Kingdom, the Koreans enjoyed a long period of relative internal peace and stability with a developed culture based on Confucianism. Since the end of the nineteenth century, however, Korea has been exposed to outside forces—emanating largely from the arrival of Westerners—and the country has gone through drastic political changes and rapid socio-economic modernization.

In the preceding one hundred years three major international wars were waged over the control of the Korean Peninsula. These include the Sino-Japanese War of 1894-95, the Russo-Japanese War of 1904-05, and the Korean War of 1950-53, which were all fought on Korean soil to determine the status of Korea in the major powers rivalry and in the balance of power system of Northeast Asia.

The old kingdom of the Yi dynasty fell in 1910, and the country was forcefully placed under Japan as a colony of the Japanese empire. In 1945, with the defeat of Japan in World War II, the Korean people regained sovereignty and welcomed the victorious allied powers as the national liberators of Korea. The country was placed under separate allied occupation forces, however, with the Soviet Red Army north of the 38th parallel and the American military forces south of the 38th parallel. The establishment of separate governments and regimes in the respective halves of divided Korea in 1948, unfortunately, led to the onset of the Korean War on June 25, 1950. The Korean War, first begun as a civil war, evolved into an international war involving outside powers—mainly the United States and China.

The political situation in South Korea was unsettling after the Korean War as the country was placed under an increasingly authoritarian rule by President Syngman Rhee. The student-led revolutions of April 1960, causing the downfall of the Rhee government, led to a brief interlude of democratic government under Prime Minister Chang Myon in 1960. The military coup led by then Major General Park Chung-hee on May 16, 1961 was carried out replacing a fledgling democracy with authoritarianism. Thus, the seemingly never-ending cycle of political change, the alternation between democracy and authoritarian rule, began in the Korean political tradition and culture.

The Koreans' ardent desire and demand for democracy are embedded in the contemporary belief and value systems of the many Korean elites. The Koreans are a highly educated and intelligent people. They are strong in the work ethic, possibly a legacy of the traditional Confucian culture. Although South Korea has been highly successful in the current drive toward industrialization, the impact of the rapid socio-economic changes through urbanization and industrialization tend to undermine her traditional social structure, values, and institutions.

The reality of South Korea's "economic miracle" is now widely recognized: the possibility of South Korea's attaining democracy, reflected in the recent series of political changes and developments, is a hopeful sign in Korean politics today. If successful, the Korean "political miracle" commensurate with the Korean "economic miracle" will enable South Korea to earn the coveted status and recognition as an advanced developed country in the post-1988 Seoul Olympics era.

Koreans are quite distinctive, and different from other East Asian people, such as the Japanese and the Chinese who have also taken up the tasks of modernizing their countries and continuously developing their economies. Koreans are generally regarded as more individualistic and rambunctious; they are easy to get to know as people and are also, as a rule, open and outgoing. In this sense the Koreans are often regarded as the "Irish of the Orient"; the Koreans are individualistic and contentious but they are also volatile in their political attitudes and behaviors.

In chapter one, the author discusses South Korea's search for new political order in the late 1980s by examining the nature and processes of the 1987 constitutional crisis. The origin and background of the 1987 political turmoil, the politics of constitution-making, and the presidential and legislative elections are described and analyzed in this chapter. (The editors acknowledge the contribution of Dr. James Simmons for his computation of the results of the 1987 presidential election in this chapter.) In chapter two, Gregory Henderson discusses the life cycles of the five republics from the First Republic under the leadership of Syngman Rhee, which was established in 1948, to the Fifth Republic which ended in February 1988. In the third chapter, Chong Lim Kim addresses the issues of democracy and their applicability in the context of the Korean culture. He explores the contradiction between the democratic theory and the actual authoritarian political culture of Korea.

In chapter four, Young Whan Kihl analyzes the problems of party politics in South Korea with a special emphasis on the politics of the Constitutional revision which took place in 1986 and 1987. Eugene C.I. Kim addresses the role of the military in Korean politics in chapter five. He discusses the military coup of 1961. Since then South Korea has recruited non-military technocrats from the civilian sector to operate the government and manage the economy, thus impeding the development of political parties as the instruments of interest articulation.

In chapter six, Sung Moon Pae discusses local self-government and the legislation affecting it that was worked out in 1986 through cooperation between the ruling Democratic Justice Party (DJP) and the opposition party and is scheduled to be implemented sometime in 1988. If the local self-government system is properly implemented, it will enhance the democratic process by decentralizing the authority of the central government in Seoul. One of the major problems of Korean politics has been the concentration of political and administrative power in a centralized system.

In chapter seven, Hong N. Kim discusses the relationship between urbanization and changing voting patterns in South Korea during the period from 1963 to 1985. He concludes that the more urbanized the constituencies are, the lower the voter turn out. This finding seems to confirm the hypothesis that the more urbanized a political unit with economic specialization, the less the percentage of the vote for the ruling government party.

Wonmo Dong presentes his analysis of the students' viewpoint in chapter eight. His findings show that students believe those with greater ability should receive more reward—which is not the present practice in Korea. He also found that for the Korean students the idea of ability is often infused with a moral quality to a degree far greater than for Americans.

In chapter nine, Hang Yul Rhee presents economic problems South Korea faces in the 1980s—the income inequality, the concentration of wealth in a few conglomerates, and the coming trade frictions between Korea and the United States—against the background of a high economic growth rate and the rapid development of the 1970s. Despite the student demonstrations and labor unrest, Rhee concluded, the peaceful transition to a democratic government following the first direct election of a new president on December 16, 1987 would enhance the political development commensurate to the economic development of the 1970s and 1980s.

In chapter ten, Hong N. Kim surveys the political crisis of 1987 and U.S.-Korean relations in the context of emerging issues of diplomatic relations between the two nations. The rise of nationalism, radical ideas such as the dependency theory, and the presence of foreign troops on Korean soil, which are prevalent topics among the students, intellectuals, and opposition groups, may require a certain readjustment in the conduct of diplomatic relations between the United States and Korea. Political change and democratization processes may to some extent alleviate the anti-American sentiments among the students, intellectuals, and the opposition party leaders.

In chapter eleven the editors examine the political dynamics of South Korea's Sixth Republic in the period prior to the 24th Olympiad in Seoul held September 17 - October 2, 1988. The character of the Roh Tae-woo government, his leadership and executive style, the result of the 13th National Assembly election of April 27, 1988, and the challenges confronting the Roh government during the first six months are discussed. The prospects for the Roh government continuing to carry out its pledged democratic reforms in the post-Olympic era will also be speculated upon.

Part I.
Political Democracy Under Stress

1

South Korea's Search for a New Order: An Overview

YOUNG WHAN KIHL

Korea is a country in search of a new and stable political order. During its forty-year constitutional history, since the Republic of Korea was proclaimed on August 15, 1948, the country has gone through considerable political turmoil and constitutional change.

The constitutional crisis of South Korea in 1987 was one of the most serious challenges to the Korean people's ability to govern themselves. To place the episode of the 1987 political conflict and its resolution in its proper perspective, this chapter will examine (1) the origin and background of the 1987 political crisis in terms of its historical significance and meaning, (2) the dynamics of the political forces and movements of the 1987 "democratic reform" politics, and (3) the analysis of the 1987 presidential election campaigns.

The Origin and Background of the 1987 Political Crisis

The Significance and Meaning of the 1987 Episode

From the perspective of the overall political development of South Korea since 1945, the 1987 events and political crises are important in the following senses:

- Student unrest in June 1987, followed by labor/industrial unrest, provided the impetus to political compromise then in the making.
- A popular presidential election was held on December 16, 1987, the first in sixteen years, following the ratification of the new constitution by referendum on October 27, 1987.
- The newly-elected government of President Roh Tae-woo took charge on February 25, 1988 as President Chun Doo-hwan stepped down; the first peaceful and orderly power transition in the Republic's constitutional history.
- Whether South Korea's new beginning as a popularly mandated democracy will succeed, however, remains to be seen in light of the country's long tradition and legacy of authoritarian rule.

The significance of the 1987 political changes is that a crisis was averted and the prospect for democracy was enhanced as a result of the ruling and opposition party leaders (Roh Tae-woo of the ruling Democratic Justice Party and Kim Young-sam of the main opposition Reunification Democratic Party) agreeing, in July 1987, to adopt a new constitution. To appreciate its historical significance the following facts need to be recalled.

- The Fifth Republic was founded in 1980, following Park Chung-hee's assassination on October 26, 1979 and the military coups of December 12, 1979 and May 17, 1980, which were led by then Major General Chun Doo-hwan. The latter triggered a nationwide protest movement including the Kwangju uprising which was suppressed by force; the Chun regime therefore suffered from weak political legitimacy from the outset.
- The February 1985 National Assembly election was the turning point as the ruling Democratic Justice Party (DJP) failed to receive a popular mandate and the opposition forces captured 116 seats of the 276-seat National Assembly; the New Korea Democratic Party (NKDP) was formed only one month before the election to emerge as the first opposition party.
- The opposition demand for constitutional amendment was finally heeded by Chun in June 1986, with the threat of a nationwide protest, as the ruling party agreed to work through the National Assembly Constitution Revision Committee.

However, the inter-party parliamentarian talks on constitutional revision conducted in the fall of 1986 were deadlocked on the question of the preferred form of government. Whereas the ruling DJP proposed a parliamentary cabinet system of government, the opposition NKDP insisted upon a presidential system in which president as chief executive would be popularly and directly elected.

As no progress was made to break the deadlock, the opposition party became impatient and threatened to politicize the constitutional revision issue by launching a massive grassroots campaign to obtain ten million signatures on a petition demanding a direct presidential election. The government vehemently resisted the opposition party demand on the grounds that such a mass movement would disrupt social stability and domestic peace. South Korean domestic politics in the spring of 1987 were thus deadlocked and only some drastic and bold measures would break the logjam.

Constitutional Development

In order to appreciate the episode of the 1987 political conflict and its resolution, we need to briefly trace the major highlights of South Korea's constitutional history.

The First Republic (1948-1960), under President Syngman Rhee's autocratic rule, was overthrown by the student-led revolution of April 16-27, 1960. The Second Republic (1960-1961), under the government of Chang Myon as prime minister, was a victim of incessant internal party factionalism. It was soon destroyed by the military coup of May 16, 1961 led by then Major General Park Chung-hee. The Third Republic (1961-1972), initially placed under the military rule by the junta called the SCNR (Supreme Council for National Reconstruction), was reasonably stable as the regime was gradually civilianized. A series of general elections, including popularly-held presidential elections in 1963, 1967, and 1971, were held to install Park Chung-hee as the elected president.

The Fourth Republic (1972-1979), called the Yushin (Revitalizing Reform) system, however, was imposed in December 1971 by the incumbent president in a "coup in office." The result was to perpetuate the life-long tenure of Park Chung-hee as president. In the wake of confusion following the assassination of Park by one of his top aides, Korean CIA chief Kim Jae-kyu, on October 26, 1979, a coup was engineered by then Major General Chun Doo-hwan on December 12, 1979. The hope for restoring democracy in

South Korea, ushering in the season of South Korea's "Springtime of Freedom" in early 1980, was crushed by a second military coup on May 17, 1980. This eventually led to the founding of the Fifth Republic (1980-1988) as the new constitution was approved by referendum on October 22, 1980.

The presidential election on December 16, 1987 will lead to the establishment of a new Sixth Republic when the incumbent president Chun Doo-hwan steps down on February 25, 1988. The frequent political changes and the short life span of the South Korean republic thus is a notable, record-breaking fact in the annals of constitution-making throughout the world, in sharp contrast with the well-established and advanced democratic systems of the West. South Korea's turbulent constitutional history has been telescoped into a single generation; it took almost two centuries for France to undergo a similar cycle of political change owing to the rise and fall of separate republics.

Votes on constitutional amendments were held nine times during Korea's forty-year constitutional history, between 1948 and 1988: in 1952, 1956, 1958, 1960, 1962, 1969, 1971, 1980, and 1987. (For the details, see chapter two by Gregory Henderson).

The Politics of the 1987 "Democratic Reform"

An attempt to introduce "democratic reform" to South Korea's authoritarian rule was initiated, under the shadow of worsening political violence, in the summer of 1987. Serious constitutional crisis flared up in June 1987 as the rock and fire-bomb throwing university students clashed with the tear gas canister-throwing combat police. The violent street demonstrations in the summer of 1987 could not easily be contained. The reason was that some middle class citizens began to express their sympathy with demonstrating students, and to side with the student demands for democracy.

The deepening crisis placed the fragile constitutional structure of the Fifth Republic under stress, pushing the system close to the edge of collapse. After weeks of intense political threat and maneuvering by politicians a formula of grand political compromise was finally produced to avert the political crisis. An 8-member constitution drafting committee, representing both the ruling and the major opposition parties, produced the text of a new constitution on August 30, 1987, after a four-week marathon session.

The new constitution of the Sixth Republic was subsequently approved by the National Assembly on October 12, 1987, by a vote of 254 to 4. The 1987 constitutional amendment, unlike the previous constitutional amendments, was genuinely reform-oriented in the sense that it expanded the rights of the citizenry and also restored and strengthened the power of the legislature, thereby reversing the historical trend of augmenting executive power. The constitutional referendum to adopt the new constitution was held on October 27, 1987, and adopted by a record 93.1 percent approval rate of those voting. The voter turnout rate was also high, with 78.2 percent of the total 26.6 million eligible voters.

In the summer and fall of 1987 dramatic events took place to restore democracy in South Korea. The political system of the Fifth Republic was dangerously close to the edge of an abyss, although it was rescued from total collapse at the last minute. These breathtaking and fast-moving events of 1987 need to be discussed and analyzed in detail so as to acquire the proper historical perspective and significance of the political changes occurring in 1987.

The February 25, 1985 National Assembly Election

The Fifth Republic of Korea, from the very outset, suffered from weak legitimacy. This was due to the questionable means through which the Chun Doo-hwan regime came to power, i.e., the usurping of power through a military coup led by then Major General Chun. It was also due to the bloody suppression of the Kwangju uprising of May 1980, thereby inflicting a permanent scar on South Korea's body politics. The Kwangju uprising began initially as part of the nationwide protest movement against the proclamation of the state of national emergency by the military leaders on May 17, 1980, and the establishment of a 31-member Council of National Emergency. As the protest marches in Kwangju resulted in insurrection led by radicals the Chun Doo-hwan regime ordered the suppression of the rebels with a special force unit. Casualties were high--with an official figure of 191 dead and several hundred wounded, although an eyewitness account estimated several thousand casualties. (Hwang Suk-yong).

In the political life of the Fifth Republic the Chun regime, therefore, suffered greatly from political instability in spite of its success in economic growth. The February 1985 National Assembly was a telling demonstration of how the Chun regime was unable to acquire the support of the majority of the Korean electorate, in spite of its spectacular success in holding inflationary pressure down and in restoring the momentum of the dynamic growth-oriented economic system. The ruling DJP failed to receive a popular mandate for its rule since 1980, while the opposition forces managed to capture 116 seats of the 276-seat National Assembly. The new NKDP was formed only one month before the election, as already noted, but it succeeded in emerging as the first opposition party in the February 1985 election.

A Chronology of Political Events in 1987

The "democratic reform" announced in the summer of 1987 took many observers of Korean politics by complete surprise. In view of its significance, from the standpoint of promoting South Korea's democratic political development, a step-by-step progression of political events and crises needs to be recounted. The following is a chronology of South Korea's major political events and unfolding of the political drama in 1987.

4/8 The opposition New Korea Democratic Party was split as Kim Young-sam announced the founding of a new party, Reunification Democratic Party.

4/13 Chun announced his intention to suspend the talks on a constitutional amendment until after the 1988 Seoul Olympics; this announcement followed the split of the opposition party.

6/10 The ruling Democratic Justice Party held its party convention to nominate Roh Tae-woo as their presidential candidate; the event triggered a well-timed university student protest movement, the Myongdong cathedral in downtown Seoul was taken over by radical students; student demonstrations were met by combat police but citizens generally were sympathetic with the student cause.

6/29 Roh Tae-woo announced an eight-point "Democratic Reform" measure that included fair and direct presidential elections and the release of political prisoners; two days later Chun Doo-hwan announced that he would accept Roh's recommendation; Roh Tae-woo and Kim Young-sam subsequently agreed on an 8-member working group to draft a new constitution.

8/30 The text of the new constitution was drafted and submitted to the National Assembly for deliberation.

9/2 Kim Young-sam and Roh Tae-woo agreed to hold the referendum on the constitutional amendment before the end of October and to hold the popular presidential election before December 20.

9/13 Roh Tae-woo left on a U.S. visit; also stopped in Tokyo on the way back; Kim Dae-jung tests the water by touring his home constituency in the Cholla provinces.

9/30 Kim Dae-jung and Kim Young-sam failed to agree on a single presidential candidacy issue; each urges the other to make concessions on the presidential candidacy.

10/2 Kim Jong-pil, ex-prime minister under Park Chung-hee and president of the then Democratic Republican Party, indicated his plan to run for president after forming a new party.

10/12 National Assembly acts to approve the new constitution by 254 to 4.

10/27 The constitutional referendum approved the new constitution overwhelmingly by 93.3 percent of those voting. The voter turnout rate was also high, with 78.2 percent of the total 26.6 million eligible voters.

10/28 Kim Dae-jung declared his intention of running for president and of founding a separate party, the Party for Peace and Democracy (PPD), making his split with Kim Young-sam official.

11/16 The date of the presidential election was proclaimed to be December 16, 1987. The election law stipulated that the candidates must register within seven days of the proclamation and that electoral campaigns would be allowed for 30 days; five major party candidates vied for the election.

12/16 The governing party candidate Roh Tae-woo emerged as the winner, with a plurality of 36.6 percent of those voting, followed by Kim Young-sam and Kim Dae-jung with 28 percent and 27 percent, respectively. Kim Jong-pil received 8.1 percent of the vote.

Dynamics of Political Forces and Movements

Who are the major actors and key political groups and to what extent did they play a role in the unfolding of South Korea's political drama of "democratic reform" in 1987? The individual political leaders in 1987 included the so-called "three Kims," Kim Dae-jung, Kim Young-sam and Kim Jong-pil, and Roh Tae-woo, all of whom declared their candidacy in the presidential election, and Chun Doo-hwan, the incumbent president of the republic. These individuals were at the center stage of electoral politics as they actively courted and appealed, directly or indirectly, for voter support in the presidential election. In the case of Chun Doo-hwan, he indirectly rendered his support to Roh Tae-woo as his successor. In this drama the public essentially played the role of spectators rather than as participants in the electoral process, although there were many who were actively campaigning on behalf of their respective party candidates.

Whereas Kim Dae-jung and Kim Young-sam were the opposition party leaders who failed to produce and unite behind a single presidential candidate, in spite of their repeated public pledge to do so, Kim Jong-pil was ex-prime minister and president of the ruling party during the Park Chung-hee era. Kim Dae-jung formed his own new political party called the Party for Peace and Democracy after resigning as permanent advisor of Kim Young-sam's Reunification Democratic Party. Kim Jong-pil also formed a new political party called the New Democratic Republican Party. Roh Tae-woo was president and presidential candidate of the ruling Democratic Justice Party.

Four major political parties thus contested and actively campaigned to elect their respective presidential candidates in the December 1987 presidential election. They were the ruling Democratic Justice Party headed by Roh Tae-woo, the main opposition Reunification Democratic Party with Kim Young-sam as president, the splinter Party for Peace and Democracy under Kim Dae-jung, and the New Democratic Republican Party led by Kim Jong-pil.

In addition, three other political parties and groups fielded their presidential candidates. The Korea Social Democratic Party nominated Hong Suk-ja the first woman presidential candidate. Her name was removed from the ballot, however, as she subsequently came out in support of Kim Young-sam and was thereby forced to resign from the party. The radical group nominated Paek Ki-wan as their candidate. He subsequently withdrew from the race urging his followers to support either Kim Young-sam or Kim Dae-jung. The fifth candidate, whose name remained on the ballot, was Shin Jong-il, an obscure figure who headed the Unification Korea Party.

The politically active groups in South Korea in 1987 included several anti-government organizations. These were (1) the National Coalition for a Democratic Constitution, which acted as an umbrella organization for the nationwide protest movement in the summer of 1987; (2) the Mint'ongnyon (People's Coalition for Democracy and Reunification), which is a national federation of some 23 separate organizations that include dissident writers, artists, professors, students, workers, farmers, some Buddhist, Protestant, and Roman Catholic groups, as well as some women's groups; and (3) two radical leftist student groups called *Minmint'u* and *Chamint'u.*

The politically relevant "social strata" in South Korea encompasses seven broad social groups. They emerged as key interest groups in South Korea's political arena in 1987 by expressing their political concerns and preferences on conflict issues. The political role and profile of these seven groups follows.

The first is the middle class which, in the broad sense, constitutes the majority of the population of South Korea. They became increasingly dissatisfied with Chun's authoritarian rule, especially the perceived corruption associated with members of his and his wife's family. The middle class citizens were also tired of the political turmoil and unrest associated with violent street demonstrations carried out by radical student groups. They were generally supportive of the causes of democracy, but they were also desirous of political stability and internal peace in South Korean society.

The second relevant group in South Korean politics is big business, which typically maintains close ties with the regime. The business community in Korea has been well organized as an interest group. The spokesman for big business conglomerates like Daewoo, Hyundai, Samsung, and Gold Star is called the Chonkyongyon (All Korea Federation of Economic Organizations and Industries). Medium and small businesses, on the other hand, are represented by the Korea Chamber of Commerce and the Federation of Korean Medium and Small Businesses.

The third interest group in South Korea is organized labor and the national federation of labor organizations. Working men and women in South Korea are generally not well organized, nor are they effectively represented in politics through organized labor. Whatever exists at the national level of the labor movement, such as the Korea Federation of Labor Unions, is generally weak and seems to lack political power. The reason for this is that the labor union movement in South Korea has been suppressed by the authoritarian government. Company or enterprise unions, not trade unions, have been allowed to exist in South Korea. The perceived and real inequities that prevail in the Korean labor market finally exploded into widespread labor discontent and industrial unrest in the summer months of 1987. Labor's demand for higher wages and collective bargaining rights were partly met in July-August 1987, thereby avoiding serious disruption of economic activities.

The farmers are the fourth group playing a role in Korean politics. In spite of rapid urbanization in recent decades, the rural exodus continues to supply an army of workers to be employed by industries in factories. The government has adopted generous policies and programs to enhance the rural welfare and the farmers' interest, through such projects as the Saemaul Undong. Programs of price support and subsidies for agricultural goods have also been adopted, but they are generally not effective in the face of increasingly competitive market forces derived from greater imported agricultural products.

Radical students are the fifth arm of South Korea's interest politics. Of the total of 1.2 million university students, the anti-government radical students represented a small minority of only one or two percent. But they have been well organized and positioned to exert real political pressure and to display strength. They were generally leftist in ideology, openly anti-American, and were sympathetic with the policies of North Korea on many issues. They openly advocated U.S. troop withdrawal from South Korea and condemned the Reagan Administration policy of supporting the Chun regime. They also agreed with Pyongyang's stance on the reunification issue.

Dissident clergy, intellectuals, and journalists constitute the sixth interest group in South Korean politics. They have been, as a rule, opposed to the military regime of President Chun Doo-hwan and have demanded the termination of authoritarian rule and the speedy restoration of democracy. Many of them are, in fact, identified closely with the opposition leaders Kim Dae-jung and Kim Young-sam, who represented, as co-chairs, the political group called the Council of the Restoration and Promotion of Democracy in Korea.

Finally, the military is seventh on the list of power groups in South Korea. The military has ruled South Korea, as an institution, since the founding of the Fifth Republic. Although basically conservative and nationalistic in ideology, the military has been well organized and powerful as an interest group, playing a decisive role as the "veto group" in Korean politics. So far the military discipline has been maintained, but intra-group factionalism is always a possibility and, when and if the intra-military consensus breaks down, it will inject an element of uncertainty into Korean politics.

With regard to the question of supporting the status quo or advocating political change and reform, these seven social groups are varied in their respective political positions. The balance of power among these competing groups is therefore the key to political stability in Korean politics. When these groups are distributed along the continuum, the following picture emerges as broadly reflective of an ideological scale, ranging from the right to the left. In the center of the scale may be found the middle class citizens whose support is deemed essential for the government to stay in power. To the extreme right of the center will be big business and the military, the latter acting as a powerful veto group in Korean politics. To the extreme left of the center are found the radical students and the dissident intellectuals, journalists, and clergy who refused to recognize the legitimacy of the Fifth Republic under the incumbent president Chun Doo-hwan. Also slightly left of the center may be found the working men and women in South Korea's fledgling industrial economy, and slightly to the right of the center may be found the farmers who, like the workers, are generally kept less active in politics.

With rapid progression in urbanization and the industrialization of the economy, South Korea begins to witness the emergence of social conflict and policy disputes. The population migration and rural exodus continues, for instance, to undermine the traditional social structure and value consensus. Yet, the new pattern of interest politics representing newly emerging socio-economic forces has not been fully developed or instituted, so as to replace the traditional structure and value systems. Thus, the tendencies of regional voting and the personal ties with party leaders continue to play a role in South Korean party and electoral politics.

Included in the general list of conflicts and contending issues confronting South Korea's 1987 presidential election were the following:

- democracy and human rights
- the economy and social stability
- national security and reunification
- regionalism and intra-party factionalism

Restoring "democracy and human rights" was the key theme in the 1987 presidential politics. The ruling party candidate Roh Tae-woo used the campaign slogan "democratic reform" as enunciated in his July 29, 1987 announcement as the backbone of his presidential campaign. The opposition party candidates used the theme of replacing authoritarianism with democracy as their political missions in the presidential election. Kim Young-sam claimed that he was the only one who could terminate military dictatorship and usher in the new politics of democracy, while Kim Dae-jung asserted that he would carry on his mission of establishing mass democracy to its logical end. Kim Dae-jung was actively supported by those who were released from prison under the authoritarian rule of Park Chung-hee and Chun Doo-hwan.

The continuous economic growth and socio-economic stability, such as holding inflationary pressures down, were among the key campaign issues in the 1987 presidential election. All the candidates came up with generous campaign pledges to uplift the status of the poor, including the financial support of the farmers. Resisting U.S. pressure to open South Korea's protected domestic market was a popular stance adopted by presidential candidates.

National security and the theme of reunification were also used and manipulated by the major parties and presidential candidates. The bombing of the Korean airliner over the Andean Sea near Burma en route from Baghdad to Seoul on November 29, 1987, and the subsequent apprehension of a suspect with possible North Korean connections, acted to influence voters on the eve of the election, to favor the governing party candidate.

In the end, regionalism and intra-party factionalism were the decisive factors in influencing the outcome in favor of the governing party candidate. Regions with favorite son candidates played a determining role in the outcome of the election, as was the case of the overwhelming support Kim Dae-jung received from the Cholla provinces. Intra-party factionalism in the opposition ranks, however, was exploited by the governing party candidate to his advantage. The failure of the two Kims to unite behind a single candidacy was the decisive blow to the election of an opposition candidate.

Regionalism and Personalism in the 1987 Presidential Election: An Analysis

Personalism and regionalism played decisive roles in the 1987 presidential election. Not just the candidate's personalities but also their regional support base, together with the campaign issues, were decisive in determining the outcome. The thirty days of heated campaign activities mobilized more than one million people to attend rallies by the major party candidates.

In view of the historical significance of the December 1987 presidential election, the overall makeup of South Korea's political landscape needs to be closely examined and assessed. This section will examine (1) the projective analysis of the 1987 presidential election, in terms of the historical trends of the "winnable" strategy and (2) the post-election analysis of the 1987 presidential election, in terms of the voter distribution and alignment.

Projective Analysis

The total number of eligible voters in South Korea in 1987 was 25,573,609, which is 61.9 percent of the total estimated population of 41,338,959. The voter turnout rate on election day was very high, with close to 90 percent of the eligible voters turning out.

The ecology of voter alignment and distribution in the 1987 presidential election was distinctive as the voters in South Korea generally followed historical patterns. The place of residence is a relevant factor here because voter support has varied in the past in terms of (1) an urban and rural dichotomy and (2) regional cleavages. The last presidential election, held in 1971, followed a pattern in which the governing party candidate, the incumbent president Park Chung-hee, was heavily supported by the rural voters and the Southeast region of the Kyongsang Provinces, while the opposition party candidate, Kim Dae-jung, was overwhelmingly favored by the urban voters and the Southwest region, the Cholla Provinces.

Given the four major announced presidential candidates, the large metropolitan regions and cities were expected generally to support the opposition party candidates, especially Kim Dae-jung and Kim Young-sam, while the rural areas were projected to go for the pro-government party candidate of Roh Tae-woo. The fact that the opposition party was divided between the two Kims, however, would polarize the regional support in such a way that each Kim received overwhelming support from the respective province in which they were favorite sons. While Kim Dae-jung was expected to receive overwhelming voter support in the southwestern region of the Cholla Provinces, Kim Young-sam expected to do well in the southeastern region of the Kyongsang Provinces. The Kyongsang voters, however, were under cross-pressures in the sense that they would split their votes between Kim Young-sam and the governing party candidate Roh Tae-woo, who is another favorite son of the Kyongsang Provinces. The third opposition candidate Kim Jong-pil, an ex-prime minister under Park Chung-hee, was expected to receive large support from the central region of the Chungchong Provinces where he is a favorite son.

The political ecology of South Korean politics is such that the large metropolitan cities, like Seoul and the Kyonggi Province which surrounds Seoul, were expected to emerge as the decisive arena for electoral contests. Seoul and the Kyonggi Province together constituted 40 percent of the total votes. Capturing the votes in this region would thus determine the outcome of the 1987 presidential election. The overall distribution of voting strength, in terms of the metropolitan districts and rural provinces, is as follows:

Table 1-a.
Distribution of Eligible Voters

Northern Region:		
Seoul	6.40	million
Kyonggi Province	4.20	
(Inchon city of 0.9 million inclusive)		
Kangwon Province	1.00	
sub-total	11.60	
Central Region		
Chungchong Nam Prov.	1.80	
Chungchong Buk Prov.	.80	
sub-total	2.60	
Southeast Region		
Pusan	2.20	
Taegu	1.20	
Kyongsang Nam Prov.	2.20	
Kyongsang Buk Prov.	1.90	
sub-total	7.50	
Southwest Region		
Kwangju	.80	
Cholla Nam Prov.	1.60	
Cholla Buk Prov.	1.30	
sub-total	3.70	
Chejudo (Island)	.27	
Grand total	25.67	million

Source: HANGUK ILBO; various issues from November, 1987.

Given the above distribution of voters and the tendencies of regional voting, it is obvious that a winning electoral strategy would require the voting support of the three metropolitan districts of Seoul, Pusan, and Taegu, which together constitute 9.8 million of the total votes. Alternatively, a winning electoral strategy would require majority support from the northern region, including the capital city of Seoul and the Kyonggi Province, which together constitute 10.6 million of the total votes.

Also, given the plurality of the candidates running, none of the four candidates was likely to receive the simple majority of electoral votes and the minimum winnable support might be somewhere in the neighborhood of the 35 to 40 percent mark. The fact that South Korea's next president would necessarily be elected by less than the simple majority vote. This would inject a new element of uncertainty and instability, an image of the minority president trying to depolarize divided South Korean society. The tendency of regional vote splitting between the Southeastern and the Southwestern provinces would also continue to create havoc in South Korea's body politic in the results of the polarized voting of the 1987 presidential election.

Post-Election Analysis

Of the eight presidential candidates initially registered when the 30-day presidential campaign period began, only five remained on the presidential ballot on election day. According to the new election law adopted by the National Assembly, the presidential candidates had to register within seven days after the proclamation of the date of the national election and the candidates were allowed to conduct active campaigns up to thirty days prior to the election date.

The distribution of the votes for each of the five major presidential candidates, in terms of regional breakdown, was as follows:

Table 1-b
The Presidential Election Result by Region
(% of the total)

Region	% voter turnout	DJP	RDP	PPD	NDRP	UKP
Metropolis						
Seoul	87.5	24.4	28.6	32.1	8.1	1.8
Pusan	88.4	31.6	55.2	9.0	2.6	1.6
Taegu	89.9	69.8	24.0	2.6	2.0	1.6
Inchon	88.2	38.7	29.4	20.9	9.1	1.9
Kwangju	92.5	4.5	.4	93.3	.2	1.6
Metro %		34.0	32.1	26.2	6.0	1.7
Provinces						
Kangwon	90.7	57.9	25.4	8.6	5.3	2.8
Kyonggi	88.4	40.6	27.0	21.8	8.3	2.3
Ch'ungbuk	91.1	45.7	27.5	10.7	13.2	2.9

Ch'ungnam	88.3	26.6	15.8	12.1	42.8	2.7
Chonbuk	90.4	13.7	1.4	80.9	.7	3.3
Chonnam	90.3	7.9	1.1	87.9	.3	2.8
Kyongbuk	91.0	64.8	27.5	2.3	2.5	2.9
Kyongnam	89.5	40.4	50.3	4.4	2.6	2.3
Cheju	88.5	48.6	26.1	18.1	4.4	2.8
Rural %		37.4	23.8	26.8	9.4	2.6
TOTAL	89.2	36.6	28.0	27.0	8.1	.3

Source: NEWSREVIEW; December 19, 1987, page 5.

The five presidential candidates, with their party affiliations are: Roh Tae-woo ((DJP), Kim Young-sam (RDP), Kim Dae-jung (PPD), Kim Jong-pil (NDRP), and Shin Jong-il (UKP).

The details of the election result as shown in Table 1-b above will be examined in the concluding chapter of this book.

Conclusion

South Korea's search for a new political order will not end with the conclusion of the present chapter of turbulent and tension-ridden political history in the post-World War II era. As South Korea continues to develop economically and to modernize socially, the question of constructing the ideal political order of democratic polity will remain as one of the unresolved issues for the present and future generations of Korean people.

It is clear, in reflecting upon the recent episodes of "democratic reform" that the essence of Korean politics is the moral issue of sustaining the political legitimacy of the government. The central question in Korean politics has been how to select the new leader. Such a leader must represent the public will and enjoy the broad support of the populace, perhaps as a reflection of an age-old Confucian notion of the "mandate of heaven." The ruler's "mandate" must be tested by appeals to the public through an open and fair electoral contest.

Many observers of the Korean political scene believe that political institutionalization has lagged behind socio-economic modernization of the Korean society. The time has long passed, these critics point out, for South Korea to bring about political democracy and to make the Korean society commensurate with its newly acquired wealth and status. South Korea is now widely regarded as a "success story, attaining an economic miracle," and the hosting of the 1988 Seoul Olympics will make South Korea eligible to join the ranks of the advanced industrial countries. For a Third World country this newly acquired status will be a source of great pride for the present generation of South Korean people.

South Korea's GNP in 1987 surpassed the $100 billion mark, with an estimated 1987 GNP PC of about $2300. This is a remarkable accomplishment because the GNP was only $10 billion in 1970 and the GNP PC was about $300 in 1970 and about $100 in 1960. The annual growth rate of the GNP, during the first six months of 1987, was 15.4 percent. Although the economic slowdown due to rampant labor and industrial unrest in the summer months of 1987 dampened the growth rate, the overall yearly rate of economic growth in 1987 is estimated to be close to 10 percent. South Korea's trade surplus with the U.S. in 1986 was about $7 billion. Although the accumulated foreign debt is a serious national problem, about $40 billion in 1986, South Korea has begun to pay off its loan, in the neighborhood of approximately ten percent of the total debt in 1986. In fact, South Korea is the only Third World country with a large national debt that has begun to pay back its loans.

For South Korea to continue to develop economically and politically, however, the basic condition of maintaining peace and stability on the Korean peninsula must first be assured. The heightened tension and conflict that have prevailed on the Korean peninsula in recent decades must be lessened. By taking steps toward peace and adopting concrete measures of deescalation, such as redemilitarization of the DMZ, both governments of North and South as well as the major powers surrounding the Korean peninsula renew their efforts to institutionalize the peace process on the Korean peninsula. The suspended inter-Korean dialogues and negotiations, halted in 1985 must soon be resumed and resuscitated in order to make progress on the question of Korea's reunification.

Finally, South Korea's continuous struggle for democracy in recent years should be placed in its broader historical context and in the context of prevailing world trends. Is the wind of democracy blowing in Asia, as in Latin America? Is South Korea's "political miracle" in the making broadly reflective of global trends? Some say "yes" and others "maybe." It remains to be seen, obviously, whether South Korea's current search for democracy will succeed, but the trendline seems to be on the rise and we are hopeful that South Korea's march toward democracy will not fail. Even if future prospects are only dimly perceived at this time, we can safely say that Korean politics will continue to be full of excitement and surprises. That's what makes Korean politics dynamic and interesting, and therefore worthy of continuous investigation.

2

Constitutional Changes from the First to the Sixth Republics: 1948-1987

GREGORY HENDERSON

The Rose Tree

by William Butler Yeats
(A paradigm of the Korean student's dream)

'O words are lightly spoken,'
Said Pearse to Connolly,
'Maybe a breath of politic words
Has withered our Rose Tree;
Or maybe but a wind that blows
Across the bitter sea.'

'It needs to be but watered,'
James Connolly replied,
'To make the green come out again
And spread on every side
And shake the blossom from the bud
To be the garden's pride.'

'But where can we draw water,'
Said Pearse to Connolly,
'When all the wells are parched away?
O plain as plain can be
There's nothing but our own red blood
Can make a right Rose Tree.'

Constitutionalism at the Starting Line

The Dilemma

Korea in 1948 was a newly liberated nation which, though one of the world's oldest continuous polities, had never known written constitutional rule. A land inured for over a millennium to mountingly intense political activity, Korea in 1948 was a state institutionally divorced from its political past, tempest-tossed by a chaotic, modern, reborn, partly liberated politics which had blossomed since American forces had ended Japanese rule in 1945: three ebullient years. As an unusually continuous, homogeneous, united culture within her well-delineated peninsular boundaries, Korea had long achieved sharp linguistic, ethnic and cultural identity. But here constitutional identity remained undefined and the political life and institutions she needed to discover this identity in a modern sense were inchoate.

Sadly for Korea's political stability—ironically as an accompaniment to her sensational economic and kaleidoscopic social revolutions—the search for constitutional and, behind it, political identity still lurches on forty years later. The issues are now sharpened, hostilized and, perhaps, slightly altered, but not resolved. These forty years, moreover, have churned a tumultuous wake of five ever-changing constitutions, altered priorities, uprooted political institutions and hectic and discontinuous political life which has challenged, disillusioned, antagonized, and disquieted aspiring urban Koreans, intensifying as the penetration of education, communication, enhanced wealth, and political expectation has deepened and, in part, politically riven South Korean society.

The Past's Constitutional Blank Slate

The Confucian tradition, dominant for half a millennium until this century, not only countenanced no constitution; it abhorred the idea of one as 'legalist,' the signboard of its ancient philosophical *bete noire*. The neo-Confucians governed by sage insight and edifying example, not by chapter and verse, check or balance. Written laws were more for the 'lower castes' who were deemed to be beyond exemplary admonishment—their employment to be as sparing as possible. "The sage," declared a founding Korean Confucianist, "proclaims law not to rule with law but to rule without the aid of law." [1]

The Colonial Mirage of Japanese Constitutionalism

Japanese colonial rule (1910-1945), while introducing a modern, authoritarian civil legal system, governed through an omnipotent military Governor-General of prime ministerial timber who enacted decrees (*seirei*) and ordinances (*furei*) almost automatically sanctioned by the Japanese Emperor through the premier. His legislative powers equaled those of a parliament. Even the Japanese questioned whether legislative authority—so despotically exercised by an unelected official operating without a Korean parliament and, until 1919, not even answerable to the Japanese Diet—could be regarded as Japanese constitutional rule.[2] Though greater technical subordination to the Japanese constitution came after 1919 with the Governor-General's membership in, and formal answerability to, the Japanese Diet and with Korea's technical control by the Home Ministry after November 1942, the Governor-General's rank reserved his independence and hardly a single Korean thought of the distant Japanese constitution as a resort against arbitrary or unjust government, a hope for mildening repressive colonial rule.

Korea's constitutional experience on coming of second age in 1945's liberation was hence an almost completely blank page and what little was written thereon repelled more than it invited.

The KILA, 1919, 1944, and 1948 Constitutional Drafts

As a people with an already fairly advanced educational standard, however, and with western connections through missionaries and education, Koreans were aware that a constitution was a prerequisite for the modern democratic state which would lead them to their liberation from Japanese military fascism. It was, *inter alia*, part of a fledgling, reborn Korea's de-Japanification and desired independent identification with the United States and Europe.

Work to this end was in abeyance from 1945-1948, however. The first two years were expended in the tumultuous American occupation and the search for a politics of unification—a lengthy time in which it was unclear what form or direction—left or right—politics in the South would take or more precisely to what form and texture of democratic government a constitution should seek to conform. Delays in the last year centered around the weakness and lack of legitimacy in the initial jerry-structured "legislature" —the (South) Korean Interim Legislative Assembly ([S] KILA) (1946-48).

Despite its weakness, it partially formulated and debated at length a draft constitution which was then vetoed by the acting military governor on the grounds that it would "hinder the work of the UN Commission" (*vide infra*). Instead KILA drafted an election law (later heavily amended) for a national "election under the United Nations of a National Constituent Assembly to form a national provisional government and draft a constitution for Korea." [3]

In the late spring and summer of 1948, a far-better-elected and more legitimate and effective legislature emerged from the May 10, 1948 UN-observed elections. It convened for the first time on May 31, 1948, turning its attention to the drafting of Korea's first constitution.[4] The text was adopted on July 12 and promulgated on July 17, 1948. The first constitution was thus drawn up in only forty-two days under circumstances of minimal reflection, but with the wise and informed technical leadership of Korea's main constitutional expert, Dr. Yu Chin-o.

Since the exiled Korean Provisional Government's revised but abortive Chungking Constitution of 1944 all thought of compromise with the left had been abandoned. Also, all thoughts of coalescing with them to form a unification framework were abandoned after the attempts of 1946-47. The United States' decision to end the military government and to withdraw all active military units left conservative rightists (headed by the elderly, U.S.-educated patriot, Syngman Rhee) with a virtual monopoly of South Korean politics and of the 1948 Assembly elections that had been boycotted by most leftists or middle-of-the-road elements.[5] Dr. Rhee was elected Assembly chairman on May 31 by 188 votes out of 198. His election to President on July 20 was by 180 to 16—the latter going to former president of the exile government, Kim Koo.

The 1948 Constitution

The Content of the First Constitution

The framers of the constitution numbered some thirty in a Constitution Drafting Committee headed by constitutional law expert, Dr. Yu Chin-o. They were aware of the old and new (1947) Japanese constitutions, the KILA draft, the US, the Weimar, and other constitutions. US Military Government experts, though competent and available for consultation, were consulted very little and were counseled not to give unsolicited advice.[6]

For the first three weeks, the drafters were in agreement on a cabinet-responsible system for the new government. But on June 20, 1948, the drafters were called to the mansion of Dr. Rhee, who had strongly advocated adoption of a presidential system. In the next two days, key features of the cabinet system were hastily dropped and a presidential system substituted and adopted despite some views that the seeds of authoritarianism were being sown.[7]

The lengthy resulting document sought to establish " a democratic and republican state" whose "sovereignty...shall reside in the people" whose "liberty, equality and initiative" should be guaranteed. Wide liberties were guaranteed but with two exceptions: "except as specified by law" and in situations "when necessary for the maintenance of public order or the welfare of the community." The President, elected for four years, had strong powers but was elected by two-thirds of the National Assembly: Two-thirds of a quorum of two-thirds of the membership could override a presidential veto. Though the President could call an "extraordinary" Assembly session, so could one-fourth of the legislators and no provision was made for the Assembly's dissolution until the end of its four-year term. Assembly members, as well as those in the executive branch, could introduce legislation and institute impeachment against the President or any chief official.

The independence of the judiciary was qualified by making constitutional review subject to a constitutional committee (never appointed) on which justices were a minority. Judges' appointments were limited to ten years, thus making their renewals subject to the executive branch. Only the appointments of the Prime Minister and the Chief Justice required assembly approval, but it was not required for their removal; both were, in effect, servants of the President, as Rhee wished. As in the Weimar Constitution, the President was given emergency powers "to issue orders having the effect of law." [8]

Rhee's Assaults on the 1948 Constitution

It is easy to say that an uneasy mixture of democracy and autocracy emerged from the first constitution. Much the same could be said of many constitutions, even that of the United States. Yet looking back almost forty years, the first constitution emerges as probably the best-balanced of any in Korea so far amid a landscape where the 1960 constitution proved too libertarian and the 1962, 1972, and 1980 constitutions too authoritarian.

It soon became apparent that in 1948 the fault lay less in the constitution than in Rhee's—and Korea's—inability to live with any concept of the balance of powers, even the small degree of balance inherent in the Assembly's powers. No clear break with the excessive, centralized executive power of the past had ever been made by Korea, Japan, or by the American Military Government. Rhee soon took advantage of this unwobbling monopoly. He doubled and redoubled the bureaucracy that, by 1953, employed three times as many officials, for less than half the peninsula, as the Japanese had employed for their rule over all of it. Police and army forces expanded the most and a Local Autonomy Law, though passed over Presidential objection in 1949, was unimplemented until 1952, and even then meaninglessly. Land reform, long discussed and in draft, had to be passed over a Presidential veto and implemented, in part, only in 1950—slower than in North Korea. After a rebellion in October 1948, tyranny swelled. A tough and ill-defined National Security Law—the first of a bristling series—was promulgated December 1 while back in November a press control law was passed making disturbances of state tranquillity a criminal offense. Between September 4, 1948, and April 30, 1949, 89,710 people (including future President Park) were arrested; seven newspapers and one news agency were closed; the army and educational institutions were purged; censorship and kangaroo trials proliferated; and Rhee's chief political opponent, Kim Koo, was assassinated. The Assembly, feistier than at any time since, reacted not only by turning down one prime ministerial appointment but by twice passing resolutions for the resignation of the cabinet—which were ignored. They then began to pass laws over presidential vetoes and ended by introducing, in January 1950, a constitutional amendment, barely defeated, for a clear-cut cabinet-responsible system.

This proved to be the high-water mark of constitutional and Assembly rebellion against executive excesses in South Korea. Rhee reacted by arresting sixteen Assemblymen (over 7 percent of the body) and on May 14, 1950, he convicted thirteen of them on trumped-up charges of communist conspiracy after an outrageously unfair trial. Thus the captive judiciary was used to emasculate opposition politics and the powers of the legislature and this was not the only time it happened. Popular reaction to Rhee rule, however, came two weeks later in the elections of May 30, 1950, when many Rhee opponents won seats, only to be tragically removed into North Korean captivity soon afterwards.

Defeat in the early war months and miserable conditions endangered Rhee's re-election in 1952 so he reluctantly decided to form the Liberal Party in December 1951. Almost concomitantly with its founding, Rhee proposed a constitutional amendment mandating an easily manipulable popular—instead of Assembly—election of the president. The Assembly promptly and decisively rejected this on January 18, 1952, by a vote of 143 to 19. Further arrests of Assemblymen on false "Communist conspiracy" charges followed, these being suddenly dropped when the accused were marched to the Assembly hall in Pusan and forced to vote for the amendment at gunpoint on July 4, 1952. Strangely, the amendment the opposition struggled to oppose in 1952 is precisely the one the opposition of 1986-87 fights to obtain!

In 1954, looking ahead to 1956 when his second term was to end, Rhee again demanded a constitutional amendment removing the barrier against more than two presidential terms. Its defeat by two-thirds of a vote was announced on November 27, 1954, but reversed the next day by eliminating the fraction through a sleight-of-hand rounding off. Finally, in 1958, a constitutional amendment abolished the light and ineffective local autonomy reluctantly implemented from 1952-58. Since then, except for an abortive attempt in 1961, officials down through township chiefs have been appointed, thus undermining the process of building local interests and political identities which an assembly could articulate and represent.

As a result, after starting in 1948 with considerable democratic ideals which had already inspired previous Korean drafts from 1919 to 1947, the Korean constitution soon was laid under siege by amendments, evasions and repressive legislation which continued, solidified, extended, or centralized the increasingly autocratic power of the executive position.

The Turn to Democracy: The 1960 Second Constitution

The Political Background

The worst was to come. Fundamental changes of an explosive character were breaking over Korea's ancient polity. The war jolted vast segments of Korea's population loose and started a process of urbanization and centralization which has proceeded relentlessly ever since. Seoul, which had 394,200 people in 1930, 935,500 in 1940, and 1,446,000 in 1949, had 2,445,400 by 1960 (and 10,000,000 in 1987). Urban population, which had been 11.4 percent in 1940, became 33.2 percent by 1960 (and 80 percent by 1987). Communications of every sort, including international, boomed with urbanization. So did education which, from 1948 to 1960, saw a doubling of colleges (almost quadrupling their enrollments), almost a quadrupling of high schools and their students, and a rapid overall literacy explosion. Seoul became—and remains today—one of the largest and most violent educational centers in the world. Dislocation, broadened knowledge of conditions elsewhere, and enormous population concentrations deepened, and still deepens, grievances, while sharpening ambition and desire for social and political change.[9]

Such forces, colliding with Rhee's authoritarianism, built up an increasingly powerful and united opposition Democratic Party that elected its candidate, Chang Myon, as Vice President in 1956, cut Rhee's electoral majority, increased opposition Assembly seats in the 1958 elections and even gave 2,000,000 votes to a (soon executed) socialist, Cho Pong-am.[10] The opposition was within striking distance of victory in the 1960 presidential elections against the semi-senile, octogenarian President and his physically debilitated Vice President, Yi Ki-pung. When the government shamelessly manipulated the ballot counting in the March 15, 1960, election, the forces of urban violence were called to the stage. Massive student demonstrations, turned violent by government police fusillades, brought the Rhee government down (April 19-26, 1960), soon destroyed the Liberal Party, seated a moderate interim government under an able, moderate Rhee associate, Huh Chong, and cleared the way for a democratic constitution and governance.[11]

The Framing of the Democratic Constitution

An atmosphere of intense and emotional reform ensued in which even Liberal Party Assemblymen, as their dying shot, collaborated. Again too rapidly, as in 1948, the Constitution was extensively amended by a Democratic-led Assembly. In reaction against the long and extensive violation of basic civil rights during Rhee's rule, the 1960 constitution's rights were made unconditional, all "except as provided by law" escape clauses being removed. Provisions for the impartiality of officials and police were added. A full cabinet system of government was then erected in clauses making the President simply "head of State," elected to a five-year term by a two-thirds vote of a now newly-created Senate meeting in joint session with a far more powerful and numerous (233 members) House of Representatives.

Executive power was vested in a state council headed by a Prime Minister, responsible as a body to the House of Representatives. The Prime Minister was to be nominated by the President but approved by majority vote of the House, which could elect him in case of a deadlock with the President. The state council had either to resign *en bloc* if a non-confidence resolution was passed or it had to dissolve the House and call for new elections. All presidential acts required prime ministerial countersignature. A majority of cabinet members had to be selected from the National Assembly. A Central Election Committee was established for fair elections and a Constitutional Court for constitutional review. Again, after only a month and a half of work, "the Second Constitution" was adopted on June 15, 1960, by a vote of 208 to 3. Elections on July 29, after considerable, but not very successful, socialist-reformist campaigning, carried the Democratic Party triumphantly to power (with over 160 of the 220 seats) after over a decade of frustration and struggle.[12]

The Disintegration of the Democratic Enterprise

Unfortunately the process of nominating the prime minister pitted the two almost equal 'Old' and 'New' Democratic factions against each other, factions only the Rhee autocracy had been able to weld together. The latter's leader, Dr. Chang Myon, barely emerged prime minister in August with three votes over the majority. The two factions then split into two parties in September 1960, with 86 'old' (New Democratic Party) and 95 'new'

(Democratic Party) assemblymen. Though Chang gradually raised his adherents to 118 by October 19 and 133 to the New Democrats' 62 by the end of his regime, this factional split caused instability, delays in decision-making and public disenchantment. Disputatiousness and the vote bribery which accompanied it was aggravated by the two-house Assembly. Demonstrations became endemic. Most were peaceful, but some in the fall of 1960 at Yonsei University and at the National Assembly (who were terrorized into passing unwise ex-post-facto legislation) were not. The government, having come to power by demonstrations, balked at curbing them and was deemed to face them with excessive caution. Robbery and gang terrorism increased citizen apprehension. Student attempts in the spring of 1961 to debate North Korean students at Panmunjom caused gnawing queasiness.

None of this was, in itself, fatal, irreversible or beyond what many societies like Colombia's, are routinely used to. A new Security Law and an able Home Minister in the spring of 1961 gave promise of better control; demonstrations attenuated somewhat. But the military, already ready to pounce against Rhee in 1960, now pounced on the Democrats after only nine months. The coup of May 16, 1961, reinforced a then growing judgment that the short-lived 1960 constitution had excessively loosened controls and that a return to greater stability and decisiveness was called for.

The Turn to Military Authoritarianism: The 1962 Third Constitution

The Coup

The reaction came with a vengeance in the May 16, 1961, coup by Major General Park Chung-hee, his nephew, Colonel Kim Jong-pil, and some 250 officers and 3,500 men from the 600,000 man armed forces. The Government, surprised, intimidated and overthrown without resistance—was replaced by a military junta of 30 colonels and brigadier generals under Major-General Park. The government leaders were arrested, the National Assembly dissolved, the 1960 Constitution sidetracked. The junta itself, clothed in the majestic title 'Supreme Council for National Reconstruction' (SCNR), 'legislated' a comprehensive "Law Regarding Extraordinary Measures for National Reconstruction" on June 6, 1961, which superceded the constitution in essential respects and appropriated executive, legislative, and judicial powers to itself.[13]

Extensive purges and 'purification' measures from the streets on up throughout the government were initiated at once. Thousands of politicians, civil servants, military officers, journalists and entertainment business operators were arrested or retired and most news organs closed. A Political Purification Law of March 1962 banned 4,367 politicians from politics, though most were cleared within two years. Thousands were given kangaroo court trials under special court-martial. The results of recent local elections were, in effect, cancelled and local administration was again, as in 1958, killed off. A large and ubiquitous Central Intelligence Agency (KCIA) deepened internal (and external) controls and surveillance.

A third constitution now became necessary to normalize rule and return the country to partly civilianized control. This constitution was drafted *in camera* by December 1962 without public contact. It called for the election in 1963 of a President heading a strong presidential system with power to appoint and dismiss the prime minister and the cabinet without legislative consent. The Assembly was downgraded to a weak, unicameral body reduced from 233 to 175 members unempowered to revise basic SCNR legislation that had been decided by military men arguing in secret. As a reaction against what the military regarded as 'chaotic' or 'corrupt' politics, candidacy for the Assembly as an independent was forbidden and "a person shall lose his membership...when he leaves or changes his party or when his party is dissolved." [14] The Coup Constitution turned out to be a politically more restrictive form of the later Syngman Rhee constitution.

In its wake another government-organized party without local roots soon arose: The Democratic Republican Party (DRP), secretly formed in late 1962 and unveiled in January 1963 when the ban on political activities was at last lifted. With some controls, massive government support, mounting government economic success, and a proportional representation system of 44 out of 175 seats (which cushioned any plurality), the DRP succeeded in engineering narrow election victories for Park in 1963, 1967, and 1971. It also controlled the assembly with a minority of total votes in 1963 (32 percent) and 1971 (47.7 percent), achieving just over a majority in 1967, after admitted illegalities.[15] The proportional representation system not only cushioned government pluralities, it also gave military men without local political roots a chance to serve in—and retire into—the legislature.

Park Out-Rhees Rhee: Assault, Amendment and Laceration: The Yushin Constitution

The Park era saw the rebirth of a kind of Japanese colonial-style politics of firm, somewhat militarized control, decisive economic planning, widespread mobilization techniques, and political desiccation. Park's Assembly had chiefly censorial and limited consultative powers, but narrow legislative powers. Park's drive toward ever greater authoritarianism deepened. In 1969 the much battered constitution was amended for the 6th time, in Rhee fashion by removing the third-term limitation, the opposition boycotting. This still failed to sate Park's lust for unobstructed power even though he received a shock with Kim Dae-jung's great crowd-getting popularity in the 1971 elections in which urban areas voted 51.4 percent for Kim (though Park took 51.2 percent of the national vote). Park then declared a quite unjustified state of emergency on December 6, 1971, and martial law on October 17, 1972. In a bloodless coup against his own constitution, he used soldiers and tanks against the Assembly and other civilian centers, proscribed all politics once again, and lacerated the constitution with some seventy-two amendments—cutting away any remaining muscle the mangled legislature and judiciary still possessed.

This constitution also proved to be innovative—instituting direct elections by an electoral college which Park headed and which then dutifully re-elected him on December 23, 1972, by a Pyongyang-style majority of 2,357 of 2,359 delegates, to an expanded six-year term. Government control of the further-weakened Assembly was assured by the presidential appointment, via the same dutiful electoral college, of one-third of its members. Draconian 'Emergency Measures' then supplemented even these taut controls, suppressing student movements, demonstrations or any criticism. From 1972 to 1975 repression reached its highest point since the worst wartime colonial days. Park euphemistically called this monstrosity the 'Yushin' ('Revitalizing') reforms, a phrase which, not insignificantly, he drew from Meiji Japan. The economy had boomed, but politics, like a starved and frightened waif, quaked at the edge of a totalitarian precipice.

Murder, Twilight Glasnost, and the Chun Fifth Constitution

The Park Goetterdaemmerung

Korea has yet to take a decisive step back from the precipice that plunges a society with repressed politics toward violence. The main author of the Yushin Constitution's repressed politics was himself consumed by violence. On October 26, 1979, Major General Kim Jae-kyu, Park's CIA chief, shot the President and his chief bodyguard at dinner. The nation was stunned but calm. An interim government was assembled under Park's prime minister, Choi Kyu-hah, a conservative career civilian bureaucrat whose chief experience had been in foreign affairs. While cancelling one egregious Park emergency decree, he moved with excessive caution and unwisely used the unpopular, rubber-stamp National Conference for Unification to get himself elected President on December 6, 1979. The military lurked constantly in the background.

After Park's death there was an outpouring of intellectual and media zeal for the abolition of the Yushin Constitution and its provisions that exceeded socialist constitutions in repressiveness. However, the Commander of the Defense Security Command, Major General Chun Doo-hwan staged a coup against his commanding officers on December 12, 1979, placing the Army Chief of Staff under arrest. He subsequently retired him and virtually all of Park's senior officers, some 30-40 generals. Students and intellectuals feared (with good reasons even though there was a general tide of hope) that continued martial law and a slowed down pace of constitutional revision might well write another chapter in the thick volume of obstructions and frustrations to Korean democracy.

Their fears mounted on April 14, 1980 when General Chun made himself National Security Planning Agency (old KCIA) Director while retaining, apparently illegally, the Defense Security Command, itself a kind of armed forces gestapo. Student demonstrations now escalated. Chun and the military responded with Martial Law Decree No. 10 on May 17, 1980. It closed universities, prohibited demonstrations, reimposed censorship and allowed the arrest of chief opposition politicians Kim Dae-jung, Kim Young-sam and Park's three closest associates. The riots which followed in Kwangju and South Cholla, (Kim Dae-jung's home province) were then repressed by special forces that Chun had trained for brutal warfare behind the North Korean lines. The ferocity induced by their aggressive training wreaked cruel havoc on the originally unarmed civilians of Kwangju, costing hundreds of lives. The national tragedy of this May 18-26, 1980, massacre of students and civilians has yet to be exorcised from the Korean national conscience and is regarded by many of today's students as a catastrophe outranking the distant Korean war. With resistance broken and with martial law, Chun's coup was essentially complete, bringing with it another extended military regime dominated by younger military academy classes.[16] He has, however, never achieved legitimacy.

The Staging of the Fifth Constitution

On May 31, a Special Committee for National Security Measures was established with a junta-like 31-member Military-Civilian Standing Committee behind it that, with subcommittees, made all key state decisions. On October 22, 1980, it was replaced by the 81-member Legislative Council for National Security, appointed by Chun, which lasted until it was replaced by the newly elected National Assembly, on March 25, 1981. These elections were held with heavily restricted campaigning and little time to recover from the recent months of suspended politics and continual political bans.

Shortly after the resignation of the short-lived post-Park government of President Choi Kyu-hah on August 16, 1980, General Chun (rapidly promoted to full General) resigned and was elected President by the rubber-stamp National Conference for Unification with all but one of its 2,525 votes. He was sworn in as President on September 1, 1980. In his inaugural he announced that a new constitution would soon be drafted. In the meantime, however, politics was again proscribed, all parties were uprooted, the media was censored and partly closed down, 8,000 government employees fired, and 40,000 "hooligans" rounded up and subjected to arrest and re-education.

Celerity again characterized the drafting of the constitution. A government-appointed committee, working behind the scenes, delivered the eighth revision of the constitution on September 29, 1980. It was approved in a national referendum—under martial law and without debate or an alternative—on October 22, 1980. Compared to the hopes of eleven months earlier, it represented only a decidedly lukewarm improvement on the unparalleled rigors of the Yushin Constitution.

The Content of Chun's Fifth Constitution

In the 1980 Chun Constitution a number of the worst features of the Yushin Constitution were removed: forced labor can only be imposed as a consequence of criminal conviction; *habeas corpus* and the exclusion of coerced confession from evidence are guaranteed.[17] Freedoms of residence, occupation, correspondence, speech, the press, assembly and association are now guaranteed without "except as provided by law" clauses, though the needs of security and public welfare still permit ill-defined exceptions. Some newly conferred rights appear, but largely as ornaments. In fact, numerous rights violations in the 1980 trial of Kim Dae-jung and his 23 codefendants, the banning of 600 journalists, the closing of 172 periodicals, the forced unification of all news services, the elaborately minute controls specified in the Basic Press Law, and the six restrictive labor laws all give the impression that, in essence, freedoms have advanced little since Yushin.[18]

The Chun Constitution contains new presidential provisions for an expanded seven-year term. The president is allowed to serve only one such term and no amendment favoring the incumbent can be submitted. This greatly improves on the Yushin Constitution and its terms continue (1987) to be reiterated. Amendments removing these barriers to another term are conceivable, however, under the real or imagined pretext of a *force majeure.*

The president continues to be elected indirectly by a "presidential electoral college" of 5,278 members who cannot be recommended by political parties and are fated to be manipulable unknowns. Campaigning in elections is strictly controlled: candidates may not "barnstorm" and must campaign "only through posters and mass media" and only twice in each medium. Campaign funds, rigidly controlled in a separate law, are, in essence, provided by the government.[19]

The president continues to have greater powers. He no longer appoints all judges—only the chief justice and Supreme Court justices, the latter not requiring Assembly approval. All other judges are appointed by the chief justice. Emergency powers are slightly reduced and require National Assembly concurrence but the martial law provisions remain the same as in the Yushin Constitution. Presidential appointive powers remain much the same as in former 'strong president' constitutions.

Also, the constitution provides for a new Advisory Council on State Affairs. Its chairman is to be the "immediate former president." Though now advisory, it is currently rumored that—if, and when President Chun steps down from the presidency and chairs this council—the government Democratic Republican Party may pass a law making it a policy clearance body.

The Chun Constitution's Assembly remains weak but it has recaptured the ability to override a presidential veto by a two-thirds majority and to inspect state affairs and demand documents and witnesses. It can call for the removal of ministers after the first year of tenure. Its budgetary powers cannot strangle the government, however: the executive branch may continue to disburse funds in accordance with the previous budget if no new budget is passed. Yushin provisions limiting regular sessions to 90 days a year and to 30-day extraordinary sessions called by the president or by one-third of the Assemblymen remain. The Assembly follows Yushin in being limited to 150 days of meetings a year—to avoid pestering the executive branch.

The Yushin Constitution's weakening of the judiciary essentially continues. The 1963-72 power to review the constitutionality of laws was not restored to the courts. As a result, their supine and craven refusal to acquit guiltless political defendants has, as in the conviction of Kim Dae-jung and his 23 co-defendants, continued.

By far the most repressive part of the Constitution lies in its supplementary provisions that were legislated, sometimes at a clip of twenty laws a day, by the unilaterally Chun-appointed Legislative Council for National Security. The laws once passed, many with the provisions noted above, were extremely repressive and "may not be litigated or disputed for reasons of this constitution or other reasons." Prominent among these was the Law on Political Purification (November 3, 1980), under which 587 politicians were barred from political activities, without trials or a chance for defense in an apparent violation of the Constitution. However, in most of the cases that occurred on or before March 6, 1985, all political rights deprived under this law were restored.

From late November through December 1980, eighteen essentially government-created political parties miraculously appeared. One was a firmly trussed government party—the Democratic Justice Party (DJP) in the Liberal and Democratic Republican party tradition—while the other seventeen were opposition groups sedulously sliced into small pieces by the government knife. Seeing through this tactic, the Korean public has retired two-thirds of these parties and only four parties have any importance. In the March 25, 1981, general elections the DJP won only 35 percent of the votes but, through the proportional representation system, was able to control 55 percent of the seats, the opposition's division counting heavily against it. In the second election on February 12, 1985, the three opposition parties received 58 percent of the popular vote to the ruling party's 35.4 percent, but the apportionment system continued the government's 55 percent control. However, a revived opposition party, fortified with senior politicians released from bans, won 29 percent within a few weeks of its creation and has since expanded opposition unity. This degree of unity, however, is always fragile and it has since ebbed. On April 8, 1987, the dominant Kim Dae-jung and Kim Young-sam opposition factions both broke away from the New Korea Democratic Party (NKDP) and left it as a shell of some 18 assemblymen members, who apparently were willing to compromise with the government's proposal for parliamentary government. The two Kim factions then formed a die-hard Reunification Democratic Party (RDP). Further defections to the RDP in November 1987 have still further reduced the NKDP and, unfortunately, it seems this most recent division and weakening won't be the last.

The RDP's formation prompted surveillance and legal harassment from the Chun government. President Chun, losing hope of any possibility for compromise with the new party, made a fatefully miscalculated announcement on April 13, 1987, calling for an end to the debate on constitutional reform until the completion of the Seoul Summer Olympics in October 1988. Far from quieting the situation, in every major city the announcement precipitated concerted and violent demonstrations of protest. These were fed by still further disclosures about the torture which had earlier killed the student Park Chong-chul. The RDP and its associates formed a "National Council for Democratic Constitution Reform" with the purpose of repealing the April 13 announcement, investigating the Kwangju incident and the Park torture case, releasing political prisoners, and freeing the press. Almost no one expected success.

But on June 2, Chun recommended the nomination of retired General Roh Tae-woo as the DJP's next presidential candidate, the nomination being ceremoniously approved on June 10. This move immediately instigated demonstrations of some 60,000 in eleven cities, opposed by 60,000 police. Another student death fired the populace. Seoul's Myongdong Cathedral was occupied and held for days and the participation of many non-students from the middle classes was clear.

Seeing no hope for political tranquility, a smooth transition, a legitimate government or a peaceful Olympic Games, the new candidate, General Roh, made a historic announcement on June 29. In essence he conceded to the opposition that constitutional reform should allow direct presidential elections; that the presidential election laws should be revised; that non-criminal political prisoners should be released and Kim Dae-jung's political rights restored; that human rights be respected and freedom of the press allowed; that educational institutions should be self-regulating; and that full political party activities be encouraged. Though it was not clear whether all these measures had the enthusiastic support of the President, Chun nonetheless accepted them two days later. Demonstrations, though they have not ceased, have since quieted considerably and though some 3,000 labor strikes, large and small, erupted soon afterwards in July and August, these, too—after some difficulty and with the acceptance of higher wage levels—had subsided by early September. Euphoria swept the country and, though old laws and enforcing agencies continued in place, citizens commenced acting as if already liberated.

Denouement and Epilogue: Constitutional Reform and Political Problems

The Chun Constitution was the Yushin Constitution mildly corrected; it had remained more authoritarian than the post-coup 1963 constitution. It clung to an extremely centralized, authoritarian, and undemocratic ethos and expanded repression whenever it saw fit. Chun had, in 1986, agreed to the revision of his constitution, which even the DJP desired. Deadlock, however, ensued between the opposition's desire for direct elections and the government's desire for a parliamentary system. With this deadlock dramatically and unexpectedly removed on June 19th, the terms of the announcement have been gradually implemented: Kim Dae-jung and all parties have been restored to full political activity, all but some 900 political prisoners have been freed, and the Constitution, through long summer committee sessions, has been successfully revised in a compromise version agreed to by all parties. On October 12 the National Assembly voted 254-4 to fairly extensive constitutional revisions which, on October 27, were approved by 93 percent of the 78 percent of the electorate voting in a national referendum.

These revisions provide for direct elections for a president limited to one five-year term. They strip the president of the power to dissolve the National Assembly or to issue emergency decrees with the same legal power as the constitution or to appoint judges without Assembly approval. The Assembly gains audit powers over government expenditures and the right to investigate all administrative functions. Press censorship and licensing of publications are to be banned as are arrest, search and seizure without a warrant issued by a judge. Torture is banned, police are required to inform relatives of anyone arrested and suspects guaranteed the right of legal counsel and arraignment in court. University autonomy, a minimum wage system, and workers' rights to organize, engage in collective bargaining and strike are guaranteed. Finally, the preamble orders the military to "observe neutrality in political affairs." Though compromises were made and the constitution probably not fully restored to the first constitution of 1948, improvements have been palpable. Many laws restraining democracy outside the constitution, however, still remain (as of November 1987) incompletely revised.

An observer like myself, who has seen forty years of eight amended or recreated Korean constitutions, cannot help but remember the first one in 1948 with nostalgia. There lurked in it, for all its faults, a hopeful feeling that democracy would neither be too headlong-embraced, as in 1960, nor too curbed and waylaid, as always since, but that it might in some way be truly sought. Somehow, between the extremes of a hard-line military and students caught in passionate idealism, the thread of a viable democracy, indeed, of political moderation itself, was lost for an entire generation.

The June 29 announcement and the implementation, thus far, of most of its provisions have begun the process of substantial restoration of democratic hopes. Yet their quick fulfillment is no certainty. The two Kims have, as feared, split. Both have, as of November 1987, launched political campaigns, despite opposition promises to field a united candidate. Indeed, on October 5, 1987, a third Kim, Kim Chong-pil, revived, under the name New Democratic Republican Party, the old DRP and launched his own campaign. The party situation has been greatly worsened by the formation, on November 12, of the Peace and Democracy Party of Kim Dae-jung, comprising some 27 assemblymen deserters of the once-united Reunification Democratic Party which, with 50 members, is fielding its President, Kim Young-sam. A trail of numerous splits not only leaves the divisiveness of five competing opposition parties but breaks progress toward the institutionalization of the party system as a supporting column of democracy: it remains, in Korea, the transient vehicle and even plaything to individual leaders. Already, popular disillusion is palpable.

Thus, even before the presidential elections scheduled for December 16, 1987, shadows have begun to fall on constitutional Korean democracy. Unless one of the two main Kims concedes at the last minute, it appears that Korean politics is heading for a minority president who may not have the support of much more than a third of the electorate. Moreover, opposition splits are disenchanting the Korean electorate and raise the fair possibility of a victory by General Roh. While General Roh would command more popularity than President Chun, he cannot accomplish that distancing from the military which is desirable for Korean politics and which alone contains any prospect for quieting continued student unrest.

The political skies have been lightened by the June 29 announcement but clouds still hang in them. A highly political people packed into tinderbox urban concentrations have yet to achieve the political identity they sought with an enthusiasm so wholeheartedly in 1945; an identity which today should be a fit partner of their economic flair. Lacking proper channels and institutions, such as established and respected parties, to bear their messages, issues dissolve on the streets in violence. Such violence, though slightly dampened from what it had been, may still continue into 1988, possibly into the Olympic Games. A politically legitimate government has yet to be established. Further emotional political discontent may yet be rekindled. Such a rekindling is not the best builder of democratic stability. What will emerge from the passion, the repression, the turmoil of these months is not fully predictable. A further coup or assassinations, though their likelihood has been reduced, are not inconceivable. Yet, on the whole, hopes have revived.

The auguries for the longer run may increase these hopes. A viable political identity will not forever elude a people so well-educated, open to the world, and experienced in government. To build a system of representation will require firmer interest closures, more marked and continuous intermediary institutions. In the business world, especially among the conglomerates (chaebol), such interest closures are emerging, even if their umbilical cords to government remain uncut and perhaps never can be severed in the Western sense. For the rest, far more local administration, with local police and possibly educational controls, is needed. When a system of greater pluralism is forged, a representative system with some spirit of compromise will grow to break the ancient vortex pattern which has so long defined Korea's political life; its advent will be as welcome as its delays in arrival have been prolonged.

NOTES

1. Chong To-jon, *Sambong-jip* (Collected Works of Sambong [Chong To-jon]); *Han'guk saryo ch'ongso* (Korean historical materials), No. 13, Seoul, 1961.
2. Gregory Henderson, *Korea: The Politics of the Vortex*, (Harvard University Press, 1968), pp. 72-73; Chong-Sik Lee, *The Politics of Korean Nationalism*, (University of California Press, 1963), p. 91.
3. Gregory Henderson, *idem*, p. 157; *Foreign Relations of the United States, 1947*, Vol. VI, Sept. 18, 1947, p. 794.
4. It should, however, be observed that on April 23, 1919, during the early weeks of Korea's independence movement from the Japanese, a group of independence Koreans met secretly in Seoul and adopted a provisional constitution and a draft government organization naming Syngman Rhee as 'chief executive'. Two weeks earlier, on April 10, 1919, a provisional legislative assembly had been formed among the few hundred Korean residents of Shanghai; later that year it instituted a presidential government responsible to the legislature. In early 1944, a constitutional revision was hammered out and passed by the provisional government. Unfortunately, the provisional

government's constitutions were known to only a tiny fraction of Koreans and had, like the provisional government itself, little more than symbolic importance at the time nor much subsequent influence since neither liberated Korea nor either of its foreign liberators ever recognized the provisional government as the legitimate government of Korea and South Korea's lawyers, all trained in Japanese law, had little knowledge of or sympathy for the constitutions of the independence movement. (Chong-sik Lee, *op. cit.*, pp. 130-134; 224-225.)

5. For the 1948 constitution and the politics of the time, see John Kiechiang Oh, *Korea:Democracy on Trial*, (Cornell University Press, 1968), pp. 11-22.
6. Gregory Henderson, *op. cit.*, p. 425.
7. Oh, *op. cit.*, p. 204.
8. Gregory Henderson, *op. cit.*, pp. 158-159; Oh, *idem*, pp. 15-21.
9. Gregory Henderson, *idem*, pp. 168-174.
10. Bong-houn Choy, *Korea: A History*, (Tuttle, 1971), pp. 274-277.
11. Oh, *op. cit.*, pp. 73-76.
12. For a detailed source on this period see Sungjoo Han, *The Failure of Democracy in South Korea*, (University of California Press, 1974), (here pp. 103-123.).
13. Gregory Henderson, *op. cit.*, pp. 182-184.
14. For texts of the Law Regarding Extraordinary Measures for National Reconstruction, the Supreme Council for National Reconstruction and the December 26, 1962, Constitution, see Se-jin Kim, *The Politics of Military Revolution in Korea*, University of North Carolina Press, pp. 179-218.
15. Gregory Henderson, "The Politics of Korea," in John Sullivan and Roberta Foss (ed.), *Two Koreas: One Future?*, (University Press of America for American Friends Service Committee, Feb. 1987), p. 104; Young Whan Kihl, *Politics and Policies in Divided Korea*, (Westview Press, 1984), p. 60 (a detailed text of recent Korean politics).
16. For many details of this period see Kihl, *idem*, pp. 78-85.
17. For analysis of the Chun constitution, see Edward J. Baker, "South Korea's New Constitution: The Emperor's New Clothes," North America Coalition for Human Rights in Korea, November 1980.
18. See also International League for Human Rights and the International Human Rights Law Group, "Democracy in South Korea: A Promise Unfulfilled," 432 Park Ave. South, 1103 New York 10016, 1985.
19. Gregory Henderson in *Two Koreas, op. cit.*, pp. 108-112. The above provisions are partly in legislation supplemental to the Constitution.

3

Potential for Democratic Change in a Divided Nation

CHONG LIM KIM

No other issue is more salient in the politics of South Korea than the issue of democratic reforms. This is true today as much as it was in the past, reflecting the persistence of widespread public aspirations for a democratic rule. Seldom has the ideal of democracy ever been denied, in their public pronouncements at least, by the leaders of the past regimes. While they systematically thwarted it in their actions, they all nevertheless tried to justify their undemocratic rules in the name of democracy. When it became all too clear that their rule deviated drastically from what we commonly understand as democracy, they called theirs "the Korean style" democracy.

Nearly forty years after the beginning of the Republic, democracy still remains an elusive goal. Despite the persistence with which Korean people have pressed for it, its attainment does not seem anywhere near. Why is it that democracy has failed to take root in Korea?[1] This is the central question that this paper seeks to answer. The analysis consists of four parts: (1) a definition of the key concept; (2) a discussion of the important prerequisites of a democratic process; (3) an assessment of the present conditions; and finally, (4) a conclusion.

Democracy As a Political Process

Of the many different definitions of democracy Robert Lane's may serve as a useful starting point.[2] He states that "democratic politics embraces standard elements: competitive elections, a legitimate opposition, a relatively free (officially uncensored) press, and protection of minority rights." (Lane, 1986: 383) Competition and institutional safeguards that permit its full play are essential to democracy. The freer the competition between leadership groups, in elections, and in the market place of ideas and influences, the more democratic the process is. Competition produces three important political effects. It discourages any form of monopolistic control of power by a single leader or an institution, making it possible to establish a pluralistic structure of power. The second effect is leadership responsiveness. Leaders who depend on the continuing support of their followers for tenure in office are likely to pay close attention to the sentiments and views of their supporters. Competition is a principal mechanism which generates alternatives in policy and candidates, and citizens are free to choose their preferred alternative from among these. There is therefore incentive for leaders to be responsive if they wish to remain in power. The third effect of competition is the expansion of opportunities for popular participation. Through competition and because of it a variety of views and interests, which might not otherwise be heard, gain a public forum. This makes it possible for a broad base of society to be involved in various aspects of political life.

The presence of a legitimate opposition is another defining element. Where oppositions to the policies of government are suppressed and denied a legitimate role in the political process, the tyranny by a majority or a small minority is likely to emerge. Opposition forces institutionalized through partisan politics prevent tyranny. The interests and opinions opposed to the current policies are mobilized and articulated by opposition parties, which has an important restraining effect on the potential abuse of power by the party in power. Not only do opposition parties provide political alternatives to the people but they also serve as a training ground for future leadership. If one regards turnovers in power through elections as an aspect of democracy, a legitimate opposition plays a vital role in this. The presence of vigorous opposition is essential, for it ensures political competition, provides alternative channels of interest aggregation, and restrains the abuse of power. Furthermore, a legitimate opposition makes a peaceful transfer of power possible, contributing significantly to the democratic stability.

A free and uncensored press is a vital element of democracy. The beneficial role of a free press is beyond any doubt. It facilitates social communication, brings to the public attention the important issues of broad social concerns, helps organize and express public opinions, informs citizens of public affairs, amplifies the salience of issues latent at the grassroots, and performs a "watch dog" function over governmental actions. These multiple roles of a free press help create a viable competitive political process which is in some sense analogous to a free and open market of ideas and influence.

The protection of minority rights is a central concern in Madisonian democracy. As R. A. Dahl has so rightly seen it, the central problem of the Madisonian theory of democracy is "to bring off a compromise between the power of majorities and the power of minorities." (Dahl, 1956:4) The tyranny of a majority was the issue which received the greatest attention among the Founding Fathers of the American democracy. The solution to the problem was found in the system of decentralized powers through the adoption of the principles of separation of power, the federal system, a bicameral legislature elected from different constituencies, and a pluralistic electorate. The protection of minorities is, in a broader sense, an aspect of political competition. Where the views of a minority are not respected the majority can dominate the whole political process without any restraint, which reduces competition. It also implies that there exists a set of widely accepted rules of the game that governs political competition. These rules prescribe what a majority can do and cannot do, especially with respect to minority rights. In order to prevent the infringement of minority rights both institutional devices and behavioral norms must be developed. A legitimate opposition is merely an extension of the principle of minority rights.

What emerges from the conceptual discussion presented above is a definition which is even more parsimonious and general. All that one needs to define democracy as a process is one single distillate: an open and orderly political competition. Open competition ensures the broadest possible participation in politics by individuals and groups. It induces leadership to be accountable and responsive in their actions. It creates an atmosphere where a variety of views and interests are freely discussed and debated. Most important of all, it discourages the tyranny of a well organized minority or a majority through decentralization of power. An open competition alone does not define democracy. It must also be an orderly competition. Inherent in any competition is conflict. Competition arises when people pursue different goals. If unrestrained by a set of legitimate rules of the game, an orderly competition will break down. The attainment of the desired effects of competition such as liberty, freedom from tyranny, representation, and justice becomes possible only if the competitive process follows such rules. A democratic system, because of its competitive nature, is particularly vulnerable to the severest kinds of conflict and strife. The success of a democracy therefore depends upon how well it manages conflicts. A set of formal and informal rules, which is accepted by most members of the society, must be present if conflicts are to be restrained and an orderly process of political competition is to be secured.

Democracy is a special species of political process, distinguishable from other forms of government by its open and orderly competition. In addition to its parsimony and generality, such minimal conception has several other advantages as well. A common confusion over the meaning of democracy exists because we often fail to distinguish the properties of a process and the preconditions that sustain it. Our definition makes a sharp distinction between these two. For example, a free press is commonly regarded as a defining element of democracy (see Robert Lane). But the presence of a free press is a precondition that helps shape a competitive process and not a property of competition itself. Similarly, the autonomous structure of interest groups is often considered an essential element of democracy. This too involves confusion. The presence of active interest groups should be regarded as a precondition of political competition.

Another common source of confusion is the conceptual failure to distinguish the process from its consequences. For example, the democratic rights of individuals, such as freedom of speech and assembly, and the protection of minority rights are all the consequences of an open and orderly process of political competition. In this sense, all of the cherished democratic values should properly be considered as the consequences, not the properties of competition itself.

Prerequisites of a Democratic Process

What are the requisite conditions of an open and orderly competition? There are three general types of preconditions: socio-economic, institutional, and cultural.

Socio-economic Conditions

The principal source of political competition is socio-economic diversity. Where the social base is homogeneous in terms of values and interests, competition between groups is unlikely to materialize in the political arenas. Social diversity and complexity are a function of socio-economic development. As a society develops, its structure becomes more differentiated and creates a vast array of new and complex roles (Almond and Powell, 1978: 19-23). The process of development through rapid industrialization, urbanization, education, and the communications revolution leads to increasing social diversity.

An open competition presupposes the existence of social diversity in interests, political beliefs, and attitudes. The diversity increases as a society makes socio-economic progress. For this reason students of democracy postulate socio-economic progress as one of its essential conditions. There exists strong evidence to support this view. Studies of S.M. Lipset (1960), P. Cutright (1963), and G. Winham (1970) have disclosed strong and positive correlations between the measures of a country's socio-economic development and its level of democratic performance. What connects, it is important to note, socio-economic progress to democracy is social and political diversity which result from modernization.

However, social diversity does not always lead to a democratic process. Diversity, although a necessary condition of competition, can also engender social conflicts. These conflicts must be managed in a way broadly acceptable to citizens. Otherwise, an open and orderly process of democratic competition would not be obtained. The evolution of a set of legitimate rules by which conflicts are resolved in an orderly manner is a vitally important precondition of democratic progress.

Institutional Requisites

The viability of a democratic system stands on several key institutional devices designed to induce an open and orderly process of competition. These include: a constitutional framework appropriate for democracy, a stable two or multiparty system, autonomous interest groups, a system of local autonomy, a free press, an open and free electoral system, and an independent judiciary. Each of these institutions facilitates political competition, expands the channels of communication and participation, restrains the abuse of power, protects individual rights, and imposes a set of legitimate rules by which conflicts are peacefully resolved.

Formal institutions alone, of course, do not guarantee a competitive democracy. There are any number of countries whose constitutional frameworks are explicitly democratic, embracing the principles of separation of power, protection of minority rights, popular election, and a broadly defined bill of rights and yet whose politics fall far too short of a genuine democracy. No matter how democratic a constitutional framework may appear, if not seriously taken and practiced by both the leadership and the citizens, a competitive political process is not likely to emerge. The same may be said of other institutions such as the presence of a well organized press, interest groups, or the system of justice administration. A governing minority, unless constrained by an external pressure, could seize these institutions and exploit them to their own advantages, thwarting their proper functions of maintaining an open and orderly process of competition.

Nevertheless, these institutions are important because they constitute necessary, if not sufficient, conditions of a competitive political process. Without the safeguards of some institutional devices a democratic process, being an extremely fragile structure, is very likely to collapse, either degenerating into a ruthless dictatorship or a state of ruleless conflicts. Social and cultural norms assume importance here. If there exists a set of strong social norms of behavior consonant with a democratic process, these institutions have a greater chance to survive and perform their proper functions.

Cultural Requisites

The importance of cultural patterns for democracy has been widely recognized. The concept of "the civic culture," formulated by G. Almond and S. Verba (1965: 29-30), exemplifies this. They characterize it as a political culture in which individual citizens are well informed of public affairs, are actively involved in various aspects of the political process, and are strongly allegiant to the existing political system. Lipset, in his now classic statement on the social requisites of democracy (1959) concurs with this view. He asserts that a stable democracy is unattainable unless it is undergirded by strong behavioral norms and values that allow "the peaceful 'play' of power" (Lipset, 1959: 161). The legitimacy of a political system, which flows from the congruence between a society's value system and the kind of politics actually practiced, is crucial to a functioning democracy.

Of the many cultural requisites three are very important to fostering an open and orderly process of competition. The first is the requirement of a culture that encourages diversity. A culture which places an excessive emphasis upon homogeneity is not conducive to a competitive political process. In a homogeneous culture there exists a relentless pressure for social and political conformity, which tends to suppress the emergence of a competitive system. Tolerance of opposing views, based on the culturally conditioned habit of thinking which extends to others the possibility of their being equally right, is a basic requisite. The presence of social and cultural norms that are not antagonistic to the diversity of interests and political views and instead, embrace a broad tolerance of political heterogeneity is an essential feature of a successful democracy.

The second cultural requisite is a set of legitimate rules of the game by which conflicts are peacefully settled. Culture plays an important role in shaping such rules of the game. To be effective these rules must be seen as legitimate by a broad majority of the people, buttressed further by a cultural system which allows leaders and individual citizens to make free and pragmatic bargainings and compromises. The lack of a bargaining culture rigidifies political cleavages and often leads to an irreconcilable polarization. In cultures where social actions are judged on their "form" rather than on their substance (Kim and Pai, 1981: 11-13), where taking an inflexible stance on matters of principle, called *ch'ijo* in Korean, is a supreme virtue, where leaders and informed citizens cling to the bigotry of a sense of self-righteousness regarding their own political positions, there is no room for compromised solutions. Cultures that suppress bargaining and negotiated compromises are likely to suffer from frequent political *immobilisme*, especially when the new institutions of competition are introduced into this hostile cultural environment. Establishing a set of legitimate rules of the game is a democratic precondition of the first order, and it requires a culture of free bargaining and making compromises.

The third requisite is a strong and firm commitment both by leadership and citizens to a democratic rule. Mere aspirations for democracy, however intensely held by the people, do not indicate the degree of their serious commitment. Commitment entails political actions appropriate for a democratic citizen. Such a commitment grows out of a consistently organized democratic belief system, which Philip Converse (1964: 214-227) has called a "democratic ideology." That democratic aspirations are running high in a society should not be interpreted as an indication of their democratic commitment. Only when the citizens exhibit a consistent and well structured belief system on democracy, i.e., an ideology, is it possible to say that they have a firm commitment. Evidence suggests that those citizens who have a structured democratic belief system are capable of interpreting a wide range of issues and policies in terms of a coherent framework and of actions consistently reflecting their well formed beliefs (Converse, 1964: 214-219; Klingemann, 1979: 215-254; Hagner and Pierce, 1981: 45-46; Lee, 1985: 74-81). Hence, the prevalence of a consistently organized system of democratic beliefs among leaders and citizens is a reliable indicator of democratic commitment.

Democracy in South Korea: An Assessment

Has democracy established firm roots in Korea? Few would give an affirmative answer to this rhetorical question. Has there ever been a time when democratic politics was practiced? Some might point to the brief nine-month rule of the Chang Myon government, 1960-61 and say it was such a case. True, there was a rampant mood of democracy in the air during the period, but it is hard to believe that a genuine democracy was successfully established under the Chang regime. It did not have enough time even to consolidate its own power and establish social order, let alone accomplish the difficult task of building a democratic society. A coup d'état by a group of military officers abruptly terminated the Chang regime, and with it what good intentions and aspirations that the leaders of the Chang government might have had evaporated. Still, others might insist that each of the past regimes was a democracy because they represent in their own unique way a "Korean style" democracy. A small number of the apologists of the past regimes might adhere to this position. However, such an indiscriminate view does not deserve a serious consideration here, for it is totally incompatible with any reasonable definition of democracy.

That South Korea has not been and is not a fully functioning democracy is a view which appears to have many adherents. If not, how does one account for the rising popular demands for a democratic rule in the country today? One of the most interesting questions is: why has democracy failed to take root? The question becomes even more intriguing because there have been ceaseless outpourings of popular aspirations for a democratic rule since the days of the First Republic, at times with an explosive force strong enough to bring down a regime.

I propose to investigate the question through an analysis of the requisite conditions of an open and orderly process of competition. This amounts to the determination of the presence or absence of these conditions in South Korea.

Social Diversity and Complexity

Political competition draws its life from social diversity. Suppression of diversity is to deny competition its wellspring. Nearly two decades ago, G. Henderson (1968: 18-21) in his bold and sweeping portrayal of Korean society pointed to social homogeneity as its principal feature. Although his discussion focused on ethnic homogeneity primarily and, to a limited extent, cultural aspects that include a behavioral uniformity, it seems quite clear that more than an ethnic homogeneity is implied. If social homogeneity in its broader sense refers to the lack of social structural diversity and complexity, then the degree of homogeneity must be measured by the level of role differentiation. The complexity of occupational roles, the differentiation of class system, the proliferation of new life styles and subcultures, and role specialization through education and professionalization are all important aspects of increasing structural differentiation.

Social homogeneity might have been an accurate depiction of the society Korea was until the early sixties, but the period after that does not seem to fit Henderson's characterization well. Beginning from the early years of the Third Republic, South Korea embarked on a fast moving trajectory of socio-economic development. Remarkably quick and impressive gains were already made by the mid-seventies in industrialization, urbanization, education, and communications. Accompanying this progress were social changes of a great magnitude, involving drastic rearrangements of social and economic relationships in the society. The story of 'miraculous' Korean economic growth has been told well by economists (see, for example, Edward S. Mason, et. al., 1980; Kim and Roemer, 1979). Sociologists and anthropologists have carefully documented for us profound social changes occurring in industrial relations, in the countryside, in the urban metropolis, in the occupational structure, and in the culture (see Chang et. al., 1982; Han et. al., 1985). Suffice it to observe that social changes of a fundamental sort have occurred during the last two decades and that these changes led to a degree of social diversity and complexity. It may not be far off the mark to assert that South Korea, by the mid-sixties, was no longer the simple homogeneous agrarian society it once was.

The homogeneity thesis is no longer valid. On the contrary, a more apt description of industrialized Korea is one of social heterogeneity, diversity and complexity. No longer does it make sense to attribute the failure of democracy to social homogeneity. Korea is now a society of considerable diversity, largely the product of rapid socio-economic development in the past two decades. Since political competition arises from social diversity, the potentials that feed a vigorous process of competition already exist in South Korea.

Institutional Requisites

To keep a process of competition open and orderly certain institutional mechanisms must be in place and function effectively. Because of their close association with a stable democracy, we call them the 'democratic institutions.' A democratic constitutional framework which lays down the ground rules of the political game, a two or multiparty system that effects a regular turnover in the government, an intermediate structure of interest groups that is both autonomous and active, a free press capable of channelling broader views to the public, and an independent judiciary that administers justice free from the interferences of a powerful executive branch are some of these institutional devices.

Democratic institutions are created essentially to preserve the two vital aspects of competitive process, namely its openness and order. An open and competitive process requires at least three conditions. The first is a minimal barrier for any political point of view to enter political arenas. This guarantees a maximum opportunity for the people to express their opinions and interests. The second is the availability of institutions that facilitate and amplify social communications. A view, however compelling it may be, has no chance to be heard unless there exists a channel for it. The free press plays a prominent role as a facilitator and amplifier. The views of individuals and groups must be aggregated before they can emerge as politically salient issues. Interest groups and parties give to these public views both cohesion and organization ensuring their fair hearings in the political process. The presence of such institutions is the third requirement.

An orderly process is another requirement of a stable democracy. What institutional devices are necessary to foster orderly conduct in politics? When government leaders impose an order by force, the process may remain orderly for a while. In the long-run, however, an imposed order and restrictions are bound to break down simply because legitimacy is lacking. Ultimately, an orderly process depends upon the legitimacy of the rules by which the game of politics is played. If democratic institutions performed their 'true' functions, they would become firmly established in the popular consciousness—acquiring both respect and support. Out of the interplay of these established institutions evolve a set of rules that the people will regard as legitimate.

Democratic institutions, in all their formal aspects, do exist in South Korea. The constitutional structure has always been substantially democratic in its formal contents, despite the fact that it has been changed more than half a dozen times during a relatively brief period of forty years. In all of its numerous versions, including the infamous Yushin constitution, the principles of democracy and popular sovereignty have never been eliminated even once. That Korea "shall be a democratic and republican state" and "the sovereignty of the Republic of Korea shall reside in the people" is repeated in the first chapter of all of these constitutions. Not once has democracy, republicanism, and the sovereignty of the people been denied as the fundamental keystone of the Korean constitutional structure.

The appearance of a multiparty system, a well-organized press, interest groups, and an independent judiciary have always been present in South Korea. Whether these institutions were allowed to perform their democratic function is, of course, a different matter. In fact, they did not. Often, partisan politics was closely orchestrated and manipulated by those in power. Consequently, opposition parties seldom offered genuine choices. Some better organized interests, including labor and business associations, were sponsored and controlled directly by the government. Deprived of their autonomy organized groups acted as the principal spokesmen of the government, not as democratic institutions that articulate the interests of the grassroots. The judiciary that is supposed to safeguard individual rights and protect the constitutional principles fell prey to executive dominance.

It does not seem fair to say that Korea has failed to achieve a democratic rule because of the absence of democratic institutions, at least in their formal sense. Most of them are present, powerful, well-organized, and effective. The problem is that they were diverted to tasks that contribute little to making the process of politics open and orderly. Current institutional tinkering including the ongoing constitutional debates, although thoroughly compatible with the rising demands for democratic reforms, are not likely to produce much unless the infrastructure of the Korean political culture changes. Efforts to improve minor imperfections here and there in the formal institutions are always useful, but an excessive preoccupation with it, as seems to be the case in South Korea, might do more harm than good to the final achievement of a democratic society. After all, democracy has not failed because of the absence of democratic institutions. It has failed because they did not function in a manner consistent with an open and orderly process. What makes a democratic institution function fully is a cultural pattern or an infrastructure, as we have called it, which tolerates the diversity of views, encourages compromises and bargainings in problem solving, and fosters a consistent democratic belief system.

Political Cultural Conditions Adverse to Democracy

The crucial importance of cultural conditions has long been recognized among the students of Korean democracy. Implicit in Henderson's views (1968: 361-376) is an explanation that social and cultural homogeneity, together with centralism, conspired to defeat the goal of democratization. John Oh, in his detailed analysis of the constitutional framework, concluded that the "legal-institutional superstructure—appeared democratic and modern. The political substructure or culture, however, had been long accustomed to debilitating authoritarian rule." (1968: 191) The incongruity between formal institutions and the culture in which they function, he observed, has been a real obstacle to the steady growth of democracy. In a study of democratic failure which focused on a limited period of the Chang Myon government and its abrupt collapse, S. Han (1974: 1-6) offers a similar cultural explanation. He assumed that the Chang government, had it been given a longer period to implement its policies, would have established a genuine democratic rule. Although we will never know if the assumption is indeed true, he has in any case equated the collapse of the Chang regime with the failure of Korean democracy. The collapse of the Chang regime, according to Han, was due principally to acute ideological and social polarization. The Chang regime failed to control ideological conflicts and social polarization. So, the regime collapsed. Implicit in this explanation are two critical variables: a fractionalized political culture and an absence of a set of legitimate rules by which ideological conflicts are peacefully resolved.

While the three studies cited above offer an important insight into the causes of democratic failure, broadly hinting at the adverse role of Korean political culture, they did not however provide us with a systematic account of what specific aspects of the culture retard democracy, and in what specific ways. For this, we need to turn to more recent quantitative and survey-based research on the political culture. Much of this research, based on attitudinal data collected through mass surveys, is directed to the determination of salient aspects of the political culture. (See, for examples, Lee, 1969; Kim and Pai, 1980; Yoo and Wade, 1981; Kihl, 1984; and Lee, 1985) The systematic evidence disclosed in this type of research offers a firm empirical basis to draw some conclusions about the cultural elements most adverse to democracy. Of these we shall concentrate on three: (1) the inconsistent commitment to democracy; (2) the norms of political conformity; and (3) the norms of conflict resolution.

Inconsistent Commitment to Democracy

The first and foremost requisite of democracy is the people's support for and commitment to it. How firmly are the citizens and their leaders committed to an open process of competition? Such a commitment should be sharply distinguished from a mere aspiration for democracy. An aspiration, not supported by appropriate actions required of a democratic citizen, does not bring democracy any closer. There is no question that popular aspirations for a democratic rule are running high in South Korea. And they have always been so. However, this does not necessarily mean that Koreans have a firm and resolute commitment. The degree of commitment to democracy as we noted earlier, is related to the extent to which an individual's belief system is structured and coherent. Those who exhibit a consistently organized belief system, in comparison to those who have inconsistent beliefs, were found to be better informed, more active, and more efficacious. They are the sort of people who fully meet the requirements of a democratic citizenship: they not only aspire for democracy but also show their firm resolve by taking appropriate actions. A consistent belief system is a good measure of the degree of democratic commitment.

Evidence from survey studies shows a remarkable degree of inconsistency in the democratic belief systems of Korean elites and the public. It is remarkable because knowing for a fact the intense and often explosive aspirations for democracy in the country one would have been led to think otherwise. Nonetheless, the fact of the matter is that most Koreans hold inconsistent beliefs, indicating their low commitment to democracy.

Inconsistent belief systems are widespread in the ranks of political leadership as well as among the citizens. In a sophisticated empirical study of the democratic belief system, Nam Lee (1985: 46-89) showed that no more than fifteen percent of Korean adult citizens hold consistent beliefs even when he used a very conservative estimate. His study also included a sample of local notables. Among these groups of community elites twelve percent held a consistent democratic belief system. All in all, less than two of every ten citizens possess a coherently organized system of democratic beliefs, i.e., what Converse would call a well-structured ideology. A preponderant majority of Koreans, regardless of their status in power and social position, have inconsistent beliefs. Some support ardently the principle of a majority rule and at the same time, prefer a rule by an elite. Others profess that individual liberty must be guaranteed at all cost but at the same time, believe political competition is undesirable for it causes too much divisive conflict. To be logically consistent, one cannot subscribe to a majority rule and simultaneously support a dictatorship by an elite. Similarly, if one believes in broadly defined individual rights, the protection of which depends entirely on the effects of competition, he should not be opposed to the principle of competition. It is precisely this kind of belief contradiction that prevails in the Korean cognitive system.

Inconsistent beliefs are also held by those influential in the corridors of power. Members of the National Assembly, according to a study which analyzed legislative role orientations (Kim and Woo, 1972: 626-651), perceive their role almost without exception as a "delegate." They all profess that their sole and primary responsibility is to represent the will of the people. However, when they were asked to indicate whose interests they feel they should represent, they were generally very vague. A delegate role, which in another way may be characterized as an "errand boy" style of representation, is logically inconceivable when a legislator does not know which groups he should represent. One cannot run errands if there is no one to serve. Korean legislative elites, it appears, hold highly inconsistent beliefs about their representational role.

In a recent study of the democratic consciousness based on a national sample of 1,800 citizens, (K.W. Kim, 1985: 111-112) another type of belief inconsistency was revealed. To measure the level of the public's interest in politics the study asked the respondents if they routinely discussed politics. A majority of 65 percent replied that they did, suggesting a remarkably high level of political interest in South Korea. However, when followed up by another question asking them how they actually participate in such discussions, 64 percent reported that they were only passive listeners. On the one hand, Koreans show a keen interest in political matters and on the other, they tend to remain an uninvolved "spectator" in the important process of democratic debates and mutual persuasion.

It is a well established proposition that from a strong sense of political efficacy flow all forms of political activism (Verba and Nie, 1972). In Korea, it does not hold true in voting participation. What is striking is the fact that the sense of political efficacy shows a negative correlation with voting (Kim, 1980: 44-45): those who feel strongly efficacious vote less frequently than others who have a low sense of efficacy. A broader implication is that the best informed, best educated social stratum (equipped presumably with a coherent ideology of democracy) stays away from the key process of democracy, i.e. electoral politics.

A casual observation of Korean mass political behavior corroborates our observation of the inconsistent belief system. Discussing the cultural obstacles to democracy, Sung Pae (1986: 42-43) made the following insightful remark:

> Korean voters, if dedicated to the democratic principles faithfully, should not have voted for the constitutional amendments for the legitimacy of Gen. Park Chung Hee's military coup and his Third Republic, President Park's unlimited terms of service, and for Gen. Chun Doo-hwan's revolt against senior generals and his Fifth Republic. Time and time again, when a national referendum was held on the constitutional amendments for either the establishment of a new regime by the military force or the extension of the president's terms of service, the majority of Korean voters voted for them. Thereby, their coup and revolution are 'legitimized' and their power extended.

This is a refreshing antidote to one popular and often simple-minded view that democracy failed in the nation because the political leaders deliberately betrayed the trust placed upon them to pursue their own selfish ambitions. Of course, they did and yet, the causes of democratic failure run much deeper. Had Koreans not cooperated, although it seems clear that they did so passively and without great enthusiasm, with their leaders and sternly refused to give them overwhelming endorsements on the constitutional amendments, the outcomes might have been quite different. Although it is clearly nothing more than a tacit cooperation, it still does not absolve Korean citizens from sharing a heavy responsibility for the failure of democracy.

Another striking aspect of mass political behavior is the strong undercurrent of what may be called a "political sentimentalism" (Kim, 1981:16-18). In 1960 the corrupt and autocratic rule of Syngman Rhee was brought down by the bloody April 19 student uprising. Forced to resign from the presidency by the angry and mounting public outcries, Rhee moved his family and staffs from the presidential palace to private quarters. Tens of thousands of citizens poured out into the streets, standing several lines deep on both sides to see the final procession of the disgraced leader. What was astonishing is that they all stood in the silence of profound reverence, many with tears in their eyes, as if they were bidding the last farewell to a fallen national hero, and not a disgraced autocrat. Twenty-six years after the incident there are still a large number of well educated and well meaning Koreans who revere Rhee and regard him as a great leader. What can one make of their democratic commitment? Indeed, many of these citizens are the staunchest supporters of a democratic rule. Inconsistencies in their attitudes seem to arise from their political sentimentalism. Similar is the case with the late President Park who fell at the hands of an assassin in 1979. He was the principal architect of the infamous Yushin system, which is commonly considered as one of the darkest days in the history of Korean democracy. It is reported that a large crowd of people, young and old, appears at his grave every year on the memorial day to pay their deeply felt respects. What is startling is the number of students who show up on their own, without the urgings of their teachers, parents, or officials. There is no question that these students' intentions are pure and genuine. If there is any group in Korea whom one would expect to have the fullest exposure to democratic values, it is the students. One might wonder just how their cognitive systems are capable of incorporating these two conflicting attitudes into a single system, that is, their genuinely warm feelings toward a not-so-democratic president on the one hand and on the other, all the democratic values they have been taught to cherish at school. Very vividly, we witness here another uncritical expression of political sentimentalism that seems to run deep in the Korean political consciousness.

Political sentimentalism dulls the citizen's capacity to make critical and rational judgments about the performance of their political leadership. If just because they were once powerful national leaders, they are routinely accorded a sentimental reverence and respect regardless of how much harm they have inflicted upon the nation's progress toward democracy, it is tantamount to a total lack of capacity to critically judge the responsible performance of leadership. Where such critical judgments by the mass public are absent, the leadership will see no incentives to act responsibly and democratically. In this respect, the public's ability to judge their leadership critically assumes great importance. In the absence of such critical judgments the leaders in power are left free to do whatever they wish. Sentimentalism weakens one of the most important "external checks", i.e., rational and critical public judgment, which restrains the abuse of power by the ruling elites.

Not only does a system of inconsistent beliefs frustrate an effort to achieve democracy, it also makes a political process highly volatile and unpredictable. Inconsistent beliefs trigger behavior in which a sharply defined pattern is difficult to discern. Cycles of political violence and tranquility alternate, defying any easy way to predict future changes. Koreans are often described as a people capable of enduring in stoic submission the most oppressive rules. However, the same people also showed heroic defiance against their oppressors. Koreans say they want democracy at any cost. But the next moment they let the authoritarian leaders have their way. A majority of 76 percent participated in a recent election because they felt so strongly about their intrinsic democratic rights (K.W. Kim, 1985: 115). And yet, most of the same people showed a low sense of political efficacy. Scarcely had they ousted an autocratic leader in bloody struggles than they turned to his idolization. These contradictions and inconsistencies in mass political behavior are precisely the stuff from which volatility and unpredictability are formed.

The Norms of Conformity

The principal source of political competition is socio-economic diversity. But before this diversity is translated into actively competing interests, it must be processed through the filters of a culture. Some cultures suppress diversity by insisting on social conformity, while others are more tolerant. In a culture where social and political conformity are demanded to an excessive degree and any deviance severely punished, an open politics of competition is unlikely to emerge.

There are probably no other societies in which social conformity is stressed as strenuously and at times as harshly as in Korea. Although we do not have any systematic evidence at hand, the degree of social conformity demanded in Korea may even exceed that well-known case in the world, i.e., Japan. Consider the society in North Korea. How else could one understand the Orwellian nightmare there without a reference to the underlying dynamics of conformity? Since conformity permits neither cultural nor political pluralism, it is incompatible with a system of open competition.

The strident norms of social and political conformity are shaped, in a large measure, by Confucian beliefs and values that have influenced Korea's past. In spite of dramatic social transformations accompanying the nation's phenomenal industrial growth in recent decades, some aspects of Confucianism still persist—affecting both attitudes and orientations toward political relations. The Confucian conception of government and leadership is essentially a moral one. A ruler, whether a king or a president, must govern by the example of his moral conduct. And the rule, or any other form of leadership, must be legitimated by one's moral character. This moral conception of leadership leads, on the one hand, to a strong emphasis on obedience and conformity and, on the other hand, to irreconcilable political conflicts. A moral claim to the rule makes it difficult to oppose a ruler, for he is supposed to be an embodiment of all moral values that matter in a society. It confers upon a political leader a normative basis for demanding absolute obedience and conformity to his action. However, there is another side to the Confucian conception of leadership: any viable challenge to a ruler must be conducted on moral grounds—which has the effect of transforming all political conflicts into a kind of morality play. For this reason conflicts in Korean politics all too frequently become deadly contests over moral issues. Conflicts couched in moral terms are difficult to resolve, often leading to a severe form of political *immobilism*.

What evidence is there to assert that Korea is a society of conformity? It is instructive to examine public attitudes for political competition. Do Koreans support political competition organized at the level of partisan politics and between individual political leaders? A sizable proportion of Koreans disapprove of competition of this sort. The data derived from two nationwide surveys, one conducted in 1974 and the other in 1984, show that one of every four adult citizens rejects any form of competition. Less than one-half approve of partisan competition as well as competition among politicians (Nam Lee, 1985: 84-85). Some Koreans feel that a multiparty system is harmful because it divides the nation. They feel that politicians should not compete with each other over policies. In their view, conflicts are inherently evil and so must be avoided at any time. Fear of division, disagreement, and pluralism stems from the culture of conformity.

The same set of data cited above reveals another facet of political conformity. Asked of their views on the rights of a minority, a preponderant percentage (60 percent in 1974 and 66 percent in 1984) replied that the people in the minority should never criticize the views of the majority. The centripetal force of conformity seems formidable indeed in the Korean culture.

The norms of conformity are pervasive everywhere. In a very recent public poll conducted by the *Hankook Ilbo-Gallup Korea* (*Hankook Ilbo,* July 21, 1986: 18) a sample of Korean adults was asked to indicate their preferred form of government. Nearly forty-four percent (43.8 percent) chose a presidential system and 19.4 percent the cabinet system. The choice between the two systems is in fact the hottest issue in the current debates on constitutional amendments. Quite apart from the central question of whether or not Koreans prefer a presidential system, one can also read in it their clear preference for a system that ensures political conformity. One standard argument for a presidential system is that a strong executive enhances national unity, whereas a cabinet system is politically divisive. Ironically, the opposition party whose members suffered most under the rule which demanded an unquestioning unity and strong executive powers, now advocates the presidential system. Popular support for a presidential system may be interpreted as a manifestation of their preference, conscious and unconscious, for the politics of unity and conformity.

The pressure for conformity is also present in electoral participation. In Korea, the rate of voting has been remarkably high since 1948. On the average, nearly eighty percent of the eligible voters participated in the National Assembly elections, a rate even higher than the comparable figures obtained in the U.S. and European democracies. This high rate of voting should not be interpreted as an indication of democratic participation. Part of the real reason is that a large number of Korean voters are vulnerable to the pressure of mobilization either by the government or by other powerful social groups such as clan and kinship associations. One study, (Kim, 1980: 125-127) reports that some nine percent of those who voted are the "mobilized" voters. This estimate was based on an extremely stringent definition. If one uses a more reasonable definition, the percentage of mobilized voting could be much higher. Typically, mobilized voters are little informed of politics and issues. Nor do they exhibit any interest in matters political. Frequently, they know almost nothing about the candidate they are voting for. In short, they do not have or care to have a conscious political preference. Then why do they vote at all? They vote because they are either fearful of political reprisals or desirous of showing their personal loyalty to their social superiors. Mobilized voting is a telling example of political conformity.

The harsh treatment of political dissents in Korean society shows another level of the rules of political conformity. The severity of punishment meted out to political dissidents is common knowledge. However, the demand for conformity is by no means the exclusive preserve of those in power. The same pressure for conformity exists in the ranks of opposition politicians and antigovernment groups, who are presumably most strongly committed to a democratic rule, i.e., an open and orderly process of political competition. Perhaps no other groups insist on behavioral conformity as intensely as do some antigovernment student groups. So do the leading factions of the major opposition parties. In this important respect, there is little to distinguish those in power, those in opposition, and those who champion the noble causes of democracy and social justice. When in all forms of organization and at all levels of society the rules of conformity apply with such a strong force, political dissidents have hardly any legitimate role to play in the polity.

The pressure for social conformity exists in all societies. What distinguishes Korean society is the degree of emphasis placed upon conformity. As the rules of conformity are excessively and at times ruthlessly stressed, social behavior tends to degenerate into a form of personal loyalty which is uncritical, blind, and total. Loyalty to a leader now acquires a value of its own, quite independent of what the leader really stands for. The rationality of the object to which a person remains loyal is no longer subject to a critical judgment. As long as one remains loyal, regardless of whether or not the leader and what he stands for is truly worth being loyal to, it is regarded in the society as supremely virtuous conduct.

The norms of conformity are enforced in Korean society to such an extent that political competition suffers severely. A competitive democracy too requires a degree of conformity, but of a different kind. What it requires is a broadly based commitment by the leaders and the people to a set of rules that structure an open political competition. This commitment is qualitatively different from the conformity of the type, both encompassing and substantive, which is expected of every citizen in the Korean society.

The Norms of Conflict Resolution

Unless there exists a set of legitimate rules of the game, an open competition is likely to invite ruthlessness and chaos. This is the reason why we have defined democracy earlier as an orderly process of competition. In South Korea these rules have not yet been developed well. The strong norms of conformity, in addition to their stifling effects on competition, leave no room for a set of legitimate rules for political game to evolve. One either conforms or does not conform. In the latter case, he should be fully prepared to accept a costly sanction. There is no middle ground. Therefore, there is little need to develop the rules and procedures for rational debates, settling disagreements, mutual persuasions, bargainings and negotiations. One side gets to make a decision for the collectivity if it can muscle enough power. Yielding to the other side for a compromise is not only a sign of weakness, but it is a betrayal of the trust the members of your side gave to you.

In politics, the "stakes" involved become exceedingly high because it is a winner-take-all situation (Kim, 1971: 193-206). If you win, you win everything worth having: power, prestige, and wealth. If you lose, you lose them all or an opportunity to gain them. Elsewhere, we have called such a political system the high risk system (Kim, 1970: 879-887). In the high risk system political conflicts tend to be a deadly contest, with neither side inclined to strike a compromise.

There does not seem to be anything important in the Korean culture that is conducive to the evolution of rules of compromise, bargaining, and pragmatic negotiation. On the contrary, many of the cultural elements stand ominously in the way of the development of rules of the game. The first is a pervasive and strong sense of self-righteousness, especially among politicians both "in" and "out" of power. Sometimes, one vaguely calls it an aspect of Korean authoritarian attitudes. When a person takes a political stance, he is expected to do it with an iron inflexibility. This is a virtue to keep one's *ch'ijo* or to be a man of principle. But it destroys any basis on which a bargaining atmosphere can develop. These behavioral norms intensify political polarization for which there are no ready compromised solutions. When polarized in policies, one group resolves the differences by destroying the other groups.

Systematic studies of political conflicts are scanty. From a few studies published thus far, we may draw some tentative conclusions. One significant mechanism designed to facilitate the process of bargaining and making compromises is the activities of organized interests. In one study of the attitudes of legislative members toward the lobbying activity of interest groups, it was discovered that a majority of 51 percent denied them any legitimate role in the legislative process (Woo and Kim, 1970: 238). There is not much sympathy, let alone friendly cooperation, for lobbying in the National Assembly. This antipathy implies that bargaining and making compromises run against the grain of the core values and beliefs that the legislative elites hold so dearly to their hearts.

In two recent analyses of the informal rules of the game in the National Assembly (Kim, 1985: 108-161; Kim and Park, 1985: 162-222) it has been documented that behavioral rules that exist there are all of one kind, namely the ones that enforce a hierarchy. In a marked contrast to the informal norms of the U.S. Congress in which the rules of equality and reciprocity predominate, the rules of dominance and submission are the most salient in the Korean National Assembly. The legislative arena is commonly believed to be one in which representatives with equal status compete with each other for the adoption of their preferred policies (Loewenberg and Patterson, 1979: 9). Composed of contentious politicians with equal status, a representative assembly requires a set of legitimate rules of the game far more than do any other organizations.

The most important behavioral rules of the National Assembly include: an inviolable norm of obedience to the orders of a political superior, a duty to legitimate the policy decisions already drawn up at a higher level, a norm that prohibits any statement about the topics understood to be "political taboos," the norm of *myongbun* which prescribes a unique Korean standard for any public conduct, and the rule of conflict resolution by the brute power of a hierarchy.

Despite the relentless pressure for conformity and obedience, interpersonal conflicts do arise among legislative members. When asked how they might try to resolve such conflicts, twenty-three percent of all the members interviewed replied that the Assembly provides no mechanism, that is, a set of informal norms by which conflicts can be peacefully settled. Forty-four percent expressed a view that they would seek an intervention or an arbitration by a political superior of their own faction or party. Others felt that it is altogether better to avoid any form of conflict lest it should surface in the open (Kim and Park, 1985: 198-201). Resolving conflict by an appeal to one's superior is a practice typically seen in a hierarchical organization. Avoiding conflict and suppressing it when it arises does not remove the basic sources of interpersonal hostilities. When conflicts are allowed to play themselves out in an open arena and are restrained by a set of legitimate rules, it is possible to contain the destructiveness of intense interpersonal hostilities. Otherwise, an endless play of dark and sinister undercurrents of bad feelings and hatred may persist between members, undermining the normal and efficient process of legislative activities.

Koreans are themselves acutely cognizant of the absence of such rules. At the level of partisan politics, they often counsel their politicians not to commit the sin of *"kukhan t'ujaeng,"* which translates roughly into 'a duel until one's death.' Nevertheless, the *kukhan t'ujaeng* continues between the government and its opposition, between the factions within the opposition, between the management and workers, and between the government and students. In a political culture which lacks a set of legitimate rules by which political games are peacefully played, an open and orderly process of political competition is unlikely to evolve. This is the central problem that Koreans must confront and solve if they are determined to achieve a democracy based on political competition.

Conclusion: Democracy and the Political Culture

Although democracy is a form of government which virtually every Korean citizen wants, only a fraction of them believe that South Korea is a democracy. In one public poll (K.W. Kim, 1985: 28) less than four percent of those interviewed believed democracy is now working in Korea. And an overwhelming majority believe Korea is not a democracy. Why is it that democracy is so hard to attain in the Korean society? We have examined some preconditions of democracy. More specifically, we analyzed the conditions that sustain an open and orderly process of political competition. The results of this effort are summarized in Table 1.

Table 1
Preconditions of Democracy

Conditions	Present in South Korea
Socio-economic conditions	
structural diversity & social pluralism	Yes
Institutional conditions	
democratic constitution	Yes
well-organized multiparty system	Yes
well-organized interest groups	Yes
organized press	Yes
court system staffed with professional lawyers	Yes
electoral system	Yes
Cultural conditions	
coherent belief systems	No
norms of tolerance	No
norms for open and orderly competition	No

Several crucial conditions are adequately met in South Korea. First of all, an open competition requires a degree of social diversity and complexity. As a result of the phenomenal growth in industries, education, communications, and urban culture in the last two decades, Korean society became structurally and functionally a very complex and diverse system. Socio-economic potentials for generating a healthy political competition exist aplenty. If these potentials are not satisfied through an open competition, due to the failure of democracy, they may even pose a direct threat to the stability of the system itself.

In their formal appearances at least, most of the institutional structures one would normally associate with a functioning democracy are in place. Korea has a constitutional framework which should compare favorably even with the ones of most advanced democracies in the world. A multiparty system is alive and well. The press is well developed, large and effective in what it does. There are thousands of well organized interest groups in labor, business, agriculture, professions, and constituencies. The court system, staffed by a well trained coterie of lawyers, is operating efficiently in what it does. Now Koreans plan to add to this already long list yet another democratic institution, a system of local autonomy. No one could say that Korea does not have the necessary institutions of democracy. And yet, these institutions have not produced a democratic process. Instead, they were often diverted to perform functions contrary to an open process of competition.

One crucial condition that is absent is a pattern of political culture which makes democracy workable. We discussed three cultural obstacles: the cognitive system of inconsistent beliefs, the norms of political conformity, and the lack of the rules for conflict resolution. A minimum set of conditions for an open and orderly process of political competition includes all three. Inconsistent beliefs indicate a lack of strong resolve as well as commitment to democracy. In another sense, it means that while the people want democracy, they are not willing to pay the price for it.[3]

Even with a strong commitment to democracy, an open political competition is by no means guaranteed. The culture must relax its norms of conformity or change them altogether. An excessive conformity that the Korean culture demands of its citizens stifles the process of competition. Tolerance for different beliefs and views must be developed as an integral part of the culture. To deny political diversity and pluralism is to reject the competitive democracy itself.

The single most important obstacle is the absence of legitimate rules for the political game. The one rule by which Koreans know how to play the game of politics is the "winner-take-all" rule. It tends to make competition a deadly game. Since political games involve high stakes, sometimes even life and death, they often result in unlimited and war-like contests. It is difficult to restrain the behavior of the contestants. The end results are likely to be ruleless competition, frequent political stalemates, and ruthless oppression of losers. Compromises and negotiated agreements are what make the process of political competition open and orderly. Moreover, the logic of give-and-take involved in compromised outcomes effects more equitable distribution of political goods. Losers as well as winners all partake of a share of the goods, be it power, prestige, policy, or income. There is good reason to believe that a "high risk political system" is congenitally incompatible with democracy. The stakes involved in the Korean politics are much too high, which is one of the root causes preventing the development of legitimate rules of the game.

An open and orderly process of political competition is the heart of a democratic government. To achieve democracy, it is now obvious what Koreans must do. Koreans must learn that reforms in formal institutions including a constitutional framework, however well thought through, will not accomplish the task. This is not meant to suggest however that institutional reforms are not important. It is suggested however that institutions alone do not ensure a well functioning democracy. The principal obstacles to democracy are cultural: the belief systems and behavioral norms. Until Koreans develop a coherent belief system of democracy, replace their norms of excessive conformity with those of tolerance, and establish a set of legitimate rules of the game for an open and orderly competition, democracy will remain an elusive goal.

NOTES

1. The phrase 'the failure of democracy' is descriptively inaccurate as applied to South Korea. Something which did not exist could not fail. Since 1948, a democratic rule has never been fully practiced in Korea and therefore, it does not make sense to say that democracy has failed. Rather, it is more accurate to say that democracy has failed to take root in Korea. The phrase is used in this paper to mean the latter.
2. The evolution of the idea of political democracy is long and complex, creating much confusion and many contradictions over the concept. Recently, David Held (1987) has successfully imposed some order in his insightful analysis of various theories of democracy. He has identified nine distinctive models of democracy. Although I am aware of the full complexity of the idea of democracy, I chose to adopt one of its variants, i.e., the Robert Lane formulation, for the purpose of the present analysis.
3. The question why democracy is so hard to achieve in South Korea may be approached from another perspective. The theoretical perspective of collective action problem, à la Mancur Olson (1971), offers an interesting avenue of investigation. Democracy may be considered as a kind of public goods, which once supplied no one can be excluded from enjoying. This character of public goods causes the familiar "free rider" problems. The reason Koreans are not willing

to fully bear the costs of democratic responsibility while wanting a democratic rule so badly, seemingly a contradiction, may be due to their strong temptation for getting a free ride. In a separate paper, I plan to pursue this line of theoretical exploration.

REFERENCES

Almond G., and S. Verba. 1965. *The Civic Culture*. Boston: Little, Brown and Co.

Almond G., and G.B. Powell. 1978. *Comparative Politics*. Boston: Little, Brown and Co.

Chang, Y.S., et al., ed. 1982. *Society in Transition*. Seoul, Korea: Seoul National University Press.

Converse, P.E. 1964. "The Nature of Mass Belief Systems," in David Apter, ed., *Ideology and Discontent*. New York: The Free Press.

Cutright, P. 1963. "National Political Development: Measurement and Analysis," *American Sociological Review*, 28.

Dahl, R.A. 1956. *A Preface to Democratic Theory*. Chicago: The University of Chicago Press.

Hagner, P.R., and J.C. Pierce. 1982. "Correlative Characteristics of Levels of Conceptualization in the American Public: 1956-1976," *The Journal of Politics*, 44.

Han, S.B. et al., eds., 1985. *Sahoepyondongui irongwa silje*. Seoul, Korea: Seoul National University Press.

Han, S.J. 1974. *The Failure of Democracy in South Korea*. Berkeley: University of California Press.

Held, David, 1987. *Models of Democracy*. Cambridge, UK: Polity Press.

Henderson, G. 1968. *Korea: The Politics of Vortex*. Cambridge: Harvard University Press.

Kihl, Y.W. 1984. *Politics and Policies in Divided Korea*. Boulder: Westview Press.

Kim, C.L. 1970. "Political Attitudes of Defeated Candidates in an American State Election," *American Political Science Review*, 64.

Kim, C.L. 1971. "Toward a Theory of Individual and Systemic Effects of Political Status Loss," *Journal of Developing Areas*, 4.

Kim, C.L., and B.K. Woo. 1972. "Political Representation in the Korean National Assembly," *American Journal of Political Science* (formerly *Midwest Journal of Political Science*), 16.

Kim, C.L., ed. 1980. *Political Participation in Korea: Democracy, Mobilization and Stability*. Santa Barbara, Calif.: ABC-Clio Press.

Kim, C.L., and S.T. Pai. 1981. *Legislative Process in Korea*. Seoul, Korea: Seoul National University Press.

Kim, C.L. 1985. "Uihoegwajongul kyujehanun p'ulmunyul," in Dong-suh

Park, ed., *Uihoewa ipbupgwajong*. Seoul, Korea: Bupmunsa.

Kim, C.L. and C.W. Park. 1985. "P'ulmunhaenguiyulgwa uihoegwajong: Ildae kukhoe yongu," in Dong-suh Park, ed., *Uihoewa ipbupgwajong*. Seoul, Korea: Bupmunsa.

Kim, K.S., and M. Roemer. 1979. *Growth and Structural Transformation*. Cambridge: Harvard University Press.

Kim, K.W. 1985. "Minjuuishikgwa t'upyohaengtae," a paper presented at the 6th meeting of Korean Political Scientists and Political Scientists in North America. Seoul, August 5-7, 1985.

Klingmann, H.D. 1979."The Background of Ideological Conceptualization," in S.H. Barnes and M. Kaase, eds., *Political Action: Mass Participation in Five Western Democracies*. Beverly Hills: Sage Publications.

Lane, R. 1986. "Market Justice, Political Justice," *American Political Science Review*, 80.

Lee, N.Y. 1985. "Sanophwawa ch'ongchimunhwa: minjuuishikpyonhwarul jungsimuro," *Hankuk ch'ongchihakhoebo*, 19.

Lee Y.H. 1969. The Political Culture of Modernizing Society: Political Attitudes and Democracy in Korea. Unpublished Ph.D. dissertation. Yale University.

Lipset, S.M. 1959. "Some Social Requisites of Democracy," in R.C. Macridis and B.E. Brown, eds., *Comparative Politics*. Homewood, Ill.: The Dorsey Press.

Loewenberg, G., and S.C. Patterson. 1979. *Comparing Legislatures*. Boston: Little, Brown and Co.

Mason, E.S., et al. 1980. *The Economic and Social Modernization of the Republic of Korea*. Cambridge: Harvard University Press.

Oh, J.K. 1968. *Korea: Democracy on Trial*, Ithaca, New York: Cornell University Press.

Pae, S.M. 1986. *Testing Democratic Theories in Korea*. Lanham, New York: University Press of America.

Verba, S., and N.H. Nie. 1972. *Participation in America: Political Democracy and Social Equality*. New York: Harper & Row.

Winham, G.P. 1970. "Political Development and Lerner's Theory: Further Test of a Causal Model," *American Political Science Review*, 64.

Woo, B.K., and C.L. Kim. 1970. *Hankukipbopgwajongui jemunje*. Seoul, *Korea: The National Assembly*.

Yoo, J., and L.L. Wade. 1981. "A Study on Current Political Culture: An Interpretive Perspective," *The Journal of East Asian Affairs*.

Part II
Political Institutions

4

Party Politics on the Eve of a Gathering Storm: The Constitutional Revision Politics of 1986

YOUNG WHAN KIHL

South Korea's party politics in 1986 revolved around the question of how to revise the Constitution of the Fifth Republic. The country thus stood at the crossroads of political development, confronting prospects for either democracy or authoritarianism. After many months of frustration and abortive attempts, an interparty dialogue on the political future of Korea beyond 1988 was finally restored. In June 1986 the governing Democratic Justice Party (DJP or *Minju Jongui-dang*) and the major opposition New Korea Democratic Party (NKDP or *Shin Hanguk Minju-dang*) agreed to set up a parliamentary Special Constitution Revision Committee (SCRC), with the explicit purpose of charting a new government structure that would include the method of selecting the country's next president.

The historical significance of this interparty initiative rested on the fact that the favorable outcome of the resuscitated parliamentary dialogue in 1986 would increase the chance of institutionalizing an orderly transition of power beyond 1988, the year when the incumbent president Chun Doo-hwan's tenure in office was to end. In the forty-year constitutional history of the Republic of Korea (ROK), founded on August 15, 1948, no president has ever stepped down from office voluntarily. President Chun will thus have made history, if his announced policy is carried out in February 1988. The failure of interparty negotiations on constitutional revision in 1986, on the other hand, would likewise increase the danger of radicalizing domestic politics in South Korea.

It is clear, in retrospect, that both dangers and opportunities were exploited by key political actors and groups in South Korea's party politics in 1986-87. The initial failure in 1986 to produce an interparty agreement on the new constitution, for instance, was turned into a political "miracle," the successful "grand compromise" attained by the ruling and opposition party leaders in 1987. To provide some background for South Korea's political crisis in the summer of 1987 this chapter examines the dynamics of party politics in 1986, subsequent to the February 1985 National Assembly election, on the eve of a gathering political storm in the summer of 1987.

Weak Legitimacy and Strong State

The root cause of political instability in South Korea throughout the 1980s was the weak legitimacy of the regime of President Chun Doo-hwan going back to the very beginning, the founding of a new authoritarian political order in 1980.[1] South Korea's Fifth Republic under President Chun Doo-hwan's rule was established by the military coup led by then Major General Chun Doo-hwan on May 17, 1980. From its inception, therefore, Chun's regime was marred by the question of doubtful political legitimacy.

What aggravated the situation further was the bloody suppression of Kwangju riots by Chun's Special Forces. The Kwangju uprising, lasting from May 18 to May 27, 1980, began as a popular protest movement against the proclamation of a nationwide martial law. It was led initially by the militant university students at Chonnam National University but they were subsequently joined by the concerned citizenry in Kwangju. As the fourth largest city, with a population close to one million, Kwangju was the provincial capital of South Cholla Province which, in turn, was the home province of dissident politician Kim Dae-jung.

The forceful suppression of the city of Kwangju resulted in 191 dead and a few thousand wounded, although an eye witness account put the figure much higher. This Kwangju episode of 1980 left a deep scar on, and schism in, South Korea's body politics. The political symbol of Kwangju was identified with an anti-regime political protest and was said to be a political albatross hung around the neck of President Chun.[2]

In spite of weak legitimacy from the very outset, Korea's Fifth Republic under President Chun enjoyed the popular expectation and residue of a broad support for the promise of socio-economic progress.

Most Koreans in 1980 seemed to welcome the end of political uncertainty, following the assassination of President Park Chung-hee on October 26, 1979, and looked forward to the resumption of political stability and rapid economic growth. In 1980, after nearly two decades of continuous rapid economic growth, South Korea registered a negative growth rate of -5.2 percent in GNP, for the first time. This was no doubt affected by the worldwide economic recession abroad and the widespread domestic violence and political turmoil.

Both liabilities and accomplishments were clearly identified with regard to Korea's Fifth Republic under President Chun's rule. Part of the negative legacy of President Chun's authoritarian rule included political repression of the student activists, suppression of the opposition forces, the exclusion of organized labor, denial of the free press, and a poor record on the human rights front.

On the more positive side, however, the state "autonomy and capacity" continued to be strong in South Korea's Fifth Republic. Even if the legitimacy of the regime was weak and questionable, the state capacity had grown and expanded in several crucial and important areas. The Chun Doo-hwan regime had managed to restore and sustain the dynamic growth of the economy, to strengthen the security through an increased alliance partnership with the United States and Japan, and to resume the inter-Korean negotiation and dialogue on unification.

The political recipe of Chun's rule in 1986, anticipating an orderly transfer of power in 1988, consisted of a program of revitalizing party politics through strengthening the ruling Democratic Justice Party, which he served as party president. His subsequent strategy was to promote interparty dialogue with the major opposition New Korea Democratic Party on the matter of revising the constitution, which he hoped would be put into referendum in 1987, and would be followed by an anticipated general election either in late 1987 or in early 1988. From the vantage point of Chun Doo-hwan in the summer of 1986, the process of South Korea's party politics had finally become revitalized and lively, because the arena of politics was shifted from confrontation outside the parliament to interparty negotiation within the National Assembly.

Electoral Contests in Bureaucratic Authoritarianism

The Fifth Republic began with a military coup d'état, and the regime subsequently became civilianized through the sponsoring of popular elections and the coopting of civilian bureaucracy and technocracy into the ruling coalition. In this sense, "bureaucratic authoritarianism" best approximates the character of South Korea's Fifth Republic since 1980.[3]

The constitution of the Fifth Republic was approved by a national referendum on October 22, 1980, but the writing of the constitution and the referendum took place under conditions of national emergency and extended martial law, proclaimed by the military regime on May 17, 1980. The junta-like body—the Special Committee for National Security Measures and the 31-member Military Civilian Standing Committee led by Lt. General Chun Doo-hwan—acted as the decision-making body soon after the coup of May.

The 81-member Legislative Council of National Security, appointed by Chun Doo-hwan once he became president, in turn, acted as an interim legislative body empowered to enact various important bills, including the election law. The legislative council produced 226 pieces of legislation in 156 days including the National Security Law, the laws governing the press, laws governing assembly and demonstrations, and laws governing the labor unions.

Chun Doo-hwan was inaugurated as president of the Fifth Republic on March 3, 1981 to serve a seven-year term. He was elected president by a 5000 member electoral college that, in turn, was chosen by popular and direct election. Two general elections took place to select the members of the National Assembly: the 11th National Assembly on March 25, 1981, and the 12th National Assembly on February 12, 1985. Of these two popular elections, the

1985 National Assembly election was more competitive, open, and fair. More importantly, the February 1985 general election provided a turning point in the recent political development of South Korea.

The electoral law enacted in 1980 stipulated a medium-sized electoral district system whereby each of the 92 districts would send two representatives to the National Assembly, totalling 184 elected members of parliament. The remaining one-third of the 276 member seats, that is 92 seats, would be allocated proportionately to political parties: the other two-thirds of these to be assigned to the party that has won the most seats in the direct election. The legislative intent here was to fashion a working majority for the ruling party.

The governing DJP, through manipulation of the electoral laws, managed to control the majority of seats in the National Assembly in the February 1985 election. As the party winning the largest number of seats in parliament, it received additional plurality seats of at-large members. But its party strength was eroded as a result of the emergence of the NKDP as the first major opposition party in parliament.

The DJP received only 35 percent of the popular vote in the general election, but managed to control a total of 148 seats (54 percent) of the 276 member National Assembly. The first opposition NKDP, although established only one month prior to the general election, was able to win 29 percent of the total popular vote and 67 seats in the National Assembly, followed by a second opposition People's Korea Party (Minhan-dang), which received a total of 35 seats in the National Assembly.

The subsequent merging of these two opposition parties soon after the general election produced a formidable NKDP with 102 seats (37 percent) in the National Assembly, denying the governing party the two-thirds majority in parliament. The February 1985 election, in short, legitimized the NKDP as the major opposition party and polarized interparty relations between the governing and the opposition parties.[4]

Fresh from their impressive electoral victory, the NKDP leadership pressed political reform measures which were crystallized in their demands for revising the constitution to enable direct popular election of the next president. The DJP and President Chun resisted the opposition pressure by refusing—until May 1986—to engage in dialogue on the constitutional revision. Frustrated by its inability to conduct parliamentary debates on the new constitution, the NKDP decided to boycott the National assembly sessions and to rely on extra-parliamentary tactics to pressure the government party.

Radicalization of Party Movements

Prior to the 1987 grand compromise on "democratic reform" measures, interparty wranglings assumed the confrontational style and posture of politics. The NKDP decided to mobilize popular support—fresh out of the major electoral victory in February 1985—by launching a nationwide campaign to obtain ten million signatures for the constitutional revision by the end of 1986. This would allow for the direct election of the president.

This confrontational approach led to the worsening of the political situation and a serious undermining of political stability. The student movement to restore democracy became radicalized with the organization of antigovernment protests and violent street demonstrations. It also took the form of anti-Americanism because of U.S. support of the Chun government. The Chun government in turn, insisted that some radical student groups were revolutionary and communist sympathizers.

Throughout the first few months of 1986 a series of violent demonstrations were waged in the major cities and provincial capitals. These events were perhaps fueled by the well-timed NKDP mass rallies. One such rally was held in Inchon, provincial capital of the Kyonggi Province, on May 3, 1986. This turned into a riot of large-scale violence and destruction. The rioters directed their anger not only against the government and the DJP—by setting fire to the party headquarters and properties—but, more importantly, against the NKDP. The radical elements of the Inchon rally were accusing the NKDP leadership of betrayal of the democratic cause and collusion with the Chun dictatorship.

The heightened political tension created by the opposition movement was further fueled by a series of developments within and outside Korea. The fall of the Ferdinand Marcos regime and the rise of the Corazon Aquino government in the Philippines gave the opposition movement in Korea a ground for hope that a similar grassroots movement could grow in Korea to oust the Chun government. But the U.S. government refused to draw an analogy between the conditions in the Philippines and those in South Korea, thereby strongly dissuading the NKDP from pursuing such a risky strategy.

The student movements for democracy and demonstrations against the government grew out of hand. Three Seoul National University students, on two separate occasions, burned themselves to death during campus demonstrations calling for democracy. The U.S. Secretary of State, George Shultz, paid a brief visit to Seoul in early May of 1986 and made an unexpected statement that praised the efforts of the Chun government to bring about peaceful political change instead of admonishing the Chun government as the opposition leaders desired. The president of the NKDP, Lee Min-woo, visited the U.S. at the end of May 1986 to converse with and seek the support of U.S. congressional leaders for his party's campaigns for democracy in Korea. Suddenly though, in the midst of the heightened tension, the political atmosphere in Korea began to thaw at the end of May 1986, coinciding with the return of Lee from the United States.

Building an Interparty Consensus on Constitutional Revision

Following a series of meetings held in early June of 1986 between President Chun and each of the two opposition party leaders, a consensus emerged on a way to overcome the political crisis. The DJP yielded to the NKDP demand for the creation of a basic law-revision committee in the National Assembly. The 45-member Special Constitution Revision Committee was set up in the National Assembly, to be led by a ruling party member as chair, but divided equally between the ruling and opposition parties in parliament. Under this formula the membership consisted of twenty-three from the DJP, seventeen from the NKDP, four from the second opposition Korea National Party (KNP), and one from the independents.[5]

On the substantive issues of how to revise the constitution, however, the fragile interparty consensus would naturally break down, unless a quid-pro-quo solution were attained. The ruling DJP was seeking a cabinet-responsible parliamentary form of government, while the NKDP subscribed to a presidential form of government based on direct popular election. The Fifth Republic constitution, of course, was based on the presidential government system and the power was concentrated in the executive branch, with a weak legislature and a subordinate judiciary, with the president chosen indirectly by an electoral college.

It is ironic that the positions of the ruling and opposition parties on constitutional revision were sharply in contrast with their earlier stands. Historically, the minority parties in Korea tended to support the cabinet form of government and the ruling majority party the presidential form of government. During the First Republic (1948-1960) the ruling Liberal Party adopted the constitutional amendment that brought about a presidential form of government, while during the Second Republic (1960-61) the Democratic Party, as the predecessor of the subsequent NKDP, had an opportunity to put the parliamentary system into effect. During the Third and Fourth Republics (1961-79) the presidential form of government was enshrined in the constitution, while the opposition held its preference for the cabinet system of government. But in 1986 the positions of the respective parties on the structure of government were completely reversed from their earlier historical stands.

It is also ironic that the DJP, in criticizing the NKDP's demand, argued that a direct election of the president would undermine "our genuine democratic process and long-term national development" and that the presidential system would bring about "a cleavage of national consensus, political corruption and turmoil, and a waste of national powers.[6]

In supporting the cabinet form of government the DJP pointed out that a "presidential government is mostly adopted by underdeveloped countries with dictatorial regimes." It also claimed that, although France was one of the advanced countries with direct popular voting for president, the French system was really "dual executive government" with the president and the prime minister occasionally coming from different political parties.[7]

The NKDP insisted that presidential government with a direct election system was the way that would most faithfully guarantee the people a free choice of government.[8] The opposition KNP also pursued presidential government under a direct election system, although it indicated a willingness to compromise in favor of a parliamentary system.[9]

In spite of these pronounced official policy stands, the real intention of the respective parties on constitutional revision might have been the opposite. At least some factions of the NKDP were rumored to favor the cabinet form of government, while the DJP wished to retain a presidential form of government, if the party would have its way. Opposition party leaders such as Kim Dae-jung and Kim Young-sam were in favor of the direct election of the president because they believed they would have a good chance of election, but their position could change if the tide of political fortune would turn against them.

One possible outcome of the interparty negotiation on the constitutional revision, from a theoretical standpoint, would be a compromised settlement in substance if not in appearance. Such a compromise that reflects rational calculation might include a system that attempts to combine some features of both presidential and parliamentary cabinet forms of government. This "rational-choice" model might be called a system of dual executives, as explained below.

The reason this scenario for a rational solution would emerge is based on both reality and logic. The incentive structure of both ruling and opposition parties in regard to the constitutional amendment question was naturally varied. Whereas the ruling party wished to avoid a political crisis and deadlock as much as possible, the opposition party was attempting to escalate the political crisis and force a showdown with the government party on matters of constitutional revision. From the logical standpoint, there is also a limit to what the formal government is able to accomplish and, indeed, neither a presidential nor a parliamentary system, if adopted, will guarantee genuine democracy in Korea. It is, more importantly, the willingness to practice democracy irrespective of the governmental forms that matters, and this attitudinal change must precede any institutional experimentation.

The Logic of the Dual-Rule System

The system of dual executive rule proposes to divide administrative authority during peaceful times. Under this system, the president would exercise power over security and diplomacy, while the prime minister would have power over matters of general administration. During a crisis, however, the president will assume emergency powers. Austria and Finland are representative examples of such a dual-rule structure of government.

Although it is referred to as a decentralized form of government, it is more accurate to characterize the dual-rule structure as a system of unified power during the process of its implementation. In a country like South Korea, where the security threat from North Korea is often invoked, this system is likely to strengthen and perpetuate the presidential power at the expense of the prime minister's administrative power.

The president under this system will be elected directly by the populace, although he may also be chosen indirectly by an electoral college. The president will appoint the premier, subject to approval by the National Assembly. The unique feature of this system is that the president is not responsible to the National Assembly. The National Assembly and the cabinet are also mutually checked and balanced because they can exercise a vote of no confidence against each other.[10]

This system of dual-rule government, or any variation of it, was considered a reasonable and feasible compromise for both ruling and opposition parties. In fact, there were foreign speculations that the dual-rule system could eventually become a viable and workable alternative open to the SCCR for its possible adoption.[11]

Like any rational plan calling for mutual compromise, the dual-rule system would present some practical difficulties to both ruling and opposition party leaders. And, for this reason, the plan was not adopted by those responsible for the settlement. Since the dual-rule system was less than what each political party desired, its adoption would present a dilemma to the respective political parties. Both DJP and NKDP, if this system were accepted, would naturally want to capture both presidency and premiership in the elections. Barring such a possibility of sweeping both offices in the election, however, they would want to share power with the rival party by capturing at least one of the two offices, either presidency or premiership.

The dilemma for the ruling party was that it might be forced to relinquish full control of the government. Anticipating possible defeat in the next presidential election, however, the DJP wanted at least to capture the premiership of the government. In order to gain sufficient experience prior to the forthcoming election, it was rumored that an anticipated cabinet reshuffle in August 1986 might very well involve a large number of DJP leaders, including the possibility of the then party chairman, Roh Tae-woo, serving as the next prime minister. Roh, as a classmate of Chun's at the military academy, played a key role in Chun's rise to power on December 12, 1979, and was widely viewed as Chun's preferred political successor.

The dilemma for the opposition parties in accepting the compromise solution of a dual-rule government was equally difficult to reconcile. There was always the possibility of internal discord over the compromise, in view of the incessant factional tendencies within the NKDP. The opposition parties' inability to use the restoration of democracy as the principal weapon against the regime in power would be condemned by some party faithful and ideologues as a betrayal to the cause of the opposition movement. The radical elements of the opposition forces would especially be alienated from the movement for restoring democracy which, in turn, would significantly reduce the level of grassroots support.

The Prospects for Democracy in South Korea

South Korea's political development in 1985-86 was directly related to the results of the February 1985 parliamentary election. The more conciliatory stance of the Chun government on the question of constitutional revision was largely influenced by the outcome of the electoral contests and demonstrated the surprising strength of the NKDP. Leaders of both ruling and opposition parties failed, however, to subsequently resolve the political deadlock and impasse in the Fifth Republic in the form of charting a new course for democracy in South Korea.

The real test of "democratic" political development in South Korea was the question of how to harmonize the contending political forces of the ruling coalition and the opposition movements, while at the same time promoting the general interest and welfare of the growing number of middle class citizens. As the pace of industrialization and urbanization accelerates, South Korea is turning increasingly into a complex, pluralistic society where competing group and sectional interests are vying for influence and power. Under these circumstances, both ruling and opposition party leaders were urged by the middle class to fashion a workable and efficient system of government, whereby the creative energy of the working population in Korea could be channelled positively, rather than negatively, as in the wasted form of the radical anti-system revolutionary movement.

From the militants' standpoint, the political debates over constitutional reform (including direct or indirect presidential elections) were immaterial and "quite beside the point."[12] They were concerned with more salient policy issues, such as the widening urban-rural gap, the regional imbalance in distribution, the relative poverty of farmers and slum dwellers, the slow rise in industrial wages, and the reunification of the nation. U.S. pressure on Korea to make concessions on trade negotiations and the opening of the Korean market for U.S. products, including agricultural commodities, while threatening to legislate protectionist measures at home against the Korean products, was interpreted by the Korean youths as an unfriendly discriminatory act against an ally. These economic pressures fuel anti-American sentiment among the radical university students in Korea.

The radical reformers were pressuring both the ruling and opposition parties to begin to take measures to rectify these problems of socio-economic inequity arising from the rapid pace of industrialization. Their patience and confidence with the regime were running out. They were openly preaching for a revolution based on the Minjung ideology, that is, a government founded on the interests of the workers and peasants.[13] At the time of the May 1986 Inchon riots, U.S.-educated Reverend Moon Ik-hwan, as chairman of the so-called *Mint'ong* noted approvingly the radical students' demands for the ouster of the U.S. military and economic presence in Korea.[14]

Mint'ong or *Mint'ongnyon* stands for "People's Movement for Democracy and Unification" in Korean. This grassroots organization, of which Reverend Moon Ik-hwan served as chairman, comprised twenty-three separate organizations representing a variety of umbrella groups that included dissident writers and artists, professors and students, workers and farmers, Buddhist, Protestant and Roman Catholic groups as well as women's groups. The police were not able to destroy Mint'ong because survivors of government crackdowns on its component parts would resurrect their groups and new recruits would replace members arrested and imprisoned. Two radical student groups, *Minmint'u* and *Chamint'u*, were well organized and also operated underground. Even if their number was small, only one or two percent of the entire university student population of 1.2 million, the radical students were unashamedly leftist in ideology and openly anti-American and sympathetic with North Korea.

What concerned the ruling elites in South Korea in 1986 was the successful hosting of the 1988 Summer Olympics in Seoul, after the successful 1986 Asian Games also hosted in Seoul. The image of South Korea's political instability, and the prospect of North Korean sponsored terrorism disrupting the sporting events, would not help the cause. The determined efforts of the Chun government to assure peace and security for sports festivals would act to restrict any excessive measures on the part of the regime of President Chun.

In the larger sense, however, the reconciliation of the rival interests must be worked out between the radical and the conservative groups in the Korean society. Political impasse, due to competing interests and demands, remains an unresolved dilemma and challenge for the government and opposition party leaders. The civilian politicians of both governing and opposition parties were, unfortunately, sandwiched between the radical student reformers on the Left and the conservative military faction on the Right.

The incessant demands by the radical university students, clergy, and intellectuals for democratization, together with dissident opposition leaders, including Kim Dae-jung, would trigger strong, anticipated reaction by the nationalist-minded faction of the young officers within the military. The latter group would insist upon harsher repressive measures as a response to the mounting pressure of the radical reformers. When and if the rightist reaction materializes—in the form of political intervention by the military faction—the timetable for democratization of South Korea will have been delayed, and the Korean people will have suffered another round of political setbacks and tragedies on their march toward, and their yearning for, democracy in South Korea.

Conclusion

Time was running out for both ruling and opposition party leaders to fashion Korea's political future with the fragile political consensus attained in the early summer of 1986. The parliamentary Special Constitution Revision Committee was constituted in July 1986 but would expire by the end of 1986, in accordance with the terms of a prior agreement. If no interparty agreement on the new form of political structure was agreed upon by then, the political situation in South Korea would once again be thrown into turmoil and chaos. In fact, this was precisely what took place in the spring and summer of 1987. North Korea's endeavor to profit from political instability in the south, by launching propaganda and peace offensives, would also complicate the issue further and make its resolution that much more difficult, thereby enhancing tensions and increasing the danger of war on the Korean peninsula.

The political situation of South Korea's party politics and the peoples' campaign for restoring democracy may now be placed in their proper historical perspective. The Korean people clearly deserve greater respect and better treatment from their political leaders during the difficult time of democratization of Korean society. As South Korea has moved forward economically—emerging as one of East Asia's successful newly industrializing countries (NICs)—the country must also move forward politically. By establishing democracy the Korean people can look forward to building a brighter and more prosperous country for tomorrow, thereby eventually joining the ranks of the advanced industrialized and democratic countries in the West. The time is ripe for South Korea's advance along the path of democratic political development.

Postscript

Since this essay was written in July 1986, a number of surprising developments occurred in South Korea's political landscape, moving the process of "democratic reform" forward. The parliamentary SCRC became ineffective, as anticipated, with the failure of an interparty dialogue and negotiation to produce any meaningful compromise—especially on matters of the form of government and the method of choosing the next president. The antigovernment student demonstrations continued on campuses and in the streets throughout the academic year of 1986-87. The violent confrontation between the combat police with tear-gas canisters and university students armed with rocks and molotov cocktails was a familiar scene in South Korea's political landscape throughout 1986-87.

The NKDP, at the same time, was experiencing internal factional strife over the question of party hegemony between the moderates represented by party president Lee Min-woo and the hardliners who sided with the position of two party advisors, Kim Young-sam and Kim Dae-jung. Disagreeing with NKDP president Lee's stand on the possible compromise with the ruling DJP on the question of direct presidential election, the hardliners eventually withdrew from the party to form a separate political party. The Reunification and Democratic Party (RDP) was set up early in April 1987 and Kim Young-sam was elected as its president.

Sensing the futility of efforts to realize a compromise settlement on the constitutional amendment through the SCRC, President Chun and his DJP announced, on April 10, 1987, the suspension of the interparty dialogue and the postponement of the constitutional amendment until after the 1988 Seoul Olympics in 1989. The DJP also held a party convention on June 10, 1987, to nominate Roh Tae-woo as party president and also as presidential candidate for the subsequent national election, presumably under the existing Constitution and election laws of the Fifth Republic. This unilateral measure by the ruling party angered many opposition politicians and concerned middle class citizens. The radical students and opposition forces used the occasion to launch a massive anti-government demonstration in Seoul which led to a well-coordinated, large-scale nationwide protest movement. The National Coalition for a Democratic Constitution emerged as an umbrella organ to coordinate activities of the various political organizations and groups during the 1986-87 mass campaigns against the Chun regime.

The political crisis of June 1987 triggered by the massive student demonstrations also faced labor and industrial unrest caused by the demands for higher wages and the right to collective bargaining throughout the country. Chapter one of this volume recounts the story of an escalated confrontation between the government forces of combat police and the militant university students and the following announcement by the ruling party and the government of the acceptance of opposition demands for political reform.

Suffice it to say that the dynamics of the 1986 interparty struggle, in the form of the controversy over the constitutional revision issue, provided the context within which the subsequent "grand compromise" of August 1987 would be worked out. In this sense the constitutional revision politics of 1986, as detailed in the present chapter, was a prelude to the 1987 political crisis. The 1986 constitutional revision politics served as a bellwether of things to come and as a useful forecast of the gathering political storm forming over South Korea in 1987.

NOTES

1. Young Whan Kihl, "Korea's Fifth Republic: Domestic Political Trends," *Journal of Northeast Asian Studies* Volume I, No. 2 (June 1982), pp. 37-56.
2. The events of the Kwangju uprising are vividly described in Hwang Suk-yong, ed., Jukomul Nomoso Sidaeui Odumul Nomoso (Crossing over Death, Crossing over the Darkness of Time) (Seoul: P'ulbit, 1985).
3. See: Young Whan Kihl, *Politics and Policies in Divided Korea: Regimes in Contest* (Boulder, Co.: Westview Press, 1984), chapter 4 and especially pp. 101-104. Also, see: Kim, Yong-myong, *Chaesamsaegeui Gunbut'ongch'iwa Chongch'i Kyongje* (Third World Military Rule and Political Economy) (Seoul: Hanul, 1985).
4. For a perceptive analysis of the February 1985 National Assembly election in South Korea, see: B.C. Koh, "The 1985 Parliamentary Election in South Korea," *Asian Survey* Vol. 25, No. 9 (September 1985), pp. 883-897.
5. *Korea Herald,* July 10, 1986.
6. *Korea Herald,* July 2, 1986, p. 3.
7. *Ibid.*
8. *Korea Herald,* June 10, 1986.
9. *Korea Herald,* July 17, 1986.
10. On the discussion of a variety of democratic forms of government now in existence, see: Arend Lijiphart, *Democracies: Patterns of Majoritarian and Consensus Government in Twenty-One Countries* (New Haven: Yale University Press, 1984).
11. *Sankei Shimbun* (Tokyo), July 15, 1986.
12. *The Far Eastern Economic Review* (Hong Kong), July 10, 1986, pp. 36-41.
13. Minjung stands for the "masses" in Korean.
14. *The Far Eastern Economic Review* July 10, 1986.

5

The South Korean Military and Its Political Role

C. I. EUGENE KIM

Introduction

In August of 1986, a mood of optimism and euphoria appeared to be afloat in South Korea, in spite of deep national concern with unceasing student activism and increasing radicalization. Both the ruling and opposition parties had agreed to work on a new constitution, the sixth since South Korea became an independent republic in 1948. According to the *Korea Herald*, "The unanimous passage of a resolution (by the National Assembly) on the formation of the Special Constitution Revision Committee on Tuesday (June 24, 1986) testified to the viability of the current mood for 'grand compromise.' "[1] To cite further from the same paper:

- Some political observers interpreted the passage as a valuable opportunity to replace politics of confrontation and conflict with politics of compromise and harmony.
- Other political observers hailed it as the starting point for working out a compromise bill for constitutional reform for the first time in the nation's history.
- The majority of the people are excited at the prospect of having a

new constitution in the near future.

- Well aware of the people's aspirations for democracy, rival political parties are fully poised to initiate the historical work of rewriting the present basic law.[2]

The concept of the so-called "Grand Compromise" is indeed an extraordinary development. The party in power had agreed with opposition forces to rewrite the constitution in order to bring about a peaceful transfer of power when the term of the incumbent President Chun Doo-hwan expires in 1988. This paper is an attempt to analyze these events within South Korea and to discuss the role (potential and possible) of the military in South Korean politics. Such roles have been historically decisive since President Chun came into power through a military coup, as did the late President Park before him.

The Rise of the South Korean Military to Power

As early as 1962, S.M. Finer pointed out:

> The Armed Forces have three massive political advantages over civilian organization: a marked superiority in organization, a highly emotional symbolic status, and a monopoly of arms. They form a prestigious corporation or order, enjoying overwhelming superiority in means of applying force. The wonder, therefore, is not why it rebels against its civilian masters, but why it ever obeys them.[3]

True to Finer's assessment, as well as to others, Eric Nordlinger stated in 1977 that more than two-thirds of the countries of Latin America, Asia, and Africa have experienced varying levels of military intervention since 1945.[4] Furthermore, according to Kenneth Fidel, "In the 1970's, that list is being continually lengthened as hardly a month goes by without new reports of coups or military discontent and unrest having the potential for culminating in revolt."[5] Indeed, as Ferrel Heady has concluded: "One of the most dramatic of recent political phenomena has been the spread, on almost a global basis, of regimes in which the military bureaucracy is dominant, nearly always in close association with the civil bureaucracy." [6] According to Irving Louis Horowitz, James M. Malloy and others, military authoritarianism in the Third World has become a new political modality that has been able to endure in the face of many developmental crises and has been able to carry out planned socio-economic changes.[7]

Korea was liberated by the Allied Powers in the wake of World War II, but its liberation was followed by the establishment of the two zones of occupation along the 38th parallel, North Korea and South Korea, each respectively occupied by the Red Army of the Soviet Union and American troops. The immediate purpose of these Allied occupations was to disarm Japanese troops still stationed in Korea, but the two occupation authorities failed to establish a unified government for all of Korea as they had promised during the war. Instead, in 1948 they sponsored the establishment of two separate governments—the Democratic People's Republic of Korea in the North and the Republic of Korea in the South.

The misfortune of the Korean people following their liberation in 1945 did not stop here. As often recounted, the North and South Koreans were soon engulfed in an internecine war. North Korean forces waged a massive attack on South Korea in June 1950, ostensibly to reunify the country by force. During the initial weeks of the war, South Korea was rendered defenseless when their frontline forces were quickly overrun by North Korean forces equipped with Soviet-made tanks and heavy artillery pieces. Seoul was captured within a week and North Korean forces were quickly penetrating further to the south. The North Korean technical advantage from Soviet equipment had opened a South Korean window of vulnerability ripe for exploitation. North Korea's plan was to wage a blitzkrieg, overrun South Korea, and establish its occupation and control there as a *fait accompli* before any intervention by a foreign power. Branding North Korea an aggressor, however, the United States and other members of the United Nations soon came to the aid of South Korea and effectively raised the stakes to a regional conflict with global implications.

By the time of the Korean War, South Korea had only about 100,000 men serving in the military. The Korean War, however, soon mobilized the whole South Korean society. All the available, able-bodied young men were hurriedly inducted into the service. The United States became the major contributor to this rapid military buildup. Furthermore, since the war ended in truce, South Korea, though assisted by the Untied States, was obligated to maintain an oversized armed forces.[8] (From the beginning of the war, South Korea's armed forces were placed under the operational control of UN forces, but in 1978 they were placed under the control of the Combined Forces Command of the United States and the Republic of Korea). American military aid to South Korea from 1950 to 1979 (grant-in-aid, excess defense articles, foreign military sale credits, and military education and training) amounted to nearly $6 billion. Moreover, the concern for eventual U.S. troop withdrawal from South Korea in recent years has led the South Korean government to undertake a large-scale modernization program of the defense establishment (the Force Improvement Plan). The first five-year improvement plan in the 1970s amounted to $5 billion, which was jointly funded by the United States and South Korea. The American share amounted to $1.5 billion.

The rapid growth of the South Korean military during and after the Korean War was due largely to American military aid and investment. The primary purpose of this American involvement was military preparedness against any North Korean aggression. No consideration was given to the social, political, and economic impacts which would spur an independent growth of the South Korean military apart from the rest of the society.[9] In addition, where there is no modern tradition for well established civilian and military boundaries and where the country was experiencing a rapid process of transition, the American orientation of military professionalism and political neutrality became unsustainable. By the same token, given the stability engendered by enormous power and resources, the military has been increasingly courted by political leaders for support, and has itself become drawn into the whirlwind of South Korea's highly volatile political environment.[10]

President Syngman Rhee had been able to control much of South Korea's increasingly powerful military establishment through his personal charisma. As a life-long nationalist fighting against Japanese colonialism, father of the independent republic of South Korea, and as an uncompromising anti-communist, the charismatic Rhee provided a necessary exemplar and counterweight to institutional militarism. Given the military's independent power and resources, however, Rhee remained fearful of its potential alienation and the resulting loss of control; he tried to maintain allegiance and control not only through a policy of personal favoritism but also through the skillful manipulation of factional fighting within the military. Historically, various factions can be identified as active within the South Korean armed forces. The different services have developed their own *esprit de corps* and priorities. The army, largest in size and the most powerful, has fragmented power centers with the different social backgrounds constituting the bases of factional grouping. A primary and intimate means of communication still governs the Korean pattern of interaction. Groups are formed on the basis of family relations and on the similarity of geographical and educational backgrounds. These groups are seldom formal and institutionalized groups; they operate informally, on the bases of acquaintances, friends, and relatives, and are governed by mutual trust and by an abiding sense of mutual help and obligation. The members of these groups get together frequently and exercise great power and influence.

President Rhee promoted key high-ranking military officers on the basis of personal favor. To maintain surveillance on his favorites, he utilized the Joint Military Provost Marshall (JMPM), which was created within the Department of National Defense in March 1953 with jurisdiction over all military branches and civilians. Also created within the military was the Counter-Intelligence Corps (CIC). These allegiance enforcing mechanisms proved inadequate when, in the wake of massive student uprisings in April 1960, the military deserted him, and the soldiers, enforcing martial law, refused to fire on the demonstrating students. The soldiers were then heroes. President Rhee was forced to resign, and subsequently his government of the First Republic of Korea collapsed.[11]

The Second Republic under Prime Minister Chang Myon (1960-61) followed. This well-intended and democratic Republic, however, was too unstable and ideologically fragmented.[12] Demonstrations by students continued to produce more frequent and greater demands. North Korea's menace was ever present. The national economy stayed heavily depressed with an annual per capita income of about $100. Within this atmosphere, a military coup was planned in earnest and systematically by General Park Chung-hee (Pak, Chong-hui, Brigadier General at the time) and followers led by Kim Jong-pil (Kim, Chong-p'il) and the sympathetic cohorts of the 8th Korean Military Academy class.

The 1961 Coup and Military-Civilian Coalition

The coup took place on May 16, 1961.[13] It was not unexpected: rumors were plentiful and many felt it was coming. The Second Republic of South Korea was unstable and had an unsure future. By then, as discussed previously, the military had become a powerful political force with coherent resources unmatched by civilian politicians and organizations. A successful military coup, however, needs more than the failure of a civilian government to sustain itself. Like a good Aristotelian drama, it has to accommodate many other elements, perhaps most importantly good actors. It also has special requirements in the elements of time and place. Furthermore, the failure of a coup in many instances means loss of life for the planners. It requires suicidal dedication from the participants. It must be well planned and executed. It seems, therefore, that the failure of a civilian government to sustain itself is one thing, but to wage a successful coup is quite another. The military has within it those who are capable of waging a coup and those who are not. A study of the social characteristics of the 1961 coup leaders in South Korea has shown that they maintained high indices of political socialization.[14] They had more civilian education than other military leaders. As pointed out by Morris Janowitz, they are often in extensive daily contact with civilians in their familial cultural context—particularly with their families and their old school mates—and they show definite political orientations.[15] In addition, they are strongly success-minded. Their perception of the military profession is opportunistic and non-traditional, and they choose a military career from among many other occupational alternatives as the best route for their personal success. They also feel superior to faltering civilian politicians and show their contempt for them. It was this group of young military officers in South Korea who successfully staged the coup in May 1961.

That coup was almost bloodless. Its leaders, however, realized that they were inadequately qualified to govern the country by themselves.[16] Another significant dimension lay in the fact that the coup was planned by a handful of junior officers who at the outset had no wide support within the elite military circles.[17]

Indeed, there were rumors of counter-coups during the critical few days following the initial act. Popular acceptance of the coup was also mixed.[18] The people accepted the coup as a necessary treatment for the country's deteriorating condition—a treatment announced as only a temporary remedy, not as a permanent cure.[19] Once the coup had been achieved, however, the junta leaders began to consolidate their power. They brought many senior officers into the junta government and recruited civilian and academic professionals *en masse* as advisers and councilors. The Korean CIA was quickly organized as an intelligence agency to counter any anti-revolutionary movements. To prove their worth, moreover, the junta leaders instituted many purification and austerity moves. The first Five-Year Plan in the history of the Republic was instituted during the junta period.

For slightly more than two years, the junta government ruled the country with a strong hand. The constitution was abolished; the legislature and political parties were barred. Numerous politicians were purged, blacklisted, and silenced. No demonstrations were permitted. This junta government ended in December 1963, when the Third Republic of Korea was created.

The junta's decision to return the government to civilian hands came early after their assumption of power. In their initial public pledges after the coup, the junta leaders found it expedient to promise reconstitution of a civilian government when their objectives were realized. The forces opposing their continued monopoly of power were too great to ignore or to allow to coalesce around such an issue. As an obviously unconstitutional, illegitimate assumption of power, the coup could be justified only as a transitional measure for correcting malpractices of the existing civilian regime. And only by thus declaring their government's transitory nature could the junta leaders generate support from the rest of the country's powerful armed forces and from the general populace.

The position of the United States in this situation also played a critical role. In planning and executing their action, the coup leaders were careful not to alienate the U.S. government, which has maintained a controlling influence in Korean affairs since the end of World War II. But the first reactions to the coup by U.S. authorities in Korea left the coup leaders in considerable uncertainty. The U.S. government was opposed to a military government in Korea. When it was finally forced to recognize the *fait accompli*, it did so while reiterating "the strong intent of the military leaders in Korea to return the government to civilian hands." [20]

In reconstituting a civilian government, the close alliance between coup leaders and intellectuals in legal and social science fields was revealed in the framing of the third republican constitution. Such an alliance also prevailed in the building of a political party—The Democratic-Republican Party (DRP)—as an instrument to recruit personnel into the new civilian government. The idea for this new political party, for instance, came from J.P. Kim, director of the KCIA and the number-two man in the junta lineup. However, the detailed plans for the new party were drawn up by several university professors and politicians picked by Kim. One day, according to an informant, Kim approached his secret brain trust with a question which had concerned junta leaders for some time. If civilian rule were restored, what would happen to General Park and others in the junta government? Further, who would man the new civilian government and carry out the junta's programs? The attempt to answer these questions was the effort that culminated in the formation of a new political party— one through which the junta leaders could control the new civilian government.[21]

Several alternatives were apparently considered for the future status of the junta leaders in the event of a civilian government's restoration. The junta leaders could all return to their barracks, wherein they could still fill the roles of arbiters and kingmakers in the political process—the situation so often manifested in many Latin American countries.[22] Repeated coups remained a possibility. Park, moreover, would be forced to retire soon after his return to garrison duty. Most of the core junta members were, however, still young field-grade officers and to return to their barracks would mean resumed contention with their superior officers in the Korean military hierarchy. There was yet another alternative: all junta leaders could retire and assume special advisory status for themselves in a new civilian government. Kim's brain trust, however, was unable to arrive at a suitable solution to these problems. One alternative remained: the assumption of direct political control. The junta leaders could take off their military uniforms and fill important government positions, as either appointed or elected officials. The idea for a new political party thus originated in response to the need for a vehicle by which the junta leaders could assume political power in a new civilian government.[23]

The junta leaders created a Third Republic but through a conscientious effort they also recruited many intellectuals (college and university professors, etc.) and former politicians. This so-called mixed military-civilian regime under President Park displayed an impressive rate of economic and social development and modernization for South Korea.[24] It also manifested, however, an increasingly centralistic, authoritarian tendency. It forcefully amended its original 1963 constitution, first in 1969 and then again in 1972 (Yushin reform), finally legitimizing a lifetime presidency for Park.[25] As Henry Bienen and David Morell maintain, if transition from military rule entails political decentralization, a limited resort to coercion, and a peaceful transfer of power, the Park regime indeed took a reverse course of development.[26] Park's assassination in October 1979, however, terminated his regime in a sudden and tragic way.

President Park was assassinated on October 26, 1979 by his close associate and confidant, Kim Jae-kyu, Director of the KCIA.[27] The assassination was an act of defiance, but it reflected a deep schism within President Park's inner circle of power. President Park's yushin system had come under the intense pressure of his various political opponents, which by 1979 consisted not only of opposition politicians but also of intellectuals, students, religious groups and laborers. The military did not seem to be totally united behind President Park either. The assassination took place at a dinner meeting within the KCIA compound near the presidential Blue House residence. Heated discussion was undoubtedly held among those present about the recent disquieting demonstrations and strikes in the country. President Park's credibility was increasingly questioned. Besides President Park and Kim Jae-kyu, also present at the dinner were Ch'a Chi-ch'ol, President Park's bodyguard at the Blue House, a critical opponent of Kim Jae-kyu and Kim Kye-won, President Park's Blue House Chief-of-Staff.

Given the enormous power which President Park held under the yushin system, his assassination came like an earthquake that shook the very foundation of South Korea's political structure.[28] Much political chaos had been anticipated, yet political order was momentarily kept. An interim government was organized and led by Acting President Choi Kyu-hah (Ch'oe Kyu-ha), who had been Prime Minister under President Park. On December 6, 1979, he was elected president in his own right by the National Conference for Unification, which had been organized under President Park's yushin system. President Choi's role was to ease the political transition following President Park's assassination, but he was indecisive in meeting demands for quick political liberation. Increasing student and opposition demands for a new constitution and democratic transition were unsatisfied. When student demonstrations became intense and widespread, and the government proved powerless to cope with them, the door was again left open for the military to intervene directly in politics, this time under the leadership of General Chun Doo-hwan (Chon, Tu-hwan).[29]

Following President Park's assassination, the Defense Security Command under Major General Chun was charged with the investigation of the assassination. General Chun owed his appointment to the powerful command position to the late President Park and was generally regarded as his confidant. Subsequently, General Chun's investigation was said to have uncovered "sufficient evidence" to indicate the possible complicity of some senior army officers in a conspiracy to kill President Park. General Chun then quickly led his forces to move against his superiors—arresting Martial Law Command General Chong Song-hwa (also Chief-of-Staff of the Army) and his associates on December 12, 1979. Some fighting was reported. The military was now placed under the command of General Chun. General Chun's classmates at the KMA (11th class) were mobilized and they were placed in powerful positions in the military. The country was still under martial law.

When escalating campus sit-ins and demonstrations continued into the spring of 1980, General Chun prevailed over President Choi to declare a more extensive nationwide martial law to supersede a limited martial law which had been in effect since the assassination of President Park. Ironically, the new extraordinary martial law was proclaimed on May 17, 1980, one day after the nineteenth anniversary of the 1961 coup. All the universities were closed down, any demonstration, both indoors and out, was prohibited, prior censorship of the press was imposed, any criticism of the incumbent and past presidents was outlawed, and the manufacture and spreading of rumors was heavily penalized.

Under the new martial law, General Chun was not only responsible for maintaining law and order in the country but also in charge of the government. President Choi was increasingly side-stepped in decision-making, and he could not prevent General Chun and his KMA colleagues and followers in the military from arresting and removing from the political scene many powerful opposition leaders in the name of political purification. The military seemed united behind General Chun's "conservative" coup. The arrested included dissident leader Kim Dae-jung (Kim Tae-jung), opposition New Democratic Party President Kim Young-sam (Kim Yong-sam), as well as significant yushin leaders such as Kim Jong-pil (Kim Chong-p'il), Lee Hu-rak (Yi Hu-rak), and Park Chong-kyu (Pak Chong-gyu), all of whom had been closely associated with the slain president. The arrest of Kim Dae-jung was particularly significant because it was eventually related to a nationwide protest by Kim's followers. In the city of Kwangju, the provincial capital of South Cholla (and Kim's home province), the rebellious citizenry took over the city from May 18th to 27th. The city was retaken in the end by force, but many innocent and rebellious citizens of Kwangju were killed and wounded in the process.[30]

To climax the unfolding drama of post-Park development, General Chun resigned from the army as a four-star general on August 22, 1980 and on August 30 was elected president by the rubber-stamp electoral college, the National Conference for Unification. As the only candidate General Chun received 2,524 of the total 2,525 votes, with 1 vote declared invalid. He assumed the presidency on September 1, 1980 and a new constitution, the fifth in South Korea's constitutional history, was promulgated on October 22, 1980.

Korea's Fifth Republic and 12th National Assembly Election

According to the new constitution, the Fifth Republic was: (1) to cultivate the form of democracy best suited to the political climate of Korea; (2) to promote the welfare of all citizens to the greatest possible extent; (3) to firmly uphold justice in all areas of national life; and, (4) to bring about a spiritual reform of the nation by revamping the educational system and developing higher standards of culture.

Since the inauguration of his government, President Chun and his government have significantly moved towards the fulfillment of the above mandates.[31] For instance, President Chun has intentionally tried to disassociate his government from the late President Park's stringent yushin system, relaxing and modifying many of the most rigid provisions. In this connection all political parties of Park's Fourth Republic were disbanded and 567 political leaders and former party officials who were held responsible for political corruption and social unrest were purged and banned from political activities for eight years. Also removed from the government were 232 higher government bureaucrats. Other measures have included: freeing Park's political prisoners (including the poet Kim Chi-ha); lifting the long standing 11 p.m. to 4 a.m. curfew and modifying the abusive anti-communist laws; relaxing dress codes for middle and high school students; liberalizing overseas travel by the people; and reducing the power of the KCIA, which had been known for the illegitimate use of its wide-ranging power, and renaming it the Agency for National Security Planning. Furthermore, President Chun has constitutionally limited his tenure to a single seven-year term, with no amendment to this provision to apply to an incumbent.

Also, under President Chun the economy has been returned to a condition of normalcy, since South Korea suffered a 5.7 percent decline in GNP in 1980. The successful completion of the fifth five-year plan (1982-86) was proudly announced. This plan achieved an annual growth of 8 percent in GNP; held the inflation rate to a single digit figure; promoted a welfare investment ratio of 28.6 percent; and accomplished a 20 percent annual increase in exports which reached a target of $53 billion by 1986.

In foreign relations, President Chun and his government could point to improved relations with both the United States and Japan. In his state visits to the United States, for instance, President Chun was able to secure a further commitment from the United States to the security of South Korea. President Chun also visited Japan in September 1984, the first state visit to Japan ever conducted by a Korean head of state. Reciprocating in these diplomatic activities were visits to South Korea by Prime Minister Nakasone of Japan in January 1983 and President Reagan in November of the same year. President Chun's government has also been credited with efforts to improve relations with its communist neighbors, the PRC and the USSR.

Advocating positive approaches to promote dialogue with North

Korea, President Chun on January 12, 1981 also proposed an exchange of visits between the top leaders of Seoul and Pyongyang. He has invited President Kim Il Sung of North Korea to visit Seoul and has proposed his own visit to Pyongyang, if invited. Also, on January 22, 1982 before the National Assembly he presented steps toward national unification which were "more comprehensive and specific than earlier proposals for achieving national reunification."[32] The proposal included the formulation of a unified Korean constitution and the organization of a "consultative conference for national reunification." His most dramatic approaches to Korea's peaceful reunification were the South Korean Red Cross acceptance of North Korea's offer of relief goods for South Korean flood victims in September 1984 and the consummation of a lengthy negotiation for the exchange of a limited number of hometown visitors, performing arts groups, and reporters in 1985.[33]

Under President Chun and his government, nationalist fervor was also raised to a new height in 1984 with South Korea's success in the 23rd Summer Olympic Games in Los Angeles. South Korea's athletes competing in the Olympic Games captured 19 medals—six gold, six silver and seven bronze—and occupied 10th place in the number of gold medals, an unprecedented success. South Korea then hosted the Asian Games in 1986 and will host the 24th Summer Olympic Games in 1988—events of great national pride and expectation for which much national effort has been expended with popular approval.[34]

Despite these achievements to which President Chun and his DJP supporters could make justifiable claims, there was of course no assurance in 1985 that the DJP would succeed in obtaining its stated goals in the election that year. President Chun may have gained confidence in his presidential role, but the former Commander of the Defense Security Command had never looked comfortable in his civilian suit. His legitimacy is, furthermore, always questioned. To the South Korean people, President Chun still remains "a distant figure." [35] He remains a military man. Incessant student demonstrations have been a constant reminder of his military authoritarianism. Furthermore, in his scheme of development, his just society has not been able to eliminate large scale official corruption and scandal; narrow the gap between the rich and the poor; or reduce the alienation of those who have been excluded from the benefits of national development. The ever-sprawling metropolitan centers such as Seoul, Pusan and Taegu are constantly compared with the unchanging poverty and traditionalism of rural areas. Opposition in the election was unrestrained in assailing President Chun's government as "unjust and immoral," "corrupt and illegal," "hated and distrusted," and "military controlled and dictatorial."[36] The electoral atmosphere was relatively open.

In the National Assembly election in 1985, which was to elect 184 representatives, nine political parties fielded 411 candidates. There were also 29 independent candidates. The total rate of competition was then 2.39, the second lowest in South Korea's National Assembly electoral history, but the voter turnout was the second largest in South Korea's electoral history with 84.6 percent of the total 23,987,830 registered voters participating. When all the votes were counted, they showed the following results: DJP retained a majority status (but lost the three seats which it had won in 1981), winning a total of only 87 seats. Its share of the popular vote also declined somewhat from 35.6 percent in 1981 to 35.3 percent.[37]

The fact that there was no great upsurge of support for President Chun and his DJP is perhaps no surprise and could have been predicted.[38] What surprised the observers was the emergence of the New Korea Democratic Party (NKDP) as the major opposition party largely at the expense of the opposition Democratic Korea Party (DKP). The NKDP was hastily organized on January 18, 1985, by the opposition politicians earlier banned but reinstated. As stated earlier, originally 567 politicians were put under political restriction in 1980 for their alleged roles in the political turmoil before the birth of the Fifth Republic. Since November 30, 1984, when the third round of the political ban-lifting was implemented, all but 15 remained on the political blacklist. For the NKDP, there was not time to have its national organization in place; and the best that it expected was to win about 30 seats, mostly in the urban areas. Yet it won 50 seats, receiving 29.2 percent of the popular votes. The DKP, which tried to regain its major opposition party status, won only 26 seats, a significant reverse from 1981, when the DKP had won 57 seats.

The emergence of the hard-line opposition NKDP as the major opposition party in the National Assembly must be regarded as a major defeat for President Chun and his DJP. As the only vote test of any kind before 1988, President Chun and his DJP hoped that the election would demonstrate popular support for their leadership and achievements. For President Chun and DJP, the lessons of the 12th National Assembly election appear self-evident. Despite many of their achievements in South Korea's national development, there is a strong desire among the voters to see the government of President Chun terminated when his term of office expires in 1988 and a new government elected in a peaceful transition of power.[39]

The Military Withdrawal of Power

According to Samuel P. Huntington, a military regime once in power could opt for any of the following four action alternatives:

- retaining power themselves and restricting popular political participation;
- retaining power themselves but expanding popular political participation;
- returning power to civilian politicians but restricting popular political participation; or
- returning power to civilian politicians and expanding popular political participation.[40]

In South Korea, as we have observed thus far, the Park regime followed the criss-crossing route of retaining power and/or expanding popular political participation. In the case of the Chun regime, it has retained power but expanded popular political participation. What is significant with the Chun regime is its willingness at present to return power to civilian politicians and expand popular political participation. How has this turn of events come about in South Korea? The so-called "Grand Compromise" in the politics of South Korea in 1986, as stated at the outset of this paper, is indeed an extraordinary development. It is almost axiomatic: no one, particularly in the case of South Korea, relinquishes power willingly. South Korea has not had a peaceful transfer of power throughout its independent republican history of some 40 years.

According to Ulf Sundhaussen, who has dealt with the problems of the military's withdrawal from power in his recent study, there are three sets of reasons for the military to withdraw from government responsibility.[41] The first is exogenous to the military, i.e, mounting civilian opposition to its continuing rule. The civilian groups opposed to the military regime engage in armed struggle or wage demonstrations, riots and/or strikes. These groups often consist of students, new middle classes, and a new industrial proletariat—the products of modernization which the regime might have been instrumental in creating.

The second set of reasons is exogenous to the state. Pressure—political, economic, and military—may have been applied by a foreign power to a military regime for it to withdraw from government. Both the United States and the USSR for instance, have at times exerted pressure to dispose of one military regime in the place of another or a military regime in favor of a newly elected civilian government.

The third set of reasons for withdrawal is internal within the military. Regime leaders and their military followers decide to relinquish power. They feel that they have completed their missions and/or the prolongation of their stay in power may fragment and further politicize their forces and impair their cohesiveness and fighting capacity. For this set of reasons to prevail, all the factional leaders within the military must consent to withdrawal. They must feel that their interests are best served by taking such action and they must conclude that there is a viable civilian alternative to their continued stay in power.

In reviewing the history of President Chun's Fifth Republic of Korea, we must conclude that Sundhaussen's analysis is, in many ways, applicable to the South Korean case. President Chun's rise to power was conservative in nature and it was to prevent radical liberalization of politics following the assassination of President Park. Although such a conservative coup may have been anticipated within the military, it was sudden and unexpected for the general public. It furthermore was accompanied by much bloodshed. As the legitimacy of President Chun was questioned, anti-regime demonstrations, particularly by students, have become more intense and radicalized. President Chun has not been able to shake off the ghost of the Kwangju "massacre." When President Chun's government assumed power and opted for "greater participation," its conciliatory act was only compensatory, but the government has been faced with increasing demands from various critical sectors of the population.

For President Chun's government, the outcome of the 12th National Assembly election in 1985 was an especially eye-opening experience. It also gave a new lease on life to the opposition cause. Increasingly, it has been felt by President Chun and his military followers that they must withdraw from power in 1988 as promised. Any contrary move could invite further political instability and endanger national security.

For the reasons exogenous to the state, the American official pressure must be pointed out as a critical determinant in South Korean decisions. Not only economically but also politically, there is an immense role which the United States could play in South Korea. Since the Korean War, the United States has continued with large economic and military investment in South Korea and has maintained a close relationship with the Seoul government. Given North Korea's continued military threat across the Demilitarized Zone that borders North and South Korea, American military investment and troop presence has become almost a permanent fixture in the security considerations of South Korea. Economically South Korea must depend on the lucrative American market for the sustenance of its export oriented development strategy. President Chun's government is also aware of the critical importance of American cooperation for successful completion of the 1988 Seoul Summer Olympics in which so much national wealth and prestige have been invested. North Korea must be prevented from disrupting the Olympics in any imaginable way and a firm commitment of the United States to that effect is conceived as essential in dissuading North Korea from engaging in any provocation.

Although all enumerated reasons above explain why the government of President Chun must withdraw from power, what is to be reemphasized is the fact that the military is one of the most powerful political actors in South Korea and that it can, by force, act politically. Both the late President Park and President Chun wrested power from a weak and incapable civilian government, either to protect the military corporate interests or to present a new stimulus and direction for national development. Any future civilian government must take into serious account the history of South Korean civil-military relations. The simple logic of power, furthermore, dictates that President Chun and his government would not peacefully withdraw from power unless they have some guarantee for their safety and economic security.

Further explicating the conditions which could lead to the military's withdrawal from power, Sundhaussen pointed out necessary preconditions and superstructural factors. The preconditions include a general consensus within the military that it should withdraw from power. They also include the military's conviction that their personal and institutional interests are served by withdrawal from power and that they can support a civilian alternative that is to succeed them.

The so-called superstructural factors are related to the historical and cultural inheritance of a nation, and South Korea's popular political beliefs, attitudes, and behavior may be best characterized as authoritarian, high-risk (no compromise) oriented, cynical and parochial. South Korea's political culture is best classified as authoritarian because of the tradition of dominance by self-serving elites throughout its history. The mass of the Korean people have not been able to develop the culture of political participation and meaningful interaction for decision-making necessary to a fluid democracy. South Korea's political culture is a game of high risk because it tends to be a zero-sum game, with the winner taking all the gains at the expense of the loser. The virtue of compromise has not been included in the traditions of South Korea's political culture. South Korea's political culture is cynical because, despite a great deal of interest in and knowledge about politics among the people, the people do not trust their leaders such that any affective orientation to the regime is sorely lacking. Many studies in South Korea, furthermore, have shown that the more knowledgeable the people are about politics the more likely they are to stay away from active participation in it.[42] South Korea's political culture is also parochial because the perspective of both elite and masses is limited by their own individual, family and/or small primary group orientations. In terms of political culture and in keeping with other superstructural variables, the military's withdrawal from power and democratic progress in South Korea may be faced with limited options. Indeed, as Sundhaussen stated, with all the known shortcomings of a military regime, "we cannot report the demise of military regimes."[43] To prevent recurrence of a military regime in South Korea, therefore, a formula must be found to avoid confrontation between civil and military powers and to promote their cooperation for national development. The institutionalization of a civil-military or military-civil coalition may be the most realistic approach for a country such as South Korea in the near future.[44] The politics of confrontation and reprisal can only prove counterproductive for further national development and security.

NOTES

1. "News Analysis," *The Korea Herald*, June 27, 1986.
2. *Ibid.*
3. S.M. Finer, *The Man on Horseback* (New York: Praeger, 1962), p. 6.
4. Eric Nordlinger, *Soldiers in Politics: Military Coups and Governments* (Englewood Cliffs: Prentice-Hall, 1977), p. ix.
5. Kenneth Fidel, ed., *Militarism in Developing Countries* (New Brunswick: Transaction Books, 1975), p. 268.
7. Irving Louis Horowitz, "Militarization, Modernization and Mobilization: Third World Development Patterns Re-examined," in Fidel, ed., *Militarism in Developing Countries, op. cit.*, pp. 313-314. James M. Malloy, "Authoritarianism and Corporatism in Latin America: The Modern Pattern," in James M. Malloy, ed., *Authoritarianism and Corporatism in Latin America* (Pittsburgh: University of Pittsburgh Press, 1977), pp. 3-4. See also C.I. Eugene Kim, "Asian Military Regimes: Political Systems and Styles," in Morris Janowitz, ed., *Civil-Military Relations: Regional Perspectives* (Beverly Hills: Sage Publications, 1981), pp. 26-63.
8. Some relevant literature on the South Korean military includes: Frederica C. Bunge, ed., *South Korea: A Country Study* (Washington, D.C.: U.S. Government Printing Office, 1982); Gregory Henderson, *Korea: The Politics of the Vortex* (Cambridge, MA; Harvard University Press, 1968); C.I. Eugene Kim, "The South Korean Military Coup of May 1961: Its Causes and the Social Characteristics of Its Leaders," In Jacques VanDoorn, ed., *Armed Forces and Society* (The Hague: Mouton, 1968); "Transition from Military Rule: The Case of South Korea," *Armed Forces and Society*, 1,3 (May 1975), 302-316; Kenneth Rocco, "Political Orientations of Military and Non-military Elites in South Korea," *Journal of Korean Affairs*, 4, 1 (January 1975), 16-26; "The Impact of U.S. Military Presence on the Republic of Korea," in *The American Military and the Far East* (Proceedings of the Ninth Military History Symposium, USAF Academy, 1980), 220-236; "Civil-Military Relations in the Two Koreas," *Armed Forces and Society*, 11,1 (Fall 1984), 9-31; Jai-hyup Kim, *The Garrison State in Pre-war Japan and Post-war Korea: A Comparative Analysis of Military Politics* (Washington, D.C.: University Press of America, 1978); Se-jin Kim, *The Politics of Military*

Revolution in Korea (Chapel Hill, NC: University of North Carolina Press, 1971); *Korea Military Academy, Armed Forces and National Development* (Proceedings of the First Wharangdae International Symposium, September 20-22, 1981) (Seoul: Korea Military Academy, 1981; John P. Lovell, "The Military and Politics in Postwar Korea," in Edward R. Wright, ed., *Korean Politics in Transition* (Seattle, WA: University of Washington Press, 1975), 153-199; "Professional Orientations and Policy Perspectives of Military Professionals in the Republic of Korea," *Midwest Journal of Political Science,* 13,2 (August 1969), 415-438; "Recruitment Patterns in the Republic of Korea Military Establishment," *Journal of Comparative Administration,* 1,4 (February 1970), 428-454; Robert Sawyer, *Military Advisors in Korea: KMAG in Peace and War* (U.S. Army History Series) (Washington, D.C.: U.S. Government Printing Office, 1962). See also Han-kyo Kim, ed., *Studies on Korea: A Scholar's Guide* (Honolulu: The University Press of Hawaii, 1980), Chap. 12.

9. See C. I. Eugene Kim, "The Impact of U.S. Military Presence on the Republic of Korea," *op. cit.*
10. See Se-Jin Kim, *The Politics of Military Revolution in Korea, op.cit.,* Chap. 3.
11. Se-Jin Kim, *ibid.* See also C.I. Eugene Kim, "The South Korean Military Coup of May 1961," *op. cit.*
12. Sungjoo Han, *The Failure of Democracy in South Korea* (Berkeley: University of California Press, 1974).
13. For a detailed study of the coup in the English language, see, for instance, Se-Jin Kim, *The Politics of Military Revolution in Korea, op. cit.;* C.I. Eugene Kim, "The South Korean Military Coup of May 1961," *op. cit.* See also Han-kyo Kim, ed., *Studies on Korea, op. cit.*
14. C.I. Eugene Kim, "The South Korean Military Coup of May 1961," *op. cit.*
15. Morris Janowitz, *The Military in the Political Development of New Nations: An Essay in Comparative Analysis* (Chicago: University of Chicago Press, 1964), p. 70.
16. Morris Janowitz has made a similar observation. See his *The Military in the Political Development of New Nations, op. cit.,* p. 92.
17. For an official history of the coup, see (ROK) Kunsa Hyongmyong-sa P'yonch'an Wiwon-hoe (Committee for the Compilation of the Korean Military Revolution), *Kunsa Hyongmyong-sa* (*History of the Military Revolution*) (Seoul, 1963), 2 vols. Hereafter cited *Kunsa Hyongmyong-sa (History of the Military Revolution).* See also Se-Jin Kim, *The Politics of Military Revolution in Korea, op. cit.;* C.I. Eugene Kim, "The South Korean Military Coup of May 1961," *op. cit.*
18. *New York Times,* May 28, 1961.
19. For recent, scholarly books on the Second Republic, See Sungjoo

Han, *The Failure of Democracy in South Korea, op .cit.*; Se-Jin Kim, *The Politics of Military Revolution in Korea, op. cit.*; John K.C. Oh, *Korea: Democracy on Trial* (Ithaca: Cornell University Press, 1968); and Gregory Henderson, *Korea: The Politics of the Vortex, op. cit.*

20. United Press International, Washington D.C., May 19, 1961. See also John K.C. Oh, "Role of the United States in South Korea's Democratization," *Pacific Affairs* 43, 2 (Summer 1969), 164-177.
21. This information was derived from the author's interview with an informant who was a member of J.P. Kim's brain trust. The interview was conducted in summer 1969.
22. S. E. Finer, *The Man on Horseback, op. cit.*, pp. 151ff., 168.
23. Jae Souk Sohn, "Political Dominance and Political Failure: The Role of the Military in the Republic of Korea," in Henry Bienen, ed., *The Military Intervenes* (New York: Russell Sage Foundation, 1968), pp. 115-116. Professor Sohn argues that the military revolutionaries were reluctant from the outset to transfer the government to civilian control.
24. See for instance Young Whan-kihl, *Politics and Policies in Divided Korea: Regimes in Contest* (Boulder: Westview Press, 1984), especially Tables 6.1 and 6.2. See also Leroy P. Jones and Il Sakong, *Government, Business and Entrepreneurship in Economic Development: The Korean Case* (Cambridge: Harvard University Council on East Asian Studies, 1980); Edward S. Mason *et al.*, *The Economic and Social Mobilization of the Republic of Korea* (Cambridge: Harvard University Council on East Asian Studies, 1980); David I. Steinberg, the *Economic Development of Korea: Sui Generis or Generic?*, USAID Evaluation Special Study No. 6 (Washington, D.C.: USAID, 1981); Roy Hofheinz, Jr. and Kent E. Calder, *Eastasia Edge* (New York: Basic Books, 1982), Harold C. Hinton, *Korea Under New Leadership: The Fifth Republic* (New York: Praeger, 1983); Jon Woronoff, *Korea's Economy: Man-Made Miracle* (Seoul, Korea: Sisayongo-sa Publishers, 1983).
25. See C.I. Eugene Kim, "Korea at the Crossroads, The Birth of the Fourth Republic," *Pacific Affairs*, 46, 2 (Summer 1973), 218-231. See also Y.W. Kihl, *Politics and Policies in Divided Korea, op. cit.*, Chap. 3.
26. Henry Bienen and David Morell, "Transition from Military Rule: Thailand and Nigeria," paper presented at the Inter-University Seminar on Armed Forces and Society, October 11-13, 1979.
27. Chong-sik Lee, "South Korea 1979: Confrontation, Assassination, and Transition," *Asian Survey*, XX, 1 (January 1980), 63-76; "South Korea in 1980: The Emergence of a New Authoritarian Order," *ibid.*, XXI, 1 (January 1980), 125-143.
28. *Ibid.*
29. *Ibid.*

30. *Ibid.* For the Kwangju rebellion in particular, see *Sindonga* (monthly), July 1985 and *Choson* (monthly), July 1985.
31. See for instance, Hinton, *Korea under New Leadership, op. cit.*; Woronoff, *Korea's Economy, op. cit.*
32. Y.W. Kihl, *Politics and Policies in Divided Korea, op. cit.*, p. 218.
33. Chae-jin Lee, "South Korea in 1984: Seeking Peace and Prosperity," *Asian Survey*, XXV, 1 (January 1985), 80-89.
34. *Ibid.*
35. Clyde Haberman in *New York Times*, April 16, 1985.
36. *Hanguk Ilbo*, January 20-February 12, 1985, especially February 5, 7, 11, 14 and 15.
37. For a good analysis of the 1985 election, see for instance B.C. Koh, "The 1985 Parliamentary Election in South Korea," *Asian Survey*, XXV, 9 (September 1985), 883-897; C.I. Eugene Kim, "The Meaning of Korea's 12th National Assembly Election," *Korea Observer*, XVI, 4 (Winter 1985), 363-379.
38. C.I. Eugene Kim, "The Meaning of Korea's 12th National Assembly Election," *ibid.*
39. *Ibid.*
40. Samuel P. Huntington, *Political Order in Changing Societies* (New Haven: Yale University Press, 1968).
41. Ulf Sundhaussen, "Military Withdrawal from Government Responsibility" *Armed Forces and Society*, 10,4 (Summer 1984), pp. 543-562.
42. See for instance C.I. Eugene Kim and Young Whan Kihl, *Party Politics and Elections in Korea* (Silver Spring: Research Institute on Korean Affairs, 1976); Y.S. Chang, et al., eds., *Society in Transition* (Seoul: National University Press, 1982); C. L. Kim, ed., *Political Participation in Korea: Democracy, Mobilization and Stability* (Santa Barbara: ABC-CLIO, 1980); N.Y. Lee, "The Democratic Belief System: A Study of the Political Culture in South Korea," *Korean Social Science Journal*, 1985; Y.H. Lee, *The Political Culture of Modernizing Society: Political Attitudes and Democracy in Korea*, Ph.D. Dissertation, Yale University; S.M. Pae, *Testing Democratic Theories in Korea* (Lanham: University Press of America, 1986).
43. Sundhaussen, "Military Withdrawal from Government and Responsibility," *op. cit.*
44. *Ibid.*

6

Institutionalized Local Self-Government in South Korea

SUNG MOON PAE

Local self-government, if properly implemented and well institutionalized, may relieve the central government of its heavy duties and tasks. It also may diffuse political powers between the central government and local governments, thereby preventing control of the entire nation by one political leader and his political party and subsequently reducing the potential for a zero-sum game between the government party and the opposition parties. This in turn may promote political stability. Local self-government may enhance the level of citizen participation in local affairs and programs. Safe experimentation of a variety of governmental structures, functions, and programs may be made available to the central government as well as to other local governments. Local self-government indeed enhances the inculcation of the democratic values, expectations, and behaviors into the hearts and minds of citizens. These may be just a few of the major reasons why all of the democratic countries in Western Europe and North America have long been implementing local self-government. In short, implementation of local self-government and its institutionalization are widely accepted as a prerequisite for a successful democracy.

One may wonder, then, to what extent local self-government lacks institutionalization in South Korea; what may be the real reasons for the postponement of its implementation since 1961 up until now; and what issues are to be taken into account to institutionalize local self-government, if it is to be implemented in 1988, as officially planned by the government political party.[1]

Lack of Institutionalization

Samuel P. Huntington defines institutionalization as "the process by which organizations and procedures acquire values and stability." [2] When this definition is applied to the case of South Korea, it goes without saying that the local self-governments have failed to acquire values and stability. Since a chronological age may be an indicator to measure the level of institutionalization, one may suggest that the longer an organization or procedure has been in existence, the greater the potential for its adaptation to environmental changes, and subsequently the higher the level of its institutionalization becomes.[3] Local autonomy in South Korea, however, experienced a short life span and changed too frequently in its structures, functions, and the modes of operation.

The Local Autonomy Law, which was adopted by the National Assembly on July 4, 1949, for example, was amended five months later on December 15, 1949 (1st Amendment) without the implementation and the subsequent evaluation of the original law. In 1956 the law was amended twice—on February 13 (2nd Amendment) and July 8 (3rd Amendment), respectively. Two years later on December 26, 1958 the law (4th Amendment) was amended again. Despite the four amendments to the law during the First Republic, local autonomy remained mere lip service. The Korean government flatly admitted the lack of local autonomy as follows:

> ...However, the principle of local self-government is still a novel idea to Korea. Traditionally, the country was ruled by a strong central government through central government officials. Thus there has been *no autonomy of local government in the true sense of the term.*
>
> ...These legal provisions on local self-government, however, were *virtually non-functional during the First Republic* when the central government held firm control over the local units.[4] (emphasis added)

Upon the inception of the Second Republic following the April 19, 1960 student uprising, a complete overhaul in the Local Autonomy Law was made on November 6, 1960 (5th Amendment) to warrant full local autonomy. No sooner than six months following its implementation the law was nullified by a coup on May 16, 1961 and was replaced by the Law Concerning Temporary Measures for Local Autonomy. The temporary measures called for an immediate suspension of local self-government.

The 1962 Constitution of the Third Republic clearly states that "local self-government bodies shall deal with matters pertaining to the welfare of local residents, manage properties, and may establish, within the limit of laws and ordinances, rules and regulations regarding local self-government" [Article 109-(1)] and that "a local self-government body shall have a council" [Article 110-(1)]. Nevertheless, these two provisions on local autonomy in the Constitution were violated and thereby not implemented. Finally, the 1972 Constitution of the Fourth Republic made it explicit that "local councils under this Constitution shall not be formed until the unification of the fatherland shall have been achieved" (Supplementary Rules, Article 10). This provision definitely dissipated the dreams of tens of thousands of opposition leaders and citizens' for the restoration of local self-government.

Local autonomy, which had been briefly implemented during the First and Second Republics, reveals further evidence of the lack of institutionalization. Following are a few major highlights:

1. Legislative councils were established belatedly for the first time in the republic in 1952—about three years after the Local Autonomy Law was officially chartered. However, their counterparts in the provinces, cities, and counties "north" of the Han River, namely in the Special City of Seoul, Gyeong Gi province, and Gang Won province, were postponed for four additional years until August 8, 1956, and survived until 1961. Therefore, the councils in the areas "south" of the Han River had lasted for only nine years and their counterparts north of the Han River for only four years and nine months throughout the entire history of the republic.

2. During the council's short life-span the number of years for councilmen's service was changed from four years to three years in the second amendment (2/13/56) and then changed to four years in the fourth amendment (12/26/58).

3. The council had 30 days per session, two sessions a year, but it

was changed to 90 days for provinces and 50 days for cities and other local governments in the second amendment. The session was further changed to 80 days for Seoul, 50 days for provinces, and 30 days for the remaining local governments in the fifth amendment (11/6/60).

4. The number of councilmen was decided originally in proportion to the population, uniformly reduced by 10 percent in the second amendment, and then in the fifth amendment changed into the number corresponding to the number of Lower House members elected in their respective local districts.

5. A vote of nonconfidence was originally prohibited, restored in the first amendment to apply only to the mayor of Seoul and provincial governors, and then applied to the chief executives of all the levels of local government—provinces, cities, counties and towns.

6. The right of chief executives to dissolve the council was originally granted, denied in the first amendment, and then restored from 1956 until 1961.

7. Governors and the Seoul City mayor have been consistently appointed by the President of the republic except during the six months of the Second Republic.[5]

8. Other local chief executives were elected by the council, directly elected by popular votes in the second amendment, and then consistently appointed by the Minister of Home Affairs except during the six months of the Second Republic.

In short, the absence of local self-government in the true sense of the term raises the following important question: On what grounds was the belatedly established local autonomy continuously changed in its structures and functions, and finally prohibited without its restoration up until now?

The Government's Justifications for the Postponement

Since 1961 there has been a hot debate on the question of whether local self-government should be reinstated. Those who are opposed to its reinstatement argue that the concentration of authority in the national government may have a significant advantage in facing the problems of modern society. Since the national government has more professionally trained and qualified technocrats, it is only the national government that can use clear lines of authority, marshall human and material resources, and coordinate multi-year economic development planning and implementation. It is the aggressive and energetic initiative of the national government that rescued the nation and the Korean people from persistent economic stagnation (with below $100 per capita GNP throughout the first two republics during which local self-government had been partially implemented) and that has finally enhanced the status of South Korea as a "newly industrializing country" (NIC) with over $2,000 per capita GNP as of spring 1986. Its taxation powers can also be broadened so as to make the task of financing social welfare programs much easier.

Opponents further contend that national leaders and planners are more concerned with the well-being of the nation as a whole and, therefore are able to alleviate the gap between the local governments resulting from their relative economic and financial strengths. This indeed becomes the main thrust of the Sixth Five-Year Economic Development Plan that started in 1987.

The unanticipated, dysfunctional consequences, which were derived from the partial implementation of local self-government from 1952-1961, provide the opponents with a mile-long list of additional justifications against its reinstatement. A few major highlights are: intense competition between political parties, factional and clan strife, the exacerbation of patron-client politics, and related mismanagement of personnel and finances.

Competition between political parties at local governments, for example, resulted in political crisis when two political parties—the government and the major opposition—secured a relatively equal number of legislative councilmen. Furthermore, competition between political parties was often intensified when the legislative council and the chief executive were occupied by the two contending parties. This is why the Legislative Council in the city of Taegu, under the domination of the government political party, deliberately failed to approve the budget appropriations recommended by the city mayor of the opposition party. Therefore, the city administration had been nearly frozen for six months.[6]

Different types of corruption and abuses of power were derived from different election systems. When local chief executives were elected by their legislative council, there were many incidents in which councilmen were likely to be bribed by the candidates for local chief executive. On the other hand, when chief executives were directly elected by the voters, the elected heads were likely to dismiss local government officials who did not campaign for or financially contribute to them. In order to pay the debts incurred from campaign expenditures some elected chiefs, like the cases of the city of Taegu and the town chief of Hahm Duk, Dahm Jim County, South Choong Chung province, misappropriated the local government funds.[7]

Opponents contend that democratic cultural values, norms and related behaviors such as neutrality of the government employees in partisan politics and elections, free and open debate and competition, respect for majority rule, and compromising and bargaining without resorting to extreme confrontation have not been inculcated and socialized in the hearts and minds of Korean voters. Therefore, the above-mentioned dysfunctional consequences of local self-government unfolded and in turn disappointed many Koreans. In fact, a survey conducted under the auspices of the Ministry of Home Affairs in 1962 indicated: only 11.0 percent showed an interest in elections at the local level; about 17.3 percent responded that they tried to articulate their opinions or concerns to their local government offices once in a while; and about 54 percent answered they did not care about local self-government.[8]

When the Fourth Republic was overthrown and the Fifth Republic was embarked upon in 1980, all of the above excuses, which had long been used by the government as officially justifiable against the restoration of local self-government, were brushed aside. Rather, local governments' lack of financial self-reliance was selected as the primary excuse for the postponement of local autonomy. Thus an article was included in the Supplementary Provisions of the 1980 Constitution. Article 10, for example, stipulates that "local councils prescribed by this Constitution shall be established on a phased basis taking into account the degree of financial self-reliance by local governments and the dates for their establishment shall be determined by law."

Table 1
Percent Financial Self-Reliance as of 1980 and 1981

Local self-gov't to be implemented during the first half of 1987		Other cities excluded from the implementation in 1987	
Cities and Provinces	**Percent Self-Reliance**	**Other Cities**	**Percent Self-Reliance**
Inchon	94.17	Ulsan	90.91
Seoul	93.87		
Pusan	93.37		
Taegu	88.10	Weon Ju	89.09
		Chung Mu	82.62
		Mog Po	81.80
		Sung Nam	80.79
Kwang Ju	71.37	Masan	73.51
		Dae Jean	73.06
		Gun San	70.82
Gyeong Gi Province	65.46	Cheong Ju	65.33
North Gyeong Sang		Gang Reung	64.85
Province	61.88	Jin Ju	63.81
		Chon Ju	63.28
		Yeo Su	62.90
		Chun Cheon	61.79
		Je Ju	60.40
South Gyeong Sang		Ui Jong Bu	55.02
Province	51.56	Jin Hae	54.52
Je Ju province	48.69	Geong Ju	47.99
South Choong		Po Hang	47.35
Chung province	45.97	Sog Cho	43.82
North Jeon Ra prov.	41.41		
South Jeon Ra prov.	38.60	Sun Cheon	39.80
Gang Won province	36.30	Choong Ju	35.91
North Choong Chung	35.91		

Source: Adapted from Table 5-2 in Sung M. Pae, Testing Democratic Theories in Korea (Lanham, MD: University Press of America, 1986), pp. 129-30.

The Hidden Objective Behind the Government's Blueprint

Partly due to the mounting pressures from opposition parties and students, and partly due to the purpose of enhancing the legitimacy of the regime, the government party (Democratic Justice Party) grudgingly agreed with the two major opposition parties in November 1984 that local autonomy would be implemented during the first half of 1987. In the 1985 New Year message to the National Assembly as well as to the Korean people, President Chun confirmed the Democratic Justice Party's (DJP) promise to restore local autonomy. The DJP finally promised the implementation of local autonomy as one of the key campaign issues for the February 12, 1985 National Assembly election. The same commitment was repeated on several occasions by Prime Minister Loh Shin-yong in his appearances at the National Assembly.[9] In short, the Chun Administration and the DJP now have no option but to execute their repeated promise of local autonomy as officially announced. Thus, a Research Committee on the Implementation of Local Autonomy was formally commissioned under the auspices of the Prime Minister in March 1985. Nevertheless, the committee has not been fully utilized and its deliberation focused primarily on the implementation of local autonomy to a limited scope in a few selected areas away from the large cities that are considered the strongholds of the opposition political party.

Prime Minster Loh shocked the members of the committee by not consulting them before making a visit to the Blue House on April 28, 1986 and then announced the administration's blueprint for local autonomy. Its major highlights are:

1. The government plans to implement the local autonomy system in five major cities—Seoul, Pusan, Taegu, Inchon, Kwang Ju, and nine provinces.
2. City and provincial councils will be formed by the popular election. However, councilmen will be elected not from single-member districts but from multimember districts in which two to five councilmen per district are elected.
3. Multimember districts will be based on a combination of the existing units of local governments without

redistricting the existing local governmental boundaries.

4. A councils' vote of nonconfidence in local heads will be substantially limited or restricted. Local councils will be granted only the power of investigation over the administration without the auditing power.
5. The central government will continue to appoint heads of those city and provincial governments "for the time being" instead of allowing elections for them.
6. The operation of the system will be subsequently extended into other cities and counties as a second-phase project.[10]

As is shown in Table 1, while the five major cites and the three provinces chosen for the implementation by the administration have at least over 50 percent financial independence, the remaining six provinces have financial independence far below 50 percent of their operating expenditures. Nevertheless, the administration has thus far made no comments on what grounds these six provinces with below 50 percent financial independence were selected. On the contrary, seventeen other cities that are excluded from the list under the first-phase implementation plan have over 50 percent financial independence. Among them, five cities have over 80 percent financial independence, three cities over 70 percent, seven cities over 60 percent, and two cities over 50 percent. One may wonder why these seventeen cities that are financially equally qualified and eligible for local autonomy in accordance with the constitution are excluded from the implementation of local autonomy. In short, the administration and the DJP have thus far violated and continue to violate the constitutional provision on local autonomy. Financial self-reliance has been a mere excuse against the restoration of local autonomy.

The administration's desire to control the opposition parties, not only in the central government but also in local governments, is clearly witnessed in the second item of the administration's blueprint, namely, the endorsement of a multimember district system for the election of local legislative councilmen.

One may examine this thesis from the outcome of the February 12, 1985 National Assembly election. Table 2 shows the number of National Assembly seats contested and average percent votes received by the DJP in the seven major cities and the nine provinces in which all of the small cities were combined with the counties into election districts. All 62 seats—one candidate from each of the 62 two-member rural districts—were won by the DJP! That accounts for a whopping 40.6 percent average for the popular votes, while 24 of the 30 seats secured in the major cities received an average of only 28.9 percent of the urban popular votes. The analysis of variance also shows that there is a significant difference (at 0.1 level) between the major cities and the rural districts in terms of the percentage of popular votes the government party received in the 1985 National Assembly election. This confirms the hypothesis that the DJP is likely to receive fewer popular votes in the urban areas than in the rural districts. Nevertheless, due to the continued rapid growth of industrialization and urbanization, more and more rural people have been migrating into urban areas.

As shown in Table 3, the ratio of the urban to the rural popular votes cast in the 1952 presidential election was 13.4 percent to 74.7 percent. But the percentage of urban popular votes has been consistently increasing election after election, whereas that of the rural votes has been correspondingly decreasing. Finally, the 1985 National Assembly election shows the opposite trend: the urban votes account for 47.6 percent of the total votes actually cast, whereas the rural votes explain only 45.3 percent.

The ever-increasing number of the urban votes and the correspondingly decreasing number of the urban votes for the government party are such that a single-member district system may potentially lose almost all of the Assembly seats in the urban areas. This was the reason why a two-member district system was implemented for the National Assembly election (with the combination of an at-large election system for one third of the total Assembly seats), since the inception of the Fifth Republic. The advantage of a two-member district system can also be examined in terms of the party candidates and the actual number of primary and secondary winners. Table 4 shows that in the February 12, 1985 National Assembly election, the DJP nominated a total of 62 candidates for each of the 62 two-member rural districts. From these 55 candidates 88.7 percent were elected as the primary winners and the remaining 7 candidates, 11.3 percent became the primary winners and 17 candidates (56.7 percent of the DJP's urban candidates) were elected as the secondary winners. This suggests that the DJP was able to secure a majority of the party's urban nominees as

Table 2

Percent Average Popular Votes for the Government Party in the 2/12/85 National Assembly Election* and the Analysis of Variance

Major cities	Number of Seats	% popular votes
Overall	30	28.9
Seoul	14	27.5
Pusan	6	28.5
Taegu	3	30.3
Inchon	2	36.1
Dae Jeon	2	32.7
Kwang Ju	2	28.3
Masan	1	27.4
Rural districts consisting of counties and small cities in provinces		
Overall	62	40.6
Gyeong Gi	10	32.2
Gang Won	6	46.1
North Choong Chung	4	56.7
South Choong Chung	6	42.1
North Jeon Ra		
South Jeon Ra	9	37.3
North Gyeong Sang	10	49.2
South Gyeong Sang	9	43.8
Je Ju	1	32.5

Computations for the Analysis of Variance**

	Sums of square	Degrees of freedom	Estimate of variance	F	Probability
Total	1,138.965	N - 1 = 15.0			
Between	553.093	K - 1 = 1.00	553.093	13.216	P<.01
Within	585.872	N - K =14.0	41.848		

Source: The Dong-A Ilbo, February 15, 1985, pp. 16-17.

*The Democratic Justice Party (DJP), the government party received 35 percent of the popular votes, while the opposition parties 57.9 percent with the remaining 7.1 percent of the absentees plus invalid votes.

**For further information on computations for the analysis of variance (ANOVA), see Herbert M. Blalock, Social Statistics (N.Y.: McGraw-Hill Book Company, 1960), ch. 16.

Table 3
Difference between Cities and Rural Counties in Percent of Popular Votes in the Direct Presidential Elections of the 1st and 3rd Republics and in the 2/12/85 National Assembly Election of the 5th Republic
(unit: million)

	Total eligible voters	% absent votes			% urban votes	% rural votes	Total
		Urban	Rural	Overall			
1st Republic:							
2nd Presidential election (8/5/52)	8.26	21.5	9.9	11.8	13.4	74.7	100%
3rd term election (5/15/56)	9.60	11.5	3.8	5.6	20.7	73.6	100%
4th term election (3/15/60)	11.19	5.7	1.9	2.9	25.8	66.1	100%
3rd Republic:							
1st term (10/15/63)	12.98	19.6	12.7	14.9	26.3	58.8	100%
2nd term (5/3/67)	13.94	26.7	10.9	16.4	25.6	57.9	100%
3rd term (4/27/71)	15.75	24.6	17.0	20.2	31.8	48.0	100%
5th Republic:							
2nd Nat'l Assembly (2/12/85)	20.35	n.a.	n.a.	7.1	47.6 41.0*	45.3 52.0*	

Source: The Central Election Management Committee (CEMC), The History of the Elections in the Republic of Korea (trans. into English)(Seoul, Korea: the CEMC), Vol. 1 (1973), Vol.2 (1973), and Vol. 3 (1980). For further information on the 2/12/85 National Assembly election, The Dong-A Ilbo, February 15,1985.

*The percent ratio of 41.0 to 52.0 in the parentheses are the figures based on the seven major cities in relation to all other election districts including the small cities.

Table 4
The Government Party's Primary and Secondary Winnings in the 2/12/85 National Assembly Election

	Seven major cities	Provinces
Total seats	30	62
Loss	6	0
Victory:	24	62
Primary winners	7 23.3%	55 88.7%
Secondary winners	17 56.7%	7 11.3%
$x^2 =$	375.32	$p < .001$

Source: *The Dong-A Ilbo*, February 15, 1985

secondary winners by taking advantage of a two-member district system. To test this hypothesis, the Chi-square computation was employed. Since the computed Chi-square value of 375.32 far exceeds the table value of 10.83 at the .001 level with one degree of freedom, this rejects the null hypothesis that there is no significant difference between the major cities and the rural provinces in terms of a primary-secondary winning strategy. Rather this confirms the above finding that: a majority of the party's urban candidates won the election as the secondary winners, whereas an absolute majority of their counterparts in the rural provinces were the primary winners. This indicates that a two-member district system really helped the DJP secure a majority of the party's urban candidates as the secondary winners. This is the reason the administration's blueprint for the restoration of local autonomy equally endorses a multimember rather than a single-member district system for the election of local councilmen.

Another mechanism to offset the ever-increasing urban votes and the subsequent potential for the government party to fail in securing a majority of the Assembly seats is the maintenance of the existing malapportioned election districts.

Table 5 shows that 36 percent of the 30 major urban National Assembly districts had over 300,000 votes, while only 4.8 percent of the 62 rural districts had over 300,000 votes. About 87 percent of the 30 urban districts have over 200,000 voters, whereas 79 percent of the 62 rural districts have less than 200,000 voters. The ratio of the average number of voters in the seven major urban districts to that of the rural districts is 279,543 to 171,188. The unequal distribution of population among the local towns and sub-blocks is more significant and salient than that among the National Assembly districts. For example, the Duk Hwang town of Geong Ju City has a population that accounts for only 1.2 percent of the population of another town, Ga Zwa of Inchon City. Kim Hwa sub-block (up) in Gang Won province has a population that approximates only 8.3 percent of the population of another sub-block, Dong Bbu in Gyeong Gi province. Nevertheless, no deliberation thus far has been attempted on redistricting across the existing local governmental boundaries for the local legislative council election.

The most significant and salient element of the administration's blueprint for the restoration of local autonomy is the appointment of all local chief executives by the central government with the concurrent restriction of the power held by local legislative councils in their checks and balances against the local chiefs.

The preference of the appointment of local heads may be traced back to President Rhee's painstaking experience in the presidential election in 1956. As is shown in Table 6 Syngman Rhee was elected the second-term president of the republic in 1952 with 62.4 percent and 76.8 percent of the urban and rural popular vote respectively against the three competing candidates. President Rhee felt so secure in running for a third consecutive presidency that in 1956 the Local Autonomy Law was amended as a compromise with the opposition parties. It authorized local chiefs of cities, counties, and towns to be directly elected by the popular votes. Since the local chief executives were not appointed they no longer felt obligated to obey the instructions from the central government. Nor did they feel compelled to campaign for President Rhee in his re-election. The outcome was the drastic decline of popular votes for the presidential election, the Local Autonomy Law was revised (July 8, 1956), reverting to the old system of the appointment of all local chiefs by the central government. This has been continuously practiced up to the present.

To maximize the use of the appointed local heads to influence the voters at the lowest local level, *pan-sang-hoe*, a neighborhood meet-

Table 5
Malapportionment in Election Districts
Towns (Dong) and Sub-Blocks (Up)
The 2/12/85 National Assembly Election Districts

	Seven major cities		**Rural Districts**	
Number of Districts	30		62	
Over 400,000 votes	2	6.7%	1	1.6%
300,000-399,999	9	29.9	2	3.2
200,000-299,999	15	50.0	10	16.3
100,000-199,999	4	13.3	7	75.8
Below 100,000	0	0.0	2.	3.2
Average votes per district	279,543		171,188	

Towns with over 40,000 residents		**Towns with less than 1,000 residents**	
Ga Zwa, Inchon	48,467	Duk Hwang, Geong Ju	495
Suk Nam, Inchon	42,107	Pyong Lim #2, Chung Mu	590
Doma #1	42,095	Pyong Lim #1, Chung Mu	758
*** six other large towns in-between**		*** six other small towns in-between**	
Ung Ahm, Seoul	40,033	Back Shin, Sam Chun Po	915
Sub-blocks over 50,000 residents		**Sub-blocks with less than 10,000 residents**	
Dong Bu, Gyeong Gi	63,271	Kim Hwa, Gang Won	5,258
Song Jung, Jeon Nam	60,167	Chul Won, Gang Won	7,260
Chang Sung Po, Gyeong Nam	58,715	Sung Guh, Choong, Nam	8,300
		Chung Song, Gyeong Buk	8,843
Eui Wang, Gyeong Gi	55,003	Gan Sunk, Gang Won	9,027
Mee Gum, Gyeong Gi	53,519	Hwa Yang, Gyeong Buk	9,074
Goon Po, Gyeong Gi	52,710		
Mil Yang, Gyong Nam	51,060		

Source: Population distribution among towns (dong) and sub-blocks (up) is based on the census held as of November 1, 1985. For further information see The Dong-A Ilbo, February 15, 1985 and May 17, 1986.

Table 6

Preference for the Appointment of Local Heads to Popular Election

Votes cast for the incumbent president Syngman Rhee	First Republic of Korea				
	2nd Term (8/5/52)	Amendment to Local Autonomy Law	3rd Term (5/15/56)	Amendment to Local Autonomy Law	4th Term (3/15/60)
Cities (%)	62.4	Direct election of local chief executives in cities, counties & towns*	23.5	Their appointment by the central government	79.6
Rural (%)	76.8		72.9		91.9
Total (%)	74.6		69.9		88.6
Votes for the major opponent	11.3		30.0		0.0
Number of Candidates	4		2		1

Source: The same as in the case of Table 3.
*Mayor of Seoul and provincial governors were to be continuously appointed by the central government.

ing that consists of about ten to fifteen rural residential households, was established with its appointed head in 1976 and they have been held once a month ever since. The Minister of Home Affairs, Chung Suk-mo, recently boasted that as much as 82 percent of the total popular grievances which came up at the monthly neighborhood meetings in the last ten years have been taken care of. A total of 1,364,000 petitions and complaints thus far have been presented to the central and provincial government offices through *pan-sang-hoes* during the period.[11] The May 1986 monthly meeting, for example, discussed the necessity of wearing seat belts in cars and the need for prompt reports to investigation authorities about the presence of espionage agents or any other suspicious persons.

One should keep in mind, however, that, unlike the New England town meetings, as voluntary local democratic organizations, *pan-sang-hoes* (the smallest local units of the central administration) have made a deep penetration into rural residential areas with the help of local administrators and police. In fact, they have influenced the rural voters to vote for the government party, but not to participate in the opposition party's signature campaign for a constitutional amendment for a direct, popular presidential election.[12] Appointed local heads, by means of community meetings and other local organizations, may be able to mobilize rural voters for the government party. The Ministry of Home Affairs of the national government recently announced *pan-sang-hoes* would be organized at worksites and factory dormitories in the urban areas.[13] One may wonder about the real reason behind the expansion of the *pan-sang-hoe* system to the urban areas at a time when the restoration of local autonomy is under deliberation for its implementation in 1987. The major highlights of the blueprint for local autonomy are deliberated under the primacy of the maintenance of political power by the government party.

Three months and twenty-two days after the announcement of the administration's blueprint, upon the approval of the Blue House, the plan was revised as a compromise between the administration and the government party. The revised plan again cleared by the Blue House, is the reverse of the original plan concerning the initial stage of the implementation of local autonomy. While the original plan endorsed local autonomy for 14 high-echelon administrative units—5 major cities and 9 provinces on the basis of the area-wide/region-wide reform model—the revised plan calls for introducing the local autonomy in low-echelon units—57 small cities, 139 counties, and 40 wards in the major cities.

The administration-DJP compromise is justified on the grounds that it pays "maximum attention to public opinion" as voiced in public hearings held during the month of July 1986 in the thirteen cities across the country. The revised plan is further endorsed by the government party because it is viewed as faithful to the inherent aim of local autonomy, often described as "grassroots democracy." [14]

Nevertheless, one may identify the real reason for the government party's revision of the original plan on the basis of the thesis of the underlying objective being the maintenance of government power. The government party was very uneasy and nervous about the fact that in case local autonomy should be adopted, as suggested by the administration, in the five big cities and the nine provinces, the ruling party could inevitably face strong backlash from the urban voters in the local and national elections. As is witnessed in Table 2 and Table 3, large cities have shown inclinations to vote for opposition candidates in the parliamentary and presidential elections. Therefore, once opposition party councilmen hold a strong grip on the large urban local governments, a negative snowballing effect will be expected in the national election.

The government party is further blamed for the revised plan of low level financial self-reliance for the small cities and counties, compared with that of the five big cities and the nine provinces. According to the information on the 1986 income budget, the financial self-reliance ratio averages 61 percent for 57 small cities and 27 percent for 139 counties, compared with 95 percent for the big cities and 38 percent for the nine provinces.[15] The same constitutional justification for postponement of local autonomy based on the lack of financial self-reliance that has been used for the past six years is forsaken this time by the administration and the government party themselves.

For Institutionalization

Thus far we have examined a thesis that the administration has postponed the restoration of local autonomy primarily for the maintenance of power by the government party. The administration's original blueprint and the revised plan for autonomy in 1987 are both designed primarily for the same purpose—maintaining government party power. Thereby the importance of the institutionalization of local autonomy is neglected.

Instead the following elements should be taken into consideration, if local self-government is to be institutionalized. They are: the proper division of powers and responsibilities between the central government and the local governments; the size of local self-government—small and fragmented, area-wide or region-wide; the question of nation-wide uniform structures, procedures, and rules across all the local governments or diversity among them; the one

Table 7

Autonomy of Internal Operation of the States in the United States

Degree of Centralization within the states (1)	**Centralized**	**Partially centralized**	**Balanced**	**Partially decentralized**	**Decentralized**
# of States	6	9	24	6	5
Tenure Provisions for Governors (2)	Four-year term with no restrictions	Two four-year terms	Four-year term, no consecutive reelection	Two-year term with no restriction	
# of States	19	21	6	4	
Appointive Powers of Governors (3)*	**Very Strong**	**Strong**	**Moderate**	**Weak**	**Very Weak**
# of States	12	10	10	13	3
Budget Powers of Governors (4)	Full Responsibility	Responsibility shared with a civil service appointee	Responsibility shared with the legislature	Responsibility shared with independent office or agency	
# of States	40	5	2	3	
Governor's Veto Powers (5)	**Very Strong**	**Strong**	**Moderate**	**Weak**	**Very Weak**
# of States	27	5	11	6	1

Source: (1), (2), (3), and (5) are derived from data of Table 2.5, Table 6.2, Table 6.3, and Table 6.4, in Thomas R. Dye, Politics in States and Communities (Englewood Cliffs, N.J.: Prentice-Hall, Inc. 1981), pp. 56, 170, 172, and 177; (4) Derived from the data of Table 6.4 in Dye, ibid., (1977), p. 177.
* Two states—Kansas and Michgan were excluded due to a lack of information in Book of the States, 1978-79.

person-one vote principle in the election of local legislative councilmen; the choice of an election district system—single-member or multimember; the scope and extent of the implementation of local autonomy—an extensive and comprehensive or a limited, experimental and gradual one; the transferring of a variety of local taxes from the central government to the local governments, and financial aids by the central government for local financial self-reliance. Let us briefly examine these elements.

It is not an easy task to divide powers and responsibilities between the national government and the local governments. Even in the United States, many administrators are performing their duties partially for the federal government, and partially for the state and local governments. Their paycheck is a summation of salaries paid by the different levels of government.[16] Moreover, the federal government took over some of the jurisdictions from the states. For example, such commercial activities as manufacturing, mining, farming, insurance, business-labor disputes, and elections had long been under the prerogatives of the state governments. But they were all taken over by the federal government.[17]

Nevertheless, one can identify without hesitation the clearly drawn division of powers and responsibilities between the federal government and the local governments in the United States.[18]

In the case of South Korea, even under the full swing of local autonomy for a relatively short period of time in the past, over 80 percent of the tasks performed by the local governments were those ordered and closely supervised by the central government.[19] Local governments did have a few limited jurisdictions of their own. Some scholars and politicians of today continue to endorse such a high degree of centralization. Others would prefer a broad and comprehensive interpretation of Article 118 of the 1980 Constitution whereby the central government should be granted a few specific responsibilities in areas such as national defense, foreign relations, coinage and national treasury, and economic planning. On the other hand, the local governments should be given all of the agriculture and forestry, law and order, postal service and welfare responsibilities.[20]

Under the disguise of the promotion of autonomy and independence from local politics, several major jurisdictions have been separated from the local government and then placed under the direct supervision of the central government. In order for school administration to become independent of local politics, an independent Board of Education was established in 1952 and soon fell under the direct supervision of the central government's Ministry of Education. So did the Office of Maritime Affairs, the administration of agricultural instructions and experiment stations under the direct supervision of the Ministry of Agriculture and Fisheries, and the police under the Ministry of Home Affairs.

No less serious than the above cases is the absence of judicial organizations at the local government level. Therefore, regardless of what level of government a legal dispute occurs—national, provincial, city, county or a smaller local government, all legal disputes have been handled by the national judicial courts. It goes without saying that the central government's judicial branch should have no monopoly of all legal disputes. The necessity of local judicial courts, separate from and independent of the central ones, is beyond dispute. Thus far this question has never been given attention by the administration, the government party or by the opposition parties.

A quest for an ideal size of local self-government is another controversial issue. Concerning how big local government should be, there are two contending schools of thought. One is to establish as many small governments and as many special (functional) governments as are endorsed and financially supported by the people. The other is to endorse metropolitan area-wide or region-wide local governments, because local governments that are too small would not be able to efficiently, financially, and technically manage many complicated issues such as pollution control, public safety, region-wide economic development, and transportation.[21] Due to the relatively small size of the territory the latter is often suggested. Professor Hahn Sung-joo, therefore, recommended: two metropolitan area-wide governments such as the Seoul Metropolitan Area government combining the city of Seoul and Gyeong Gi province; the Pusan Metropolitan government incorporating the city of Pusan and the neighboring areas; and four region-wide governments, each combining two neighboring provinces.[22]

Whether or not local governments should be uniform in their autonomy and functions may be an equally important controversial issue. Both the state and local governments in the United States, for example, show a rich diversity in their structures and

Table 8
Methods of Judicial Selection in the United States

Methods	Partisan Elections	Nonpartisan Elections	Selection by legislature	Appointment	Missouri Plan*
# of States	11	15	5	9	10

Source: Derived from data of Table 7.1 in Thomas R. Dye, *Politics in States and Communities* (Englewood Cliffs, N.J.: Prentice-Hall, Inc., 1981), pp. 189-190.
*Refers to a method in which governors appoint judges on the recommendations of a select committee, and after the judge has been in office for a year or more, the voters are given the opportunity to retain or oust the appointed judges.

modes of operation. As is shown in Table 7, the degree of centralization of the state governments over their local governments vary from state to state. A governor's tenure is equally diverse among the states, so as to allow either an unlimited number of four-year terms, two four-year terms, one four-year or only one two-year term. A governor's appointive power is either very strong, strong, moderate, weak, or very weak, depending on the states. Each governor's budgeting and veto powers also vary from state to state.

The selection of the judges for the state courts depends on either partisan popular election, nonpartisan election, election by the state legislature, appointment by the governor, or a Missouri plan in which the judges, after one year or more of service in office upon the appointment by the governor, may be subject to popular votes for retention. (see Table 8)

Table 9 shows a rich diversity among the cities in the United States. With respect to the forms of city government, about 44 percent of them have a council-manager form, six percent a commission form, and 50 percent a mayor-council form. In each of these three different forms of city government councilmen are elected by one of three methods: at-large, ward, or a combination. The veto power of the mayors is granted either on specific measures, all measures, or denied.

Contrary to the United States, local self-government in South

Table 9

Autonomy in Internal Operation of the Cities in the United States

Form of City Government (1):	Council-Manager	Commission	Mayor-Council
Total Number (%)	1,207 (43.9%)	165 (6%)	1,378 (50.1%)
Council Elections (2):			
At-Large	845.0 (70%)	140.0 (85%)	606.0 (44%)
Ward	241.0 (20%)	20.0 (12%)	441.0 (32%)
Combination	97.0 (8%)	0.0 (0%)	290.0 (21%)
Other	24.0 (2%)	5.0 (3%)	41.0 (3%)
Total	100.0%	100.0%	100.0%
Method of Selection of Mayors (3):			
Directly Elected	616.0 (52%)	140.0 (85%)	1295.0 (95%)
Selected by Council	555.0 (47%)	25.0 (15%)	69.0 (5%)
Councilmen with Highest Vote	12.0 (1%)	0.0 (0%)	0.0 (0%)
Voting Powers of Mayors (4):			
Yes	869.0 (72%)	135.0 (85%)	289.0 (21%)
No	338.0 (28%)	30.0 (18%)	1089.0 (79%)
The Veto Powers of Mayors (5):			
Veto Selected Measures	157.0(12%)	26.0(15%)	813.0 (45%)
Veto All Measures	48.0 (4%)	15.0 (8%)	413.0 (23%)
No Veto	1050.0 (84%)	139.0 (77%)	565.0 (32%)

Source: (1), (2), (3), (4), and (5) are derived from data of Table 10.3, Table 10.5, and Table 10.6, respectively in Thomas R. Dye, *Politics in States and Communities* (Englewood Cliffs N.J.: Prentice Hall, Inc., 1981), pp. 290, 303 and 304.

Korea had been run under the uniform structures and functions superimposed by the National Assembly of the central government. One may wonder about the wisdom of imposing exactly the same types of structures and modes of operation on all the local governments in the name of granting local autonomy to them.

As is shown in Table 5, an unequal distribution of population becomes an important issue not only between the National Assembly election districts but also between local legislative council election districts from which the election of councilmen was held in 1987. The problem of malapportionment may become a controversial issue when the choice of either a single-member or a multimember council election district system is to be made.

Thus far, the Democratic Justice Party (DJP) and the New Korea Democratic Party (NKDP) show a consensus on the preference of a multimember district system and partisan elections of legislative councilmen. But they show contending views: The DJP would implement local self-government—in 236 small cities, counties, and wards in the first phase, extend it to the large cities and provinces in the second phase, and then elect all the local chief executives by popular vote in the third phase. The NKDP, on the other hand, insists that local autonomy should be implemented in all levels of local governments, extensively and simultaneously, and their chief executives be directly elected by the voters.[23]

Summary

In order for local autonomy to be implemented and subsequently institutionalized, the administration, the DJP, and the NKDP should address themselves to the above controversial issues such as: the division of powers and responsibilities between the central government and the local governments; the size of local self-government; nation-wide uniform structures and functions or diversity among local governments; the problem of malapportionment and the possibility of reapportionment being used to promote the one person-one vote principle; an extensive and comprehensive implementation or a limited, experimental and gradual implementation of local autonomy; the appointment or popular election of local chief executives; measures for financial self-reliance; and the establishment of local judicial systems separate from and independent of the national judicial system.

All of these issues, however, may be conducive to the maintenance and persistence of government party political powers in the central government or detrimental to an attempt by the opposition parties to secure the political power, depending upon their final outcomes. The competition between the political parties for the control of local governments is seen as a microcosm of the competition for the control of the central government. Since there is no absolute correctness on resolving these issues, they should be resolved under democratic procedural principles such as the guarantee of the basic freedoms and rights, a political atmosphere of full and open debate on the pros and cons of the issues, and the subsequent decisions on the basis of a majority rule.

NOTES

1. The government announced the implementation of local self-government within the first half of 1987. However, it was delayed by the confrontation between the government and opposition forces over presidential election methods. The ruling Democratic Justice Party stated its plan to restore local self-government in 1988. For both the original and revised plans see *The Dong-A Ilbo*, May 5 and 24, 1986 and *The Korea Herald*, August 18, 1987.
2. Samuel P. Huntington, *Political Order in Changing Societies* (Yale University Press, 1969), p. 12.
3. *Ibid.*, p. 13.
4. Korean Overseas Information Service (KOIS), Ministry of Culture and Information, *A Handbook of Korea* (Seoul, Korea: KOIS, 1979), p. 374.
5. For further information on the lack of institutionalization of local self-government, see Sung M. Pae, *Testing Democratic Theories in Korea* (Lanham, MD: University Press of America, 1986), pp. 119-24; Park Moon Ok, *Introduction to Korean Government* (transl. into English) (Seoul, Korea: The Shin-Chun Sa, 1975), pp. 378-83.
6. The Ministry of Home Affairs, *A White Paper on Local Autonomy in Korea* (Seoul, Korea: Kwang Myung Publishing Co., 1968), pp. 67-68.
7. *Ibid.*, pp. 83-84.
8. For further information, see *ibid.*, Ch. 2.
9. *The Dong-A Ilbo*, May 23, 1986.
10. *The Korea Herald*, May 3, 1986 and *The Dong-A Ilbo*, May 5, 1986.

11. *The Korea Herald*, May 27, 1986.
12. *The Dong-A Ilbo*, May 5, 1986.
13. *The Korea Herald*, May 27, 1986.
14. *Ibid.*, August 19, 1986 and August 21, 1986.
15. *Ibid.*
16. Due to the strong interdependence and overlapping of the jurisdictions across the levels of government, the United States is often called a marble cake. For further information, see Morton Grodzins, "The Federalism" in *American Federalism in Perspective* ed. by Aaron F. Wildavsky (Boston: Little, Brown and Co., 1967).
17. Michael N. Danielson and Walter F. Murphy, *American Democracy* (N.Y.: Holmes R. Meier Publishers, Inc., 1983), pp. 101-103.
18. The division of powers is based upon Article 1, Section 8 and its last paragraph, Article VI of the U.S. Constitution for the federal government, and the 10th Amendment to the Constitution for the local governments.
19. Professor Choi indicated a ratio of 63 percent to 37 percent in terms of the relative powers of the central government to the local governments. However, their overlapping functions and jurisdictions are in fact excluded in his computation. See Bong-Gi Choi, "Changing Demands and Responsive Strategies of Local Administration" in *Decentralization and Public Policies* (transl. into English) ed. by Yong Sang Cho (Taegu, Korea: Keimyung University Press, 1986).
20. Sung Joo Hahn, *Democracy in Korea and Political Development* (transl. into English) (Seoul, Korea: The Bup Moon Sa, 1976), pp. 306ff.
21. The former is called the public choice model and the latter the area-and/or region-wide reform model. For further information on the two contrasting models and related pros and cons, see Vincent Ostrom et al., "The Organization of Government in Metropolitan Areas: A Theoretical Inquiry," *American Political Science Review* (Dec. 1961), pp. 831-42; Vincent Ostrom, *The Intellectual Crisis in American Public Administration* (University Press of Alabama, 1974); Robert L. Bish, *The Public Economy of Metropolitan Areas*; Sung M. Pae, *op. cit.*, pp. 133-40.
22. Sung Joo Hahn, *op. cit.*, pp. 306ff.
23. *The Dong-A Ilbo*, May 20, 1986.

7

Urbanization and Changing Voting Patterns in South Korean Parliamentary Elections

HONG NACK KIM AND SUNKI CHOE

Introduction

The impact of urbanization on the political behavior of the electorate has been a focus of debate among social scientists since the "Chicago school" advanced the much debated paradigm that urbanization leads to alienation, anemic behavior, and political instability.[1] While the paradigm was widely accepted for a while, contemporary studies challenge both its universality and usefulness in conceptualizing the political implications of urbanization. Myron Weiner and John O. Field, for example, argued recently that urban areas differ significantly from one developing country to another, that they are affected by the rural areas around them in addition to having their own effects on those areas, and that even within a single country there are likely to be substantial variations from one city to another as to the degree of politicization, radicalization, and polarization of politics.[2] David R. Cameron and others came up with a more sweeping contention that urbanization is a relatively unimportant influence on the political behavior of the electorate, and that it is only one aspect of the continuing process of modernization.[3]

An area of special concern to political scientists has been to ascertain the relationship between urbanization and political participation, including voting. Satisfactory specification of the linkage between urbanization and political participation in democratic political systems will enhance our understanding of the impact of the community on an individual's political participation.

Three distinguishable trends have emerged in the findings of various studies dealing with the impact of urbanization on political participation, particularly voting.

First, the modernization model advanced by Lester Milbrath, Karl Deutsch, Daniel Lerner and others predicts an increase in participation as one moves from the rural periphery to the urban center. According to Milbrath's center-periphery theory,[4] some individuals are more integrated than others into political communication channels. Urban residents are not only closer to the center of society than their rural counterparts, but are also more likely to be involved in politics than the rural residents. In a similar vein, Lerner views urbanization as a vital phase of multi-stage processes for political participation because urbanization tends to raise the level of literacy which in turn increases media exposure and levels of participation on the part of the city dwellers.[5] Finally, according to Deutsch, social mobilization broadens political participation.[6] As a society becomes more urbanized, industrialized, and modernized, according to Deutsch, the people become more dependent on government and more aware of political self-interest. The increase in political self-interest leads to greater demands on the government and higher levels of mass political involvement.

Second, according to the "decline-of community" model espoused by Sidney Verba, Norman Nie, Robert Dahl, and Edward Tufte and others, participation declines as one moves from the small, intimate town or village to the massive, impersonal city. Unlike the small rural community, in which citizens know "the ropes of politics" and whom to contact, in the large city politics becomes more complicated and impersonal, and their attention becomes more diffuse.[7] As a consequence, meaningful participation is more difficult and the level of participation declines in the city. In a similar vein, Dahl and Tufte predict participation declines in the urban area: "The larger the citizen body, the weaker the sense of individual effectiveness (the greater the sense of powerlessness), hence the weaker the incentives to participate, hence the less participation."[8]

Finally, Alex Inkeles and others find little evidence that urbanization exerts any significant independent influence upon an individual's political behavior.[9] In a similar vein, G.B. Powell, Kenneth Prewitt, and Norman Nie also point out that: "It appears that living in an urban environment has no significant effect on rates of national participation." [9a]

In an attempt to test the validity of some of these theories, this paper intends to investigate the relationship between urbanization and electoral participation in Korea from 1963 to 1985. Because of her rapid urbanization during this period, South Korea can be regarded as one of the most suitable laboratories for a study of this type. This study covers six general elections in the 22 year period. The parliamentary election of 1981 is not included in this study because of its uniqueness (e.g., massive purge of opposition leaders). Furthermore, due to the unavailability of necessary data for the analysis, our study of the 1985 election is tentative.

In order to delineate the urban-rural differences among electoral districts, electoral districts are divided into four categories: 1) metropolitan districts in special cities; 2) urban districts in cities; 3) semi-urban or semi-rural districts in city-county combination; 4) rural districts in counties. For urban-rural dichotomous comparison, metropolitan and urban districts were merged into "urban districts" while semi-urban or semi-rural districts were merged with rural districts to constitute "rural districts." There were 131 single-member districts in 1963 and 1967, and 153 districts in 1971 with a plurality of votes needed for victory. In the elections of 1973 and 1978 there were 73 and 77 multimember districts respectively. In these two elections, the voter was allowed to choose only one candidate, and the top two vote-getters in each district were elected. In the 1981 and 1985 elections, 92 two-member districts were used.

The data was drawn from official parliamentary election returns compiled and published by the South Korean government socio-demographic statistics of these districts derived from census reports, and statistical data compiled by the official sources.[10] By the very nature of our data the focus of the analysis is limited to a systematic study of how Korean voters behave in the aggregate in parliamentary elections and not the behavior of individual voters. However, wherever warranted, pertinent theories and data relating to the behavior of individual voters will be utilized to supplement the aggregate data.

As will be shown in the main part of this study, the findings of this paper as a whole substantiate the validity of the "decline-of community" model on the effects of urbanization on electoral participation: the more urbanized the constituencies are, the less the voter turnout rate. Its findings also confirm the hypothesis advanced by Dahl and Tufte on the inverse correlation between urbanity and the strength of the leading party (i.e., the government party): the more urbanized a political unit with greater economic specialization, the less the percentage of the vote for the leading (or government) party.

Urbanization of Korea since 1945

Despite the long history of Korea, the process of urbanization is a relatively recent phenomenon, especially in the last three decades. Table 1 shows Korea's total population and the urban percentage for census years from 1915 to 1980. In the late 1940s, one out of every five Koreans lived in urban areas. By 1980, more Koreans (i.e., 57 percent) lived in cities. In 1955, Seoul had a population of about 1.5 million, representing only seven percent of the national total. By 1980, its population grew to nearly 8.5 million, representing 22.3 percent of the total population.[11]

The dislocation caused by the Korean War accounted for the increase in urban population during and immediately after the 1950-53 period. Hundreds of thousands of refugees, many of them from North Korea, streamed into the cities. During the post-Korean war period migration from villages to cities was stimulated by the lure of greater economic and/or educational opportunities. Accelerated migration was a post-1962 phenomenon, especially with the inauguration of a series of economic development plans.

Between 1945 and 1980 the urban population of Korea grew from 14.5 percent to 57.2 percent of the total; most of this increase was attributed to rural-to-urban migration rather than to natural growth of the urban population.[12]

The rapid urbanization of Korea was closely related to its phenomenal economic growth. By the late 1960s migration had become a serious problem not only because cities were terribly overcrowded but also because the rural areas were losing the most productive elements of their labor force. The *Saemaul* (or New Village) Movement was launched in the early 1970s largely in order to improve the economic conditions of the villages and to stem this migration. However, in the early 1980s many villages consisted largely of older persons and few young able-bodied men and women remained to work in the fields.

In the late 1940s Korea was predominantly an agricultural economy. Even as late as 1963, 63.1 percent of the labor force was engaged in primary industry. However, the proportion declined to 30.6 percent, with 22.4 percent in secondary industry and 47 percent in tertiary industry by 1982.[13] In addition, the urban areas came to have highly mobilized and vocal groups, students, intellectuals, white-collar workers, and blue-collar workers.

Korea is one of the world's most densely populated countries, having an estimated 376.4 persons per square kilometer in 1980, which is 15 1/2 times the average density of the United States. In 1975 it was estimated that the density of Korea's thirty-five cities, each of which had 50,000 or more inhabitants, was 3,700 persons per square kilometer. In 1980 the densities of the two largest cities, Seoul and Pusan, were estimated to be 13,777.5 persons and 7,310.1 persons per square kilometer, respectively.[14]

Urbanization has been an important factor not only in shaping economic development and the standard of living, but also in the development of social attitudes and human relationships. Rapid urban growth has brought about problems that are familiar. Large numbers of migrants, estimated at 8 percent of the urban population in 1973, were obliged to live in illegal shanty towns as squatters, and housing for others was most often cramped, uncomfortable, and extremely expensive. The concentration of factories in urban areas, the rapid growth of motorized traffic, and the widespread use of coal for home heating in winter months have increased water and air pollution to dangerous levels, posing a serious threat to public health as well as impacting negatively upon the quality of urban life.

Among the more important long term effects of rapid urbanization are the changing family and community structure. The overall tendency has been for social relationships to become more individualistic, economically oriented, and short-term. People have become much more mobile, both socially and geographically. In addition, contemporary urban family and social life seems to exhibit a number of novel trends. One is the tendency for the extended kinship structure to weaken with the concomitant rise of the nuclear family system. Another trend is the movement toward equality in family relations and the resulting improvement in the status of women. Thirdly, there is a movement away from lineage and neighborhood-based social relations toward interest-based relations, since urbanites these days work among unrelated people in factories, shops, and offices. Finally there is an increasing tendency for an individual's location and human relationships to be transitory rather than permanent and lifelong.

Fluidity in human relationships is becoming more apparent as people change their residences more frequently, often in line with new employment requirements (see Table 2). Moreover, an increasing proportion of the urban population lives in large, impersonal, high rise apartment complexes. Such developments could not help but affect the electoral behavior of the Korean people.

Urbanization and Electoral Participation

As in many other countries, more Koreans participate in elections than in any other kind of political participation. Compared to the United States, the voter turnout rate is higher in Korea with a larger turnout rate in rural areas than in urban areas. As can be seen in Table 3, the voting turnout rates show remarkable differences among the "locality" categories in the five parliamentary elections. An average of almost 33 percent of the voters stayed away from the polls from 1963 to 1978 in urban districts while only about 21 percent of voters abstained in rural districts. Urban and semi-rural categories fell between the two extremes, with the semi-rural closer to the rural districts.[15] Basically, a similar pattern can be seen in the 1985 general election (see Table 7).

In the theoretical perspective of the "modernization" model, we would anticipate electoral districts whose main features include a large population, high density, and a high level of industrialization to show a high level of turnout. We would also anticipate that districts characterized by a high level of education and a concentration of the postwar generation would score high on voter turnout, as the more modernized sectors are expected to participate more actively in the political process, including electoral process, under the modernization model. On the other hand, we would anticipate districts with a high level of illiteracy, a concentration of the prewar generation and of females to show a low level of turnout, given the presumption that in these areas the influence of the traditional mode of thinking and behavior is strong.

Table 4 presents correlations between voting participation rates and some selected environmental conditions or characteristics of electoral districts. It reflects the level of social development such as population size and density, percent non-farm household, percent postwar generation, percent prewar generation, percent college enrollment and illiteracy, and percent female. In all five elections the population, density, industrialization, postwar generation, and college enrollment variable show strong negative correlations while prewar generation, illiteracy, and female variables show either very weak or strong positive relationships with voting participation. Such preliminary findings clearly indicate that voting turnout in South Korea deviates from the modernization model.

An inevitable question to be asked is: Why does South Korea have lower voting turnouts in urban districts than in rural districts?

Students of Korean voting behavior have advanced several hypotheses on the urban-rural differences in voter turnout rates. First, according to the "mobilized voting" hypothesis, the urban-rural difference in voter turnout should be attributed to the rural community structure and social relationships which facilitate the mobilization of voters in rural villages.[16] Many traditionally oriented citizens, especially those living in rural villages, may participate in elections merely in compliance with, or out of respect for, the wishes of their community leaders or government officials. The act of voting in this instance expresses conformity to both traditional collective norms and authority rather than self-assertive and autonomous individual choice regarding candidates and their policies. According to Kim Chong-lim, "mobilized voters" participate in elections merely because they are pressured "to conform to the wishes of the heads of their families, their villages, their clans, or government officials in their districts." Although it is difficult to ascertain the extent of "mobilized voting" in parliamentary elections, Kim estimates that at least one out of every 10 voters in the 1973 parliamentary election was a mobilized voter.[17] Furthermore, mobilized voting is more likely to occur among the old, female, low educated voters with low class status in small towns and villages than among the young, well-educated, and politically sophisticated urbanites. According to Kim, an important aspect of the political orientation among mobilized voters is their tendency to support the government party. Another aspect of mobilized voters' political orientation is their weak commitment to democratic values.

The second frequently mentioned hypothesis is the stronger feelings of duty and obligation to vote among the rural Koreans along with their fear of retaliation if they fail to vote.[18] The rural-urban differences in voting are also attributed to the stronger feelings of community and local loyalty among the villagers and their more optimistic attitudes and instrumental orientation toward elections.[19]

Third, C.I. Eugene Kim and his associates attribute the low turnout rate in urban areas to "alienation" among well educated young voters.[20] These highly educated young people show a great deal of interest in politics but have little faith in the efficacy of elections. The more politically sophisticated they become, the more intense their feelings about the futility of electoral participation. To them, then, an election is a meaningless contest or a mechanism for the ruling party to mobilize the masses to legitimize its continued rule.

Finally, Lee Chae-jin, links the low turnout of urban voters to the "disruptive effects of over-urbanization." [21] Urban mass society, due to its anonymous and competitive social and political relations, renders atomized urbanites less susceptible to communal pressures for their electoral participation.

Although these theories are helpful in our understanding of the urban-rural differences in the rate of voter turnout in Korea, a meaningful comparative perspective can be found in the "decline-of community" model which predicts the decline of political participation, including voting, as one moves from the smallness and intimacy of the village to the massive impersonality of the city.[22]

According to the formulation of this model by Verba and Nie, unlike the villagers, city dwellers usually live in a much less socially-integrated environment. Among other things, urbanization is associated with increased geographic mobility,[23] which tends to weaken the individual's integration into community associational and personal networks. In a highly mobile urban setting these networks, typically found in a residential community, are simply not as effective in reaching out or in influencing voters. In rural settings it is much easier to mobilize voters by personal contacts. As the community grows, however, it becomes less bounded economically and socially, largely because more and more residents commute to work and partly because recreational and educational facilities are located outside the community. As community life becomes less bounded and community residents more mobile, they tend to be less involved in neighborhood affairs than do the rural residents. In addition, urban residents often work in large organizations where the pattern of human interactions, authority, and communication is more impersonal. In short, the urbanites live in an environment where tradition is less binding. With this kind of social milieu voter mobilization through personal contacts becomes more difficult and less effective.

Moreover, urban dwellers have a weaker sense of obligation toward voting than the ruralites. Unlike the ruralites who regard voting as a civic duty, the urbanites tend to regard it as a right rather than a duty. Fewer urban than rural voters feel abstention is wrong.[24] In the smaller community there exists greater conformity to norms—actions are more visible, conflicting norms are more intolerable, and participation might be thought of as less private and more social and communal.[25] By contrast, as the size of the community increases, the capacity of the community to enforce conformity to a prevailing norm tends to decline rapidly. Thus, citizens in urban areas are under less social pressure to vote.

The lower voter turnout in the larger urban areas can be attributed also to the lack of incentive to participate. As the number of citizens increases, "any particular citizen's share in power, influence, and decision making necessarily declines." Thus, according to Dahl and Tufte, "the larger the citizen body, the weaker the sense of individual effectiveness (the greater the sense of powerlessness), hence the weaker the incentive to participate, hence the less participation."[26]

In the Korean context, the lack of incentive to participate in the urban areas may have been accentuated by political alienation and cynicism. According to a survey conducted by Eugene Kim and his associates, educated Koreans tend to be alienated: The more politically sophisticated they become, the more intensely they feel the futility of electoral participation.[27] This sense of alienation could stem from their realization that no peaceful transfer of governmental power has been effected through the electoral process in the postwar period. Under the circumstances, elections maybe perceived more as rituals than as a real instrument of governmental change in South Korea.

In short, citizens in urban areas are subjected to less social pressure to vote. In large metropolitan areas, which are more impersonal and less tradition-bound than small towns or villages, voting rates are lower than in villages or towns. In terms of a comparative perspective, there is a striking similarity in the pattern of voter turnout in parliamentary elections between South Korea and Japan.[28]

Urbanization and Partisan Support

Many seasoned observers of Korean electoral politics have commented on the differences in party preference between the urban and rural inhabitants. The most striking pattern that emerges from the analysis of available aggregate voting data is the difference in partisan support along the urban-rural dimension in South Korea. Throughout the period, 1963-1985, opposition parties tended to find substantially more supporters in the more developed urban districts or areas, while the government parties have garnered more votes in less developed rural areas.

In the parliamentary elections held between 1963 and 1985 (with the exception of the 1981 election), statistically significant differences can be observed in the government party preference among the voters in the urban and rural districts.[28a] In general, the degree of support for the government party was inversely related to the degree of urbanization: the more urbanized a district, the less support for the government party (see Tables 5 and 8).

More specifically, support for the ruling DRP ranged from 54.0 percent (1963) to 41.6 percent (1978) with an average of 47.2 percent in metropolitan-urban districts, while the DRP's share of the vote ranged from 67.2 percent (1963) to 56.8 percent (1978) with an average of 61.6 percent in semi-rural and rural districts. In the 1985 parliamentary election, the urban-rural difference in partisan support was even more pronounced. The ruling Democratic Justice Party (DJP) received around 28.4 percent of the vote in the five most populous metropolitan-urban areas (i.e., Seoul, Pusan, Taegu, Inchon and Kwangju), while the major opposition party, the New Korea Democratic Party (NKDP), received substantially more votes (i.e., 40.2 percent) than the ruling DJP in these five major cities.[29] In the rural and semirural areas, however, the ruling DJP did considerably better by garnering more votes than the major opposition party (i.e., the NKDP).[29a] (See Table 8)

On the basis of the statistical analysis we can state that insofar as the parliamentary elections in South Korea are concerned, there exists what is generally known as the *yado yeochon* phenomenon (cities for the opposition, villages for the government party). The election results from 1963 to 1985 (with the exception of 1981) clearly indicate that politically awakened and conscious urban voters give greater support to the opposition parties, while the less sophisticated rural voters usually favor the government party in the parliamentary elections. Given such a consistent pattern of partisan orientation by the Korean electorate, the inevitable question is: Why do the urban voters prefer the opposition parties while the ruralities favor the government party?

Several different hypotheses purporting to explain the *yado yeochon* phenomenon have been advanced:

First, according to Kim Jae-on and B.C. Koh, urbanization serves as the basis of partisan alignment along the government-opposition cleavage, reflecting the differential commitment of the electorate to democratic values.[30] Urbanites, according to this thesis, are more committed to liberal democratic values than ruralites. Better educated and more sophisticated than the ruralites, the urbanites are less tolerant of violations or breaches of the democratic norms and constitutional rules of the game. The official ideology of political democracy in South Korea has thus provided the opposition forces with their most valuable political issues and with weapons that challenge the ruling party in elections, i.e., the legitimacy of the military regime in 1963, one-man rule, and the resulting corruption issues of 1971.

Second, as Korea has undergone remarkable economic growth in a relatively short span of time since 1960, rapid economic development and expansion, despite its general desirability, may have had a destablizing effect upon urban political complexities. It has not only disrupted traditional social values and structures, but also intensified peoples' dissatisfaction with the existing political order as they perceive "relative deprivation" as a result of growing economic inequality between the rich and the poor. Measuring economic inequality in terms of wages and income, Rhee Hang-yul hypothesizes that a high degree of income inequality in urban areas—especially in Seoul—has helped to increase anti-government votes in the elections.[31]

Furthermore, Rhee also maintains that the rapid expansion of a critical mass media was responsible for the stronger political opposition and the instability in urban centers, especially in Seoul. Many of the mass media, primarily centered in urban areas, were anti-government until 1979. Their rapid expansion created more political opposition and more instability in urban centers in Korea. Under the influence of the anti-government media, Seoulites were mobilized by the opposition. According to Rhee, there was an inverse correlation between the rate of growth in newspaper circulation and the electoral vote for the government party (DRP) under the Park regime (1961-1979).[32]

Third, there are those who believe that the government party has made concerted efforts to modernize the nation and has accomplished this goal to the extent that it deserves credit, but not without some negative consequences. Due to inadequate planning, urban centers are beset with a series of problems such as overcrowding, insufficient and inadequate housing, traffic jams, energy shortages, unemployment, inflation, etc. These urban problems breed discontent that can easily be mobilized by opposition forces to challenge the government and its leaders.[33]

Fourth, according to Kim Chong-lim, [34] the government party is stronger in the rural areas because it enjoys the advantage of "mobilized voting." By placing powerful government machinery and personnel at the service of the government party during the election period, the government party enjoys enormous advantages over the opposition parties in rural districts. Since the "mobilized voters" tend to follow the wishes of the local influentials and government officials, they tend to vote for the government party's candidates in the elections. Thus, "mobilized voting...is primarily a phenomenon closely associated with pro-government voters." Inevitably, "the party and the politicians associated closely with the incumbent regime are the usual beneficiaries of mobilized votes." In short, the government party has overwhelming advantages over the opposition parties in rural areas "where mobilized voting seems to be heavily concentrated."

Finally, according to J.C. Han, [35] in contrast to the government party's advantage of mobilizing administrative networks (e.g., police and local bureaucracy) throughout the nation, the opposition parties are largely limited to urban centers in the scope of their outreach. Operating in big cities and among circles limited almost exclusively to professional politicians, major opposition party activities tend to be centered in and around the parliament. In fact, Han contends that one of the main weaknesses of the major opposition party is the inadequate organizational infrastructure in the rural areas.

While these theories are highly useful in understanding the *yado yeochon* pattern in South Korean parliamentary elections, it seems necessary for us to place the South Korean pattern of partisan support in a broader comparative perspective. To be sure, South Korea is not the only country which has experienced the *yado yeochon* pattern in voting. In fact, a similar pattern has persisted in Japanese parliamentary elections from 1958 to the present.[35a] It is thus useful to view the impact of urbanization and industrialization on political competition from the theoretical perspective provided by Tufte and Dahl.[36]

On the basis of their study of urbanization and industrialization of political competition in several Western democratic political systems, Tufte and Dahl came up with the proposition that there is an inverse relationship between urbanization and the electoral strength of the government party. Conversely, the more urbanized and the larger the size of the district, the stronger the opposition party (or parties) would be in electoral competition.[37]

In formulating the hypothesis, Dahl and Tufte proceed along the following lines of argument. First, as the size of the community increases, its density increases. As the number of people that an individual comes in contact with increases, it becomes easier for him to find an ally.[38] Also, as the scale of the occupational and institutional associations with which the individual is involved increases, the cost of dissent decreases. In short, increased size leads to increased density which in turn facilitates the identification of shared grievances, the organization of dissent groups, and the articulation of partisan interests, thereby stimulating greater political competition. Second, as the size of the community increases, its diversity increases. The diversity and heterogeneity not only enhance the chances of finding an ally, but also enlarge the number and diversity of interests that might potentially come into conflict[39] since urbanization is associated with the processes of industrialization which entail increases in the size of production units, the growing specialization and differentiation of labor, and growing distance between functional roles played by different groups of people. Diversity inevitably produces conflict; conflict in turn stimulates the mobilization of resources and polarization of loyalties, the outcome of which is again increased political competition. In short, viewed from such a theoretical perspective, political competition becomes more intense in urban areas; and the leading party's percentage of votes declines in urban areas.

Thus, according to Tufte and Dahl, in democracies using the proportional representation system, urbanization accompanied by industrialization would increase the number of parties presented to voters in elections as well as increase the relative size of the minority party (or parties).[40] Furthermore, they hypothesized that the increased competition would result in a lower percentage of the vote won by the leading party in both plurality and proportional representation systems. As they put it, "the percentage of the vote cast for the leading party decreases," with the increase in unit size, degree of urbanization, and the degree of social differentiation in a democratic country.[41] In short, Dahl and Tufte's model predicts an inverse relationship between urbanization and the electoral strength of the government party: the more urbanized and the larger the size of the district, the weaker the support for the government party. Conversely, the more urbanized and the larger the size of the district, the stronger the opposition party (or parties) would be in electoral competition.

It should be pointed out that the modernization model advanced by scholars in the field is also useful in understanding the *yado yeochon* pattern in voting. The modernization model as articulated by Lerner, for instance, views urbanization as one of the vital phases in a multistage process encompassing, among other things, the sequential increase of education and media exposure. The various processes associated with modern social change are viewed as freeing villagers from their traditional parochialism.[42] In the Korean context, as citizens become better educated, and more sophisticated politically (with concomitantly greater commitment to modern and democratic values),[43] they become more autonomous and discriminating in making their electoral choice. The net result is increased support for the opposition which stands for the liberalization and democratization of the Korean political system.

Table 6 presents the correlations between the rates of government party support in the five parliamentary elections and our selected demographic indicators of districts along the dimensions of urbanization and modernization. Again, on theoretical grounds we would anticipate election districts whose main features include a large population, high density, and a high level of industrialization to show a low level of government party support. We would also anticipate districts, whose main features include a high level of education and a concentration of the postwar generation, would support the government party less than districts characterized by a high level of illiteracy, a concentration of the prewar generation and females. Without exception, in all elections, population, density, industrialization, the postwar generation, and college enrollment variables show strong inverse correlations while the prewar generation, illiteracy, and female variables show either no strong positive relationships with government party support or relatively insignificant correlations.

In terms of a comparative perspective, the pattern of partisan support in South Korean parliamentary elections (i.e., the *yado yeochon* pattern) bears a striking similarity with the pattern of partisan support in the Japanese parliamentary elections from 1958 to 1979 in that the government party's electoral support was inversely correlated with urbanization: the more urbanized, the less support for the ruling Liberal Democratic Party (LDP).[44]

Conclusion

From the foregoing analysis, a few basic conclusions can be drawn with regard to urbanization and changing voting patterns in South Korea from 1963 to 1985.

First, in terms of electoral participation, the voting rate of the urban electorate has been consistently lower than that of the rural or semi-rural constituencies. Clearly there is an inverse correlation between urbanity and electoral participation: the more urbanized, the lower the voting turnout rate. There is sufficient evidence to believe that the low-voting rate among the urban-metropolitan voters can be attributed to the weakening of the pressure for conformity to community norms in voting as well as the ineffective community social networks in mobilizing voters. In general, the persisting gap between the urban-rural differences in voter turnout rates in the parliamentary elections substantiates the "decline-of-community" model on the inverse correlation between urbanization and voter turnout rate.

Second, it is also quite evident that the urban-metropolitan voters deserted the government party, casting their votes increasingly for the opposition parties. Such a tendency again substantiates the hypothesis advanced by Dahl and Tufte on urbanization and political competition and on the inverse correlation between urbanization and the strength of the government party (or the leading party) in democratic countries (e.g., Switzerland, Japan,[46] the Netherlands, the United States). Not only do the number of political parties competing in the election increase in the industrialized urban areas, but also the percentage of the votes cast for the leading party (or the government party) decreases in the more urbanized electoral districts.

Third, insofar as voter turnout in South Korea is concerned, it deviates from the modernization model which predicts that urbanization, industrialization, higher literacy, geographic mobility, mass media exposure, etc., would increase political participation. This finding, however, should not be interpreted as a total negation of the validity of the mobilization model, for there are clear indications that other forms of political participation such as protest demonstrations, interest and organizational group activities, etc. are positively associated with modernization in South Korea.[45] This suggests that voting should be treated separately from other modes of political participation .

Fourth, as Korea becomes more modernized through rapid urbanization, industrialization, educational and communications development, all of which are taking place rapidly, it is fair to anticipate that the social basis of conformist electoral participation (e.g., "mobilized voting") will decrease with a concomitant increase in more discriminating voter participation. As citizens become better educated, more politically sophisticated and better prepared to make independent political decisions, they are likely to become less vulnerable to various pressures to conform to the wishes of the local influentials or government officials.

Finally, in view of the persistent pattern of *yado yeochon* in voting, one cannot underestimate the political implications of urbanization for the future of parliamentary elections in South Korea. To be sure, under the existing presidential system, the outcome of a parliamentary election by itself cannot change power relations between the government party and its opposition. However, should a genuine parliamentary cabinet system of government (as proposed by the ruling DJP) be adopted, the parliamentary election will decide which party should form a new government in the future. It remains to be seen whether the opposition would be able to utilize their advantages in urban constituencies to offset their apparent weakness in rural districts.

NOTES

1. For the Chicago school's paradigm, see Sylvia Fleis Fava, *Urbanism in World Perspective* (New York: T.Y. Crowell, 1968), pp. 11-22, & 21-81. For the paradigm's applicability for Japan, see James W. White, *Political Implications of Cityward Migration* (Beverly Hills, CA: Sage Publications, 1973), A Sage Professional Paper in Comparative Politics Series, Vol. 4, pp. 8-12.
2. Myron Weiner and John Osgood Field, "India's Urban Constituencies," *Comparative Politics*, Vol. 18, No. 2, January 1976, pp. 183-218.
3. David R. Cameron, J. Stephen Hendrichs, & Richard I. Hofferbert, "Urbanization, Social Structure and Mass Politics: A Comparison of Five Nations," *Comparative Political Studies*, October 1972, pp. 259-90. For a review of the literature on sociological theories of urbanization, see White, *loc.cit.*
4. Lester W. Milbrath, *Political Participation: How and Why Do People Get Involved in Politics* (Chicago: Rand McNally, 1965), pp. 110-40. See also, Lester W. Milbrath and M.L. Goel, *Political Participation* (Chicago: Rand McNally, 1977), pp. 86-122.
5. Daniel Lerner, *The Passing of Traditional Society* (New York: The Free

Press, 1958), pp. 43-75.

6. Karl W. Deutsch, "Social Mobilization and Political Development," *American Political Science Review*, LV (September 1961), pp. 493-515.
7. Sidney Verba and Norman H. Nie, *Participation in America* (New York: Harper and Row, 1972), pp. 230-231. See also, Sidney Verba, Norman H. Nie, and Jae-On Kim, *Participation and Political Equality: A Seven Nation Comparison* (Cambridge: Cambridge University Press, 1978), pp. 269-285.
8. Robert A. Dahl and Edward R. Tufte, *Size and Democracy* (Stanford, CA: Stanford University Press, 1973), p. 43.
9. Alex Inkeles, "Participant Citizenship in Six Developing Countries," *American Political Science Review*, LXIII (December 1969), p. 1139.

9a. Norman H. Nie, G. Bingham Powell, Jr., Kenneth Prewitt, "Social Structure and Political Participation: Developmental Relationship," Part I & II, *American Political Science Review*, LXIII (June and September 1969), pp. 368 and 819.

10. Statistics for elections are based on the *Daehanminkuk Songosa* (The Election History of Korea) and *Kukhoeuiwon Songosanghwang* (Parliamentary Election Statistics) (1978) for the 9th and 10th parliaments, published by the Central Election Management Committee (CEMC), supplemented by the major Korean newspapers. Statistics for socio-demographic characteristics of election districts are from *1966 Population Census Report of Korea* and *1970 Population and Housing Census Report of Korea*, and other statistical yearbooks prepared by the provincial and national governments. Information helpful on the administrative units of election districts was obtained from *Choeshin Hankuk Haengjong Kuyok Pyollam* (The Latest Handbook of Administrative Units of Korea) (1976). Most of the economic growth data was drawn from *Major Statistics of Korean Economy, 1980,* published by Economic Planning Board of the Korean government.
11. Frederica M. Bunge, ed., *South Korea: a Country Study* (U.S. Government Printing Office, 1982), p. 61.
12. *Ibid.*
13. ROK, Economic Planning Board, *Major Statistics of Korean Economy, 1981,* p. 19. See also, U.S. Department of State, Bureau of Public Affairs, *Background Notes: South Korea* (U.S. Government Printing Office, 1983) p. 1.
14. Bunge, *op. cit.*, p. 58.
15. In comparison the voting turnout rates in presidential elections of 1963, 1967, and 1971 were consistently higher than parliamentary elections in all categories of urbanization: 74 percent compared to 65.3 percent among metropolitan districts; 86.7 percent compared to 76.5 percent among rural districts. In terms of gross urban-rural

dichotomy, an average of 80.3 percent of presidential voting participation rate compared favorably against the average of 67.4 percent of parliamentary participation rate among urban districts, while the rural districts were 86 percent to 79.3 percent. Significant urban-rural differences in turnout rates in all elections were also ascertained through t-tests. Absolute t-values in all cases were larger than 2.0.

16. For a detailed analysis, see Young Ho Lee, "Toward a Comparative Theory of Voting Participation," mimeographed paper (Athens, Georgia: University of Georgia, 1971); Chong Lim Kim, "Political Participation and Mobilized Voting," in his *Political Participation in Korea, op. cit.*, pp. 119-114; Jae-On Kim and B.C. Koh, "Electoral Behavior and Social Development in South Korea: An Aggregate Data Analysis of Presidential Elections," *Journal of Politics*, Vol. 34 (August 1972), pp. 825-59; Sung-Il Choi and Chae-Jin Lee, "Environment, Policy, and Electoral Participation: A Comparison of Urban and Rural Areas," In Chong Lim Kim (ed.), *Political Participation in Korea*, pp. 169-171; and Jae-On Kim and B.C. Koh, "The Dynamics of Electoral Politics: Social Development, Political Participation, and Manipulation of Electoral Laws," *ibid.*, pp. 59-84.
17. Chong Lim Kim, "Political Participation and Mobilized Voting," *ibid.*, p. 136.
17a *Ibid.*, pp. 133-136.
18. Kyu-taik Kim, "A Statistical Analysis of the Elections in Korea," *Korean Quarterly*, Vol. 9 (Summer 1967), p. 67.
19. C. I. Eugene Kim, Young Whan Kihl, and Dock-Kyou Chung. "Voter Turnout and the Meaning of Elections in South Korea," *Asian Survey*, November 1973, p. 1067.
20. *Ibid.*, p. 1069. See also Myong-Whai Kim Eui-young Ham, and Hyoung-sup Yoon, "Korean Voting Behavior and Political Orientation," *Korea Observer*, 3 (January 1971), pp. 51-81.
21. Chae-Jin Lee, "Urban Electoral Participation in Korea," *Midwest Journal of Political Science*, XVI, No. 2 (May 1972), p. 308.
22. In addition to Verba, Nie and Jae-On Kim's works cited *supra* footnote 7, see also Robert A. Dahl and Edward R. Tufte, *Size and Democracy, op. cit., passim*, for a theoretical foundation of the "decline-of-community" model.
23. In 1971, slightly over 13 out of every 100 households changed their residences. However, in 1977, nearly twenty-one out of 100 households changed their residences. See Table 2 in the Appendix.
24. Soo Young Auh, "Toshihua wa Jeongchi Chamyeo: Ilbon eui Kyongwoo rul choongshim euro," *Ilbon Yeonkoo Nonchong* (Seoul: Hyundai Ilbon Yeonkoohwae, 1979), p. 265.
25. Dahl and Tufte, *op. cit.*, pp. 41-42.

26. Ibid.
27. C.I. Eugene Kim, Young Whan Kihl, and Dock-Kyou Chung, op. cit., p. 1074.
28. Hong N. Kim, "Urbanization and Changing Voting Patterns in Japan, 1958-1979," *Keio Journal of Politics* (Tokyo: Keio University Press), No. 4, 1983, pp. 33-59, esp. 39-43.
28a. In all five parliamentary elections, test results show an absolute value larger than 2.0, indicating significant urban-rural differences.
29. B.C. Koh, "The 1985 Parliamentary Election in South Korea," *Asian Survey*, September 1985, p. 891. See also, C.I. Eugene Kim, "The Meaning of Korea's 12th National Assembly Election," *Korea Observer*, Vo. XVI, No. 4 (Winter 1985), pp. 363-379.
29a. In the 1985 parliamentary election, the government party won 87 seats in the direct vote and 61 seats from the proportional representation system thus retaining a comfortable majority in the new parliament. The hard-line opposition New Korea Democratic Party (NKDP), founded less than a month prior to the election, emerged as the largest opposition party replacing the moderate opposition Democratic Korea Party (DKP) taking 50 seats in the direct balloting and 17 by the proportional representation system (Table 9). What is of special interest to us, however, is the vote distribution by political parties, especially in urban areas or districts. The DJP fell far behind the NKDP in major cities, including Seoul.
30. Jae-On Kim and B.C. Koh, *op. cit.*, p. 847.
31. Hang Yul Rhee, "Urbanization, Communication, Economic Inequality and Political Behavior: A Study of Seoul Citizens, 1952-1971," Proceedings of 3rd Joint Conference, KPSA, June 18-20, 1979 (Seoul: Korean Political Science Association, 1979), pp. 105-113.
32. *Ibid.*, pp. 97-104.
33. Chae-Jin Lee, *op. cit.*, p. 308; and Sung-Il Choi and Chae-Jin Lee, "Environment, Policy, and Electoral Participation: A Comparison of Urban and Rural Areas," in Chong Lim Kim (ed.), *Political Participation in Korea, op. cit.*, pp. 176-177.
34. Chong Lim Kim, "Political Participation and Mobilized Voting," op. cit., pp. 128-133.
35. Y.C. Han, "Political Parties and Elections in South Korea," in Se Jin Kim and Chang Hyun Cho (eds.), *Government and Politics of Korea* (Silver Spring, MD: The Research Institute on Korean Affairs, 1972), p. 138.
36. Tufte and Dahl, *op. cit.*, pp. 30-109.
37. *Ibid.*, p. 100.
38. *Ibid.*, p. 89-91.
39. *Ibid.*, pp. 30-40, and 91-98.
40. *Ibid.*

41. *Ibid.*, p. 100.
42. Daniel Lerner, *The Passing of Traditional Society* (New York: The Free Press, 1958), pp. 43-75.
43 Jae-On Kim and B.C. Koh, *op. cit.*, p. 846. See also, Chong Lim Kim, "Political Participation and Mobilized Voting," *op. cit.*, pp. 131-139.
44. Hong N. Kim, *op. cit.*, pp. 43-51.
45. Chong Lim Kim, "Conclusion: Participation and Development," in Chong Lim Kim (ed.), *Political Participation in Korea, op. cit.*, pp. 205-214, esp. 208.

Table 1
Urban* Population of Korea, Japan, and the United States
1915-1975 (1,000s)

	Korea		Japan		United States	
Year	Population	Urban %	Population	Urban %	Population	Urban %
1915	16,278	3.1				
1920	17,289	3.3	55,391	18.1	106.0	51.2
1925	19,020	3.5	59,179	21.7		
1930	20,438	4.5	63,872	24.1	122.8	56.2
1935	22,208	7.4	68,662	32.9		
1940	23,547	11.6	72,540	37.9	131.7	56.5
1945	19,369	14.5	71,998	27.8		
1950	20,167	18.4	83,200	37.5	150.7	59.6
1955	21,502	24.4	89,276	56.3		
1960	24,954	28.3	93,419	63.5	178.5	63.1
1965	28,327	33.9	98,275	68.1		
1970	31,435	43.1	103,720	72.2	203.2	73.5
1975	34,709	50.9				
**1980	37,449	57.2				

Source: Edwin S. Mills & Byung-Nak Song, *Urbanization and Urban Problems: Studies in the Modernization of the Republic of Korea: 1945-1975* (Cambridge: Harvard Univ. Press, 1979), p. 8.

*The urban population in Korea refers to the portion of population living in demographic concentration areas with a minimum of 50,000 inhabitants or more.

**Frederica M. Bunge, ed., *South Korea: A Country Study* (U.S. Govt. Printing Office, 1982), p. 61.

Table 2
Changes of Residence

	Persons moving	Persons moving per 100 population
1971	4,210,164	13.5
1972	3,687,938	11.7
1973	4,860,418	15.1
1974	5,297,969	16.1
1975	9,011,440	26.4
1976	6,773,250	19.5
1977	7,397,624	20.9

Source: Economic Planning Board, Korea Statistical Yearbook: 1978.

Table 3
Voting Participation Percentages in 4 Categories of Districts in National Assembly Elections, 1963, 1967, 1971, 1973, and 1978

Types of Districts	1963 (N)	1967	1971	1973	1978
Metropolitan Districts	62.0% (15)	62.5% (15)	64.9% (15)	66.0% (11)	70.9% (11)
Urban Districts	66.7 (9)	70.4 (9)	74.7 (10)	69.4 (4)	75.3 (4)
Semi-Rural Districts	76.2 (21)	80.6 (21)	78.2 (20)	77.8 (23)	80.7 (25)
Rural Districts	76.2 (75)	82.7 (75)	78.4 (88)	71.8 (31)	83.3 (31)
Urban Districts (Metropolitan+Urban)	68.8 (24)	65.5 (24)	68.8 (25)	66.9 (15)	72.0 (15)
Rural (Semi-Rural+Rural)	76.2 (96)	82.3 (96)	78.3 (108)	77.4 (54)	82.1 (56)
Nation	73.7 (120)	78.9 (120)	76.5 (133)	75.1 (69)	80.0 (71)

Definition: Metropolitan Districts: Districts from special cities of Seoul and Pusan. Urban Districts: Districts with 100 percent urban population. Semi-Rural Districts: Districts which combine city and county population. Rural Districts: Districts with 100 percent rural population.

Source: Official publications of the ROK Central Election Management Committee.

Table 4
Pearson's Correlation Coefficients* between Voting Participation and Socio-Economic Variables of Districts: National Assembly Elections, 1963, 1967, 1971, 1973, and 1978

District Characteristics	1963 Nation	1967 Nation	1971 Nation	1973 Nation	1978 Nation
POP (Population)	-.53	-.54	-.58	-.66	-.06
DEN (Density)	-.49	-.61	-.55	-.63	-.65
IND (Industrial)	-.71	-.82	-.65	-.67	-.73
POSTWARG (Postwar Generation)	-.64	-.73	-.66	-.66	-.77
PREWARG (Prewar Generation)	-.03	-.11	.54	.45	.23
COLENR (College Enrollment)	-.68	-.79	-.69	-.68	-.73
ILLITR (Illiteracy)	.66	.69	.67	.62	.63
FEMALER (Female)	.02	-.05	-.09	.05	-.11

*Since our analysis involves a universe of cases rather than a sample, both weak and strong correlations are theoretically significant. Our primary interest, however, is in identifying the direction of relationship in testing hypotheses.

Table 5

Percentages of Votes Polled by Political Parties in 4 Categories of Districts in National Assembly, 1963, 1967, 1971, 1973 and 1978 (Two Party Computation Only)

Party	District Types*	1963 (N)	1967	1971	1973	1978
	A	52.0 (15)	42.7 (15)	41.1 (15)	44.6 (11)	38.4 (11)
DRP	B	57.4 (9)	54.9 (9)	47.4 (10)	64.3 (4)	50.5 (4)
	C	70.8 (21)	63.0 (21)	53.5 (20)	64.3 (23)	55.4 (25)
	D	66.2 (75)	68.2 (75)	59.2 (88)	56.3 (31)	58.0 (31)
	Urban	54.0 (24)	47.2 (24)	43.6 (25)	49.8 (15)	41.6 (15)
	Rural	67.2 (96)	67.1 (96)	58.2(108)	58.8 (54)	56.8 (56)
	A	48.0	57.3	58.9	55.4	61.6
NDP	B	42.6	45.1	52.6	35.7	49.5
	C	29.2	37.0	46.5	37.8	44.6
	D	33.8	31.8	40.8	43.7	42.0
	Urban	46.0	52.8	56.4	50.2	58.4
	Rural	32.0	32.9	41.0	43.2	43.2

*A-Metropolitan
B-Urban
C-Semi-rural
D-Rural
See Table 3 for definitions.

Source: Official publications of the ROK Central Election Management Committee.

Table 6
Pearson's Correlation Coefficients* between Government Party Votes (DRP) and Socio-Economic Characteristics of District: National Assembly Elections, 1963, 1967, 1971, 1973, 1978

District characteristics	1963	1967	1971	1973	1978
POP (Population)	-.26	-.31	-.32	-.22	.13
DEN (Density)	-.21	-.49	-.34	-.32	-.47
IND (Industrial)	-.34	-.62	-.45	-.23	-.43
POSTWARG (Postwar Generation)	-.34	-.64	-.48	-.27	-.56
PREWARG (Prewar Generation)	.15	-.07	.38	-.00	-.02
COLLENR (College)	-.37	-.60	-.44	-.22	-.52
ILLITR (Illiteracy)	.35	.41	.40	.25	.36
FEMALER (Female)	-.05	.03	-.08	-.08	-.26

* See note under Table 4.

Table 7
Voter Turnout by Region: 1985 Parliamentary Election (Unit: Thousand)

	Eligible voters	Participant voters	Voting rate (%)	(1981)
Seoul	5,955	4,812	80.8	(71.1)
Pusan	2,055	1,754	85.3	(76.7)
Taegu	1,149	943	82.0	*
Inchon	814	657	80.7	*
Kyonggi	2,791	2,261	81.0	(76.1)
Kangwon	1,017	904	88.8	(88.0)
Chungbuk	831	742	89.4	(86.7)
Chungnam	1,720	1,488	86.5	(80.3)
Chonbuk	1,297	1,110	85.6	(80.9)
Chonnam	2,132	1,822	85.5	(81.0)
Kyongbuk	1,865	1,647	88.3	(81.5)
Kyongnam	2,096	1,828	87.2	(83.4)
Cheju	265	234	88.2	(85.3)
Total	23,988	20,200	84.2	(78.4)

Sources: *The Dong-A Ilbo*, February 15, 1985; and *The Korea Herald*, February 14, 1985, p. 3.

* Voting rate in the 1981 parliamentary election is indicated in the parentheses. Taegu and Inchon became special cities after the 1981 election.

Table 8
% of Votes Won by Political Parties: 1985 Parliament

	DJP	NKDP	DKP	KNP
Seoul	27.3	43.3	19.8	2.3
Pusan	27.9	36.9	23.6	10.4
Taegu	28.3	29.7	18.5	15.6
Inchon	37.1	37.4	22.0	3.4
Kyonggi	34.6	27.8	20.4	13.7
Kangwon	46.2	11.3	17.8	17.6
Chungbuk	56.7	18.3	15.8	8.5
Chungnam	39.5	21.7	20.8	10.7
Chonbuk	36.8	26.4	18.8	11.8
Chonnam	35.7	25.4	18.0	10.2
Kyongbuk	44.7	15.7	16.9	10.7
Kyongnam	40.3	23.4	19.4	11.2
Cheju	31.8	5.9	17.1	
Overall Pct.	35.3	29.2	19.5	9.2

Source: *The Korea Herald*, February 15, 1985, p.1.

Part III
Policy Issues and Processes

8

Student Activism and the Presidential Politics of 1987 in South Korea

WONMO DONG

University students have played a powerful role in the opposition politics of South Korea since the founding of the Republic in 1948. In 1960 they overthrew the authoritarian regime of Syngman Rhee and ended the First Republic (1948-1960). In 1964-1965 the students challenged the survival of the military-controlled government of President Park Chung-hee when they spearheaded a violent nation-wide campaign of opposition forces against the controversial normalization of relations between South Korea and Japan. In the early 1970s the Korean campus activists carried out well-coordinated and highly effective political campaigns against the unpopular constitutional revision for the third presidential term of President Park.

After Park established the Fourth Republic (1972-79) under the Yushin Constitution which virtually eliminated limitations on the presidential terms, the student activists remained one of the two foremost organized forces—another being the activist members of ecumenical Christian churches—that in concert with the hardened leadership of the New Democratic Party were capable of waging an effective opposition to the increasingly oppressive rule of President Park, especially during the waning years of his dictatorial rule in the late 1970s. In 1979 President Park was assassinated by his security chief, Kim Jae-kyu, after the outbreak of the student-led Puma incident, a fierce popular uprising in the Pusan-Masan region. Park was succeeded by another general, Chun Doo-hwan, who with the support of his fellow officers—including General Roh Tae-woo who was elected President in December 1987—took over the power of government after the two successive coups of December 12, 1979 and May 17, 1980.

During the hectic seven-year period of the Fifth Republic, President Chun's government was constantly beset with a worsening crisis of political legitimacy despite the impressive economic growth. All organized groups were effectively silenced with the exception of one—the university students. The student activists of South Korea's 114 institutions of higher education continued and in fact intensified their political challenge to the Chun government. The Chun government became increasingly punitive and paranoid in dealing with the radicalization of student activists whose organizational capability and action strategies were more and more sophisticated and effective. Thus, since the onset of the Fifth Republic which followed the bloody Kwangju Incident of 1980, the campus activists became the single most cohesive, persistent, and effective opposition force in South Korea. Party politics and the legislative agenda of the National Assembly often evolved around the nagging problem of radical student politics. As is well known by now, the direct popular election of the new president in December 1987 in fact was forced upon the Chun government by the unified democratic forces of the present and former student activists.[1]

The division between Kim Dae-jung and Kim Young-sam, the two obstinate opposition leaders failing to agree on a single presidential candidate, spoiled the fruits of the political struggle of Korean students—and their middle class supporters. It would be quite unrealistic to suggest, however, that the university activists in South Korea will cease to be a potent force in the "Five Point Five Republic" of President Roh Tae-woo.[2]

This study seeks to examine, first of all, the role of the university students—especially the political activists among them—in the spring 1987 struggle for democratic reform which culminated in the June 29 declaration of Roh Tae-woo to accept the main opposition demands, including the constitutional revision for direct presidential elections. The main focus of this analysis is on the change of strategy and ideological posture of the student activists during the spring of 1987 which significantly contributed to their effectiveness as a catalyst of the June Democratic Revolution of 1987. The study then attempts to explore the ways in which the student activists and the more moderate elements of the university population sought to cope with the difficult and complex political situation after June 29. How effective were they in implementing their goal of labor-student solidarity in the summer of 1987? How did they deal with the widening gap and the eventual split between Kim Young-sam and Kim Dae-jung? Whom did the student population vote for in the December presidential election? These are some of the questions the study will address. This paper will conclude with a tentative prognosis for the future of student activism in South Korea.

Renewed Oppression after the 1986 Asian Games

The spring of 1987 was one of the most opportune periods for the beginning of the democratization process in the Republic of Korea—the country which in spite of a four-decade history of continuous authoritarianism, has committed itself to the realization of a liberal democracy as "the state creed (*kuksi*)" since its founding in 1948. As in the spring of both 1960 and 1980, a combination of political events taking place before and during this volatile season of political activism in South Korea provided momentum for important political change towards democracy. Several factors seemed to be working for the success of the democratic movement in Korea. First of all, the military-controlled regime of President Chun was probably the most unpopular and the most illegitimate of the three dictatorial governments in post-Liberation Korea in the eyes of the general public in the country. One measure of the very low rating of the Chun government was the result of the May 15-19, 1985 opinion survey secretly administered by the pro-government *Kyunghyan Shinmun* indicated that 65.2 percent of all respondents (N = 1,037) and 60.7 percent of the above-average income group were dissatisfied with the government in power. Among those in their 20s and the college graduates, 73.6 percent and 85.7 percent reported their dissatisfaction with the government in power, respectively.[3]

In January 1987, Selig S. Harrison wrote that a secret poll "recently" taken for the Chun government by a leading paper in Korea showed 66.4 percent opposed to the present government and 20.5 percent "strongly opposed" it.[4] President Chun was approaching the end of his seven-year term, but two thirds of his countrymen still opposed him. One source of the frustration for Chun was that the harder he tried to improve his political popularity, the less credible he appeared.[5] Besides his lack of character and ability for effective presidential leadership, President Chun also suffered from inept management of the political crisis situation. One policy concern toward which the Chun regime showed particular weakness, which worsened towards the end of his term of office, was the nagging problem of student activism. In the summer of 1985, the Chun government proposed the abortive "campus stabilization" act to the National Assembly; it was opposed by the New Korea Democratic Party, all but the very faithful of his party followers—and the Reagan administration.[6] An all-out radicalization of student politics in the fall of 1985 and the spring of 1986 indicated the counter-productivity of the Chun regime's repressive policy towards the university population in general in the light of the increased ideological and organizational sophistication of the student activists.

After the Asian Games (September 20-October 5) the Chun government introduced once again the Draconian policy of oppression toward the dissident forces, especially the student activists. On October 20, the police announced that 30 "left-leaning, pro-communist" organizations and 10,000 dissidents would be put under surveillance for any subversive activities they might attempt.[7] The most violent and widely publicized incident in the fall and winter of 1986 was the Konguk University incident of October 28-31.[8] Some 19,000 riot police systematically sacked and assaulted a large body of students assembled at the Konguk University campus, and all but a few top leaders escaped police arrest. The 126 companies of the riot police—the "combat police" (*Chontu Kyuongch'all*) comprising the army draftees—carried out a combat-style operation throwing barrage after barrage of tear gas, with no water, food, or heat given to the students, for four days in a crunching Korean winter. When this single most violent government attack on the student activists was over, 2,225 students were rounded up in spite of the fact that the student demonstrators from 26 universities rallying at Konguk University were for the most part the rank and file members and low division students. The core group which sponsored this event was the underground Federation of the Students for the Salvation of the Nation (*Guguk haksaeng yonmaeng*), called *Guhaknyon*, and the Konguk demonstrators were there to participate in the founding of the National Patriotic Students' Committee To Struggle Against Foreign Powers and Dictatorship (*Aehaktu*), which was intended as a mass front organization of *Guhaknyon*.[9] One day after South Korea's most bloody suppression of the campus activists since Kwangju (1980) was over, Prime Minister Lho Shinyong said:

> Radical leftist and pro-communist activists deny our cherished system of liberal democracy and advocate the same cause as North Korea's in its propaganda against the South.[10]

According to the government, the student activists were pro-communist and pro-North Korean agitators intent upon destroying the Republic of Korea. But the students themselves offered an entirely different explanation for their assembly at Konguk University and the brutality of the police actions. In a November 12 statement, the Christian Federation and the Ecumenical Youth Council in Korea described the situation as follows:

> We believe the Konguk University incident was not the result of a planned occupation by the students or a riot caused by communist revolutionaries, as claimed by the authorities, but an intended action to provoke the students by the regime. The authorities intentionally forced the students into the buildings and locked them in. Through a blitz of trial by media they distorted the case as one of pro-communist action, and moved in to kill and suppress the students. This is nothing more than a part of the regime's vicious conspiracy to paint the student movement as pro-communist and destroy it from its root. The authorities knew of the plans for this combined assembly of students. It has, as always, the capacity and chance to prevent the assembly. Instead, however, it carried through a pre-planned operation as part of its thoroughly worked out scheme to destroy the student movement at once.[11]

The government pressed charges against and formally arrested

1,275 students (including 471 co-eds)—the largest single arrest in the annals of student activism not only in Korea but throughout the world.[12] Of the 1,275, 398 were indicted and 35 of them were accused of violating the dreaded National Security Law, which provide death sentences for activities supportive of North Korea.

The ruthless crackdown on the student dissidents by the violent attack and the mass arrest in the Konguk University incident was bitterly denounced by the NKDP and all opposition groups as an unreasonably punitive measure which would result in the further radicalization of the university students in South Korea. The intensified repressive actions were, however, part of the Chun regime's renewed attempts to undermine and preempt the organized efforts of the opposition to change the constitution for a direct presidential election which had been in limbo since April 1, 1986—the day President Chun announced he was prepared to go along with the interparty negotiations for a constitutional revision within the National Assembly. Subsequently, on November 29, the NKDP tried to hold in Seoul the scheduled National Conference for the Constitutional Revision for a Direct Presidential Election.

The government deployed 32,000 police—over 25 percent of the total police force in the country—and forcibly blocked this nonviolent gathering of the oppositionists.[13] Then, in the midst of these worsening government-opposition confrontations, the Democratic Justice Party (DJP) unilaterally passed the government budget for the new year in the early morning hours of November 2 with only DJP members present in their meeting room in the National Assembly. Some NKDP members proposed the mass resignation of all party members from the legislative body, but the party leadership prevailed upon them to continue their political struggle within the legislative chamber, at least for the time being.[14]

The Spring of 1987: Democracy and the Student Activists

Against the backdrop of the virtual deadlock of constitutional debates for a direct presidential election and the renewed oppression of the student movement in 1986, South Korea entered what was widely anticipated to be another crisis period in early 1987, just one year before President Chun's seven-year term of office would end. As usual, a matter of imminent concern to both the government and opposition was what the student activists were likely to do in response to the bleak political situation in 1987. In an interview with the *Dong-a Ilbo* on 1 January, Dr. Yi Yong-hi, former chairman of the political science department at Seoul National University, stated that "the most serious problem facing our country today is that of the young generation." Another interviewee, Professor Choe Sang-yong of Korea University, expressed his concern about the tendency among the Korean student activists that "the more radical and extreme, the greater the moral superiority of the activist leaders." This trend created, he said, the observable phenomenon of "selfradicalization" among the activists, that is, the activist leaders often stated their case more radically than they really believed in order to engender greater acceptance among their followers.[15] This bothersome behavior pattern of the campus dissidents led the two well respected leaders of the Protestant community, Dr. Kim Chai-choon and the Reverend Ham Sok-hun, to advise the students that "the righteousness of your students' course of action is measured by the degree to which the people respond to your actions." "You can never achieve democratization by losing the people," they warned.[16] Stephen Cardinal Kim of the Catholic Church pleaded over and over that to vindicate the righteousness of their democratic cause, the students should shy away from "the left-leaning radical ideology and the cry of the revolution."[17] After the Konguk University incident, the student activists became sensitive to the counterproductive nature of their radical actions in the face of the increasingly ruthless regime which did not hesitate to deploy vastly superior institutional violence against the students. In addition, most student activists were now convinced that their political effectiveness depended largely on the support of the reform-minded middle class, who showed their deep dissatisfaction with the Chun regime since the February 12, 1985 National Assembly elections. Furthermore, the students recognized that given the widespread support of a direct presidential election by the people, they had everything to gain by aligning themselves with the moderate cause of the New Korea Democratic Party and the people at large, especially the politically conscious middle-class.

What precipitated a political typhoon of uncontrollable magnitude for the Chun government in 1987 was the widely publicized political torture killing of Pak Jong-chul during January 14-19. Mr. Park was a linguistic student at Seoul National University and a former *Minmintu* activist, who was interrogated by police with no formal charge about the whereabouts of another campus activist. The police reported he died of shock, but questions arose in the press after an attending physician announced contradictory evidence showing the young man died of torture.[18] On February 7, the students and the people of the opposition attempted to hold a memorial rally for the victim of the vicious police torture at the Myongdong Catholic Cathedral in Seoul, but the police blocked it on political grounds. On March 3, against repeated warnings from the authorities, the NKDP and 47 other dissident religious and human rights groups joined the students in the National Peace March to End Torture. This was the third time police blocked major peaceful rallies, following those on November 20, 1986 and February 7. The Pak Jong-chul incident thus became a cause célèbre for the democratic movement, contributing to the renewed vigor of the popular opposition to the continued delay of the constitutional revision. In the meantime, the DJP government successfully organized itself with the collaboration of some splinter elements of the opposition NKDP who were now prepared to support a parliamentary system of government, as opposed to a presidential system.[19]

The most critical move of the Chun government that brought ultimate political disaster was, however, President Chun's April 13 announcement whereby he imposed a moratorium on constitutional debates on the popular presidential election until after his term of office expired in February 1988.[20] An escalating confrontation between the government and the opposition from this point to 29 June—the day Roh Tae-woo, president of the governing Democratic Justice Party, surprised his countrymen and the rest of the world with his 8-point declaration—was inevitable given the Chun government's continued lack of sensitivity to the changing political mood of the people of South Korea. The Chun government's failure to correctly assess the democratic aspirations of the majority of the people, including the newly affluent middle class, was blatantly demonstrated when on June 10 the DJP nominated Roh Tae-woo as its candidate who was sure to be elected under the existing constitution providing for the indirect presidential election by a rubber-stamp electoral college.

On both May 29 and June 10, the new Unification Democratic Party (UDP) founded by Kim Young-sam and Kim Dae-jung in early May, again attempted to hold mass rallies for a constitutional revision which were actively supported by the students and practically all oppositionists with the exception of the Constituent Assembly radicals. On June 9, the *Hanguk Ilbo* reported, in a very timely way, that according to a public opinion survey conducted May 4-13, 85.7 percent of the people interviewed responded that they considered the protection of human rights should be achieved even if it delays economic growth. Of particular significance, 81.4 percent of them said that they supported the political reforms towards democracy.[21]

The June 29 capitulation of the Chun regime to the popular demands for democratic reforms was one of the two possible choices it was confronted with, the other option being the less tenable declaration of a garrison or martial law against the nationwide protests which was opposed reportedly by the majority of the field commanders in the Korean army and by the Reagan administration, which sent Deputy Assistant Secretary of State Gaston Sigur June 23-25 to convey its objection to Chun's use of the Korean troops to suppress the growing popular rallies.[22]

The three weeks of rapidly intensifying popular resistance following Chun's nomination of Roh as the DJP candidate was coordinated by a new organization called the National Movement for a Democratic Constitution, which had been brought into being on May 27. This umbrella organization was sponsored by more than 2,000 opposition leaders and activists, including the UDP leaders and other dissidents, especially campus activists. But in every subsequent major encounter with the government police—the abortive May 29 UDP rally in Seoul, the June 10-15 mass meeting at the Myongdong Cathedral, the explosive June 18-19 Pusan rally, the June 19-20 Kwangju rally and the June 26 Grand Peace March in Seoul—the students were visibly on the forefront of the demonstration and they usually provided the organizational basis and a sizeable portion, if not the majority, of the protesting masses.[23] The June 19 issue of the *Yomiuri Shimbun* reported on the Pusan situation with the headline: "Anti-government Demonstration Spread Across the Nation; Control Over 80,000 in Pusan Given Up."[24] The June 26 rally in Seoul took place along with those held in 36 other cities throughout the nation. The number of participants in the June 26 march was variously estimated from 200,000 by the press to more than 1.3 million, a figure given by the National Movement for A Democratic Constitution.[25] Students from 69 of the country's 114 colleges and universities participated in the June 26 rallies. Clearly, these large crowds were beyond the control of the 60,000 police representing one half of the total police force in the country.[26]

The 1987 Presidential Election and the Dilemma of Student Activists

The leading force of the June 1987 Revolution was "the student centered activist sphere (*undongkwon*) and the middle class people who were united with it."[27] Since the beginning of 1987 the student activists quickly and realistically adapted themselves to the changing political environment of their struggle, thanks to their bitter memory of the bloody Konguk University incident in October 1986. Since then the activist leaders made a conscious tactical decision to move away from the former self-defined role of a superior and elitist force for social change whose main political action was concentrated in the consciousness-raising of the exploited "basic minjung" (*gich'eung minjung*) to a more or less spontaneous alliance with both the middle class and the moderate students whose aspirations for democratic reforms such as a constitutional revision for direct presidential election they now chose to support. As already discussed in this paper, the student groups such as *Sodaehyup* (Association of Student Representatives in the Seoul Region) and its counterparts in the provincial capitals were a crucial element which enabled the National Movement for A Democratic Constitution to succeed in the June 26 Grand Peace March.[28] What the student movement in general and the campus activists in particular were able to accomplish after the June 29 declaration of Roh Taewoo was, however, a completely different story, especially in terms of their impact on presidential electoral politics.

What the students learned during the spring was the important fact that despite their efforts in the labor-student solidarity movement through most of the 1980s[29], the Korean workers were neither interested in nor willing to play any significant role in almost all confrontations with the Chun regime in the spring of 1987. During the three months between June 29 and late September, a chief source of anxiety and apprehension about the course of democratic reforms was the explosive political effect of a rapid spread of labor strife and especially the politicization of striking workers under the influence of the student activists. As it happened, during the months of July, August, and September, the country experienced the worst of labor management strife since the early 1960s with 3,311 labor disputes occurring between June 29 and September 28, mostly in the industrially developed parts of the country, the Seoul-Inchon (1,560) and the South and North Kyungsan (817) regions. But the student activists were involved in very few isolated cases of industrial strife. By all indication the Korean workers were much more interested in the practical solution of labor rights and immediate rice-and-soy sauce economic issues than the political reforms of their government, let alone the promotion of labor-student solidarity.[30]

According to the detailed newspaper reports in Korea during the period of widening labor strife, there were two cases of united actions between the workers and students, both with no major impact on the worker strikes in general. In early August, the workers at the Ockpo shipyard of the Daewoo Group went on strike and one of the striking workers was killed by a tear-gar canister shot by the police. Some student activists joined a group of the National Movement members who went to the aid of the striking workers. At first they achieved limited success in their politicizing, but they were soon discouraged by leaders of the opposition Unification Democratic Party and the more moderate of the National Movement who were concerned about the damaging effects of their actions on the democratization process. Before long most striking workers were kept away from these "outside agitators."[31]

On August 23, student activists from the Seoul area, presumably in cooperation with "disguised workers," held on the campus of Yonsei University the National Workers' Conference for Unconditional Re-employment of the Dismissed Workers and Opposition to Dismissal. About 5,000 student activists and workers participated in an all-night study session to advance the goal of labor-student solidarity (*nohak yondae*).[32] A working consensus among the participants, however, suggested that as a matter of strategy the student activists should not be directly involved in labor disputes.

Their reluctance to emphasize an urgency of labor-student solidarity actions might have been caused by the seemingly uncontrollable spread of labor strife in August. One reporter summarized the prevailing opinion in the meeting as follows:

> It is necessary to strengthen solidarity between labor activists and students but we should not weaken the autonomy of the workers or cause the feeling of repulsiveness against us (the student activists) among the workers.[33]

By far the most important organizing effort of the student activists after June 29 was the creation of the National Association of the Representatives of University Students (*Chon'guk daehaksaeng daepyoja hyopuihoe*)—*Chondaehyop*—in Taejon on August 19. 89 student leaders representing 95 colleges and universities gathered with 5,000 students attending the meeting. Their main goal was to expand *Sodaehvoo* in the Seoul area into a national organization by setting up its regional counterparts throughout the nation.[34] Their stated objectives were:

1. Immediate end of the Chun government;
2. End of the government oppression of workers;
3. Warning to the Unification Democratic Party for its ineffectiveness ("We shall chastise the Party with the support of the Minjung.");
4. Political neutrality of the military; and
5. Demand to the United States for a public apology for its complicity in the Kwangju Incident and for exerting pressures for more U. S. imports into South Korea.[35]

Their action plan called for exposing the deceptive nature of the June 29 declaration of Roh Tae-woo as well as the truth of the Kwangju Incident, especially the role of the US-controlled Combined Forces Command. They demanded the establishment of a neutral interim government for the administration of the presidential election. Stating that the students basically don't trust the Chun government, the *Chondaehyop* members went on to say:

> We the students lack power at present but we shall demand the end of the military dictatorship if we can mobilize enough power even before the presidential election. The election is not the only way of ending dictatorship. . . We regard it our duty to

> continue to reveal the real nature of the dictatorial government of President Chun and to demand its end.[36]

Noteworthy in the *Chondaehyop* conference was the fact that, unlike similar organizational efforts in the past, the student leaders agreed on the open proceedings of the meeting and they declared their intention to avoid "actions based on radical ideas" in keeping with "the principle of following the general public (*Daejung ch'usu chui*). Conspicuously absent in their rhetoric was reference to the Minjung (oppressed masses) democracy as well as the role of the students as the vanguard of Minjung.[37]

The government authorities at first seemed to view *Chondaehyop* as a moderate organization, similar to the reformist *Sodaehyop*. But in early September the top three leaders—its president, Yi Namju of Korea University; and two other Seoul area leaders Woo Sang-ho of Yonsei University and Im Mi-ae of Ehwa University—were arrested after 9,000 students in 19 colleges and universities demonstrated on their campuses, boycotting the make-up examinations they were required to take due to the early start of the summer vacation in late May. Woo Sang-ho in lengthy interview with a *New York Times* reporter explained why the Korean students were radicalized (the illegitimacy of the Chun regime) and anti-American (the Kwangju complicity).[38]

The single most serious drawback in the democratization efforts of the opposition camp both during and after the nation-wide labor disputes of the summer months was the inability of the two Kims to agree on a single UDDP candidate in the December presidential election. Kim Dae-jung was persuaded to join the UDP as its standing advisor on August 8, almost a month after his political rights were fully restored. But each leader continue to argue for the merits of his own candidacy. Professor Han Sung-joo of Korea University has summarized the inflexible positions of the two Kims as follows:

> Each Kim saw himself as the hero of South Korea' political drama, and each plainly thought the other was behaving unreasonably in not agreeing to pull out of the race for the presidency. Kim Young-sam claimed he appealed to a broad cross section of an increasingly middle class public. This made him not only very electable, in his view, but also a much more

> suitable figure, once elected, to unite a politically fractious nation. Kim Dae-jung saw things differently; after exile in the United States and repeated jailings and house arrests in Korea over the years, he claimed he had suffered more in the cause of democracy. His failure to run in the presidential election, he warned, could churn up anger and frustration among his many supporters and re-ignite the potentially dangerous regional antagonism that has always bedeviled Korean politics.[39]

On September 29—exactly two months after the June 29 declaration—the two Kims finally fell apart. On October 10 Kim Young-sam declared his candidacy on behalf of the UDP. Kim Dae-jung on October 28 announced the founding of a new opposition party, the Party for Peace and Democracy (PPD), and his candidacy for the presidency for the new party. What did the student activists and others in the opposition (that is, the oppositionists who were not members of UDP and PPD) do?

The two main opposition parties were now engaged, with no more than a month and a half to the December 16 election, in a nasty regionally based zero-sum game, exactly as most DJP strategists had predicted and hoped.[40] After late October, the student activists were divided into the following three groups:

1. Leaders of the *Chondaehyop* were willing to give qualified ("critical *bipanchok*") support to Kim Dae-jung, as they were impressed with his record of anti-dictatorial struggle;
2. *Sodaehyop* leaders were in favor of the single candidacy of Kim Young-sam, as he was considered more winnable; and
3. The radical activists of the Minmintu and the Constituent Assembly (CA) at first demanded a boycott of the election but later supported an independent Minzung candidate such as Paek Ki-wan, who attempted to talk one of the two Kims into dropping out of the race.[41]

In the meantime, most of the rank and file members of the student movement were following the characteristic regional, social stratification and other lines of alignment. Some joined the election campaign for DJP's Roh Tae-woo. The October 13 issue of the

Choongang Ilbo reported that 15,000 students were recruited by the DJP's Youth Volunteer Service Corps "to help prevent the embarrassing situation of the February 12, 1985 election from happening."[42]

The student activists lost their cohesiveness and failed to capitalize on the strength of their organizational base in the fall and winter of 1987. For the most part their ranks were widely dispersed into the supporters of the contending presidential candidates. As a solidified force for democratic reforms they were no longer able to carry out effective political actions in concert with other organized groups of the democratic movement which probably would have resulted in a sweeping victory of one opposition candidate—Kim Young-sam or Kim Dae-jung.

Table 1.
The Presidential Election of 1987:
Patterns of Voter Support for the Major Candidates

Candidates		Roh T. W.	Kim Y. S.	Kim D. J.	Kim J. P.
All Voters					
Gallup Poll		34.4	28.7	28.0	8.4
Actual		36.6	28.0	27.0	8.1
Ages					
20s	(747)	20.5	37.4	31.2	10.3
30s	(622)	27.7	33.2	30.2	8.5
40s	(389)	41.0	24.4	25.6	8.7
50s +	(476)	55.3	15.4	23.4	5.5
Occupations					
Agriculture/Forestry/ Fishery	(261)	46.9	17.7	25.6	8.5
Small Business	(295)	33.3	29.3	30.5	6.9
Blue collar	(258)	29.2	28.8	33.7	8.2
White collar	(238)	22.2	45.4	24.4	5.8
Housewives	(871)	39.6	24.8	26.4	9.3
Students	(127)	6.1	43.1	34.3	15.3
Unemployed	(184)	35.9	31.7	27.1	5.0

Source: Gallup Korea, 12-14, December. (N = 2,234)

In the December presidential election the students overwhelmingly voted for the opposition candidates, in spite of the division between the two Kims which revived the regional rivalry in Korean politics. Among the university population, Kim Young-sam and Kim Dae-jung were picked over Roh Tae-woo by 43.1 percent and 34.3 percent, respectively (see Table 1), as compared to only 6.1 percent for Roh. Likewise, among those in their 20s, including a large number of college students and recent graduates, 37.4 percent voted for Kim Young-sam and 31.2 percent for Kim Dae-jung, respectively, in comparison to 20.5 percent for Roh Tae-woo. The students and young voters clearly favored the two major opposition candidates in spite of the dog fight between them. The students and young voters were decidedly against Roh Tae-woo, the DJP candidate, who received a narrow 36.6 percent plurality of the total votes over Kim Young-sam (28 percent) and Kim Dae-jung (27 percent).

It is still premature to predict how the student activists will deal with the new political situation of South Korea. However, some of them have already expressed interest in a closer solidarity with the new middle class whose support in the spring of 1987 was a crucial factor which enabled the June Democratic Revolution to materialize. Some activists have emphasized since the December election "an urgent task of conscientizing the middle class."[43]

Some student leaders agree with the assessment of some opposition leaders that given the politically destructive division of the opposition camp in 1987, the democratic opposition movement in South Korea may require from 5 to 10 years to regroup themselves to the June 1987 level of effectiveness. Unless some unforeseeable events take place, some argue, it would be very difficult, if not impossible, for the opposition to reach that level of effectiveness in the near future.[44]

Conclusion

As one astute observer of the Korean political scene has put it,[45] the Korean student activists in the context of the presidential politics of 1987 were essentially "the event-making generation (*sakon'eul mandeuneun sedae*)"—the facilitators of democratic change—who successfully brought about the June Revolution. But their pre-June 29 efforts were for all practical intents and purposes nullified due to their inability to link up or "synchronize" their actions with the necessary follow-up measures of "the organizing generation (*chojikhaneun sedae*)"—the professional politicians. In short, what was critically lacking was the "institutional" and "organizing" opposition groups which could take up where the young students left off.[46] The opposition had very little time for consolidation of myriad divided democratic forces, but it wasted most of what little time it had because of the widening gap between the Sangdodong faction (the followers of Kim Young-sam) and the Dongkyodong faction (the supporters of Kim Dae-jung). When the election results were tallied, the two opposition parties led by the two Kims garnered a combined 55 percent popular vote but their "combined majority votes" were useless in defeating the Democratic Justice Party which captured a 36.6 percent plurality.

1987 was in fact the second time "an asynchronous democratization process" took place in South Korea without including the spring of 1980 in which the military carried out a coup before the democratization process was allowed to follow its natural course.[47] In 1960 the students forced Syngman Rhee out of the presidential office, but they were virtually powerless once the professional politicians of the Democratic Party took hold of the government power and started a self-destructive factional struggle between the two boss-dominated factions of the Democratic Party. Within less than a year General Park Chung-hee overthrew the impotent civilian the government of John Chang. It took twenty-six years from 1961 to 1987 before South Korea's student activists successfully coalesced with the alienated citizens—mainly the middle classes in their 20s and 30s—to force the military-controlled government of the Fifth Republic to surrender to the popular demand for democratic reforms. The main difference in the political situation of 1987 from that of 1960-61 was the fact that the opposition politicians were not able to agree on the standard bearer of the democratic opposition in the election.

The most disappointing aspect of the democratization process in 1987 was the fact that professional politicians of the mainstream opposition camp (UDP and PPD) didn't learn from their critical mistakes of 1960-61 and 1980. The student activists, church leaders, and disaffected intellectuals kept alive the momentum of opposition politics through their continuing extra-parliamentary confrontational tactics. But leaders of the "institutional opposition movement" were more effective in *opposing* the government in power than in *coalescing* and *uniting* themselves when another rare opportunity for the transfer of power arrived. A South Korean political scientist correctly assessed the political situation in Korea last year, an assessment which was widely echoed by many of his countrymen, when he said to me: "A full-course dinner is ready to be served" for the electoral victory of the civilian opposition. Unfortunately for the successful civilianization of South Korean politics, however, the happy dinner guests turned out be the "born-again democrats" led by Roh Tae-woo, his former military colleagues, and their supporters who were given a limited and fragile yet undisputable mandate of governance in 1987-1992 under the new Sixth Republic.

NOTES

1. For the radicalization of student politics since 1980, see Wonmo Dong, "University Students in South Korean Politics: Patterns of Radicalization in the 1980s," *Journal of International Affairs* Vol. 40/No. 2 (Winter/Spring 1987): pp. 233-255.
2. Due to the continuity of a large number of office holders from the Fifth Republic—e.g., about one third of the cabinet members—the Sixth Republic of President Roh Tae-woo is now referred to as "The Five Point Five Republic" among some political commentators in Korea.
3. A 12-page summary of this survey is given in *Dongrip Shinmun*, September 26, 1986.
4. "Is South Korea Going To Be Next Philippines?", *Washington Post*, January 25, 1987.
5. One serious flaw of this former head of the Korean government which several American professors have often noticed is: "Chun simply talks too much [and never listens enough to others]."
6. The proposed legislation was intended to isolate and re-educate the campus activists in a dozen or so of the internment camps which the government was to set up to stem the tide of student activism.
7. See Dong, *ip. cit.*: pp. 247-254.
8. *Dong-a Ilbo*, December 1, 1987.
9. For a cogent analysis of the background, the excessive nature of police actions and the political implications for the subsequent change of strategy among the student activists, see Shin Haeng-lee, "Kon'gukdae Nongsong Satae (The Konguk University Seizure Incident) in *Shindong'a* (New East Asia) "Hondae han'guk eul

dwiheundeun yuksipdae sagon (The Sixty Major Events That Have Shaken Modern Korea" Seoul: *Dong-a Ilbo*, 1988.

10. *Korea Herald*, November 1, 1986 (underlined by the author).
11. "Korea: A Statement of the Situation" (November 12, 1985) in North American Coalition for Human Rights in Korea, *Korea/Update* No. 81 (January 1987): pp. 4-8.
12. *Hanguk Ilbo*, November 21, 1986.
13. *Dong-a Ilbo*, December 1, 1986.
14. *Choong-ang Ilbo*, December 3, 1986.
15. *Dong-a Ilbo*, January 1, 1987.
16. "Letter to the People," January 19, 1987.
17. *Sae Gae Ilbo*, April 1, 1987.
18. Ilsu Kim, "Pak Jong Chol Gun Gomunsagon (The Torture Incident of Pak Jong-chul)," Dong-a Ilbo, *Hyundae Han'guk* (1988), pp. 340-345.
19. *Ibid.*
20. The main reason he offered for his action was that the opposition was hopelessly divided on this matter and that the country had to get on with the preparations for the 1988 Olympic Games.
21. *Hanguk Ilbo*, June 9, 1987.
22. Byung Tung Ahn, *op. cit.*, p. 350.
23. Gap Je Cho, et al., "Yuwolhyokmyong eu daedrama (The Great Drama of the June Revolution)," *Wolgan Chosun* (August 1987): pp. 142-177.
24. *Yomiuri Shimbun*, June 19, 1987.
25. *Choong-ang Ilbo*, June 28, 1987; *Dong-a Ilbo*, June 29, and June 30, 1987.
26. Police arrested 3,467 demonstrators throughout the country, and in many places the police simply controlled the demonstrating crowd. *Dong-a Ilbo*, June 30, 1987.
27. Byung Yung Ahn, "Yuwol minju hangchaengkwa 6.29 son'on (The June Democratic Revolution and 6.29 Declaration)," in Dong-a Ilbo, *Hyondae han'guk*, (1988), p. 348.
28. In Seoul 7,000 students from 32 schools participated in the March and they led the demonstrated in six different locations. A similar pattern of the student-led rally was repeated in all other cities. *Dong-a Ilbo*, June 29, 1987.
29. Dong, *op. cit.*,: pp. 249-250.
30. Hwa Choo Kim, "Chondaehyop taepung eu nun'in'ga (Chondaehyop: Is It the Eye of Typhoon)?", *Wolgan Chosun* (October 1987): pp. 319-322.
31. Kim, *op. cit.*, pp. 319.
32. *Ibid.*
33. *Ibid.* pp. 314-315.
34. *Ibid.*: p. 318.
35. *Dong-a Ilbo*, June 25, 1987.

36. Kim, *ibid.*: p. 318.
37. *Ibid.* pp. 321-322.
38. Woo's widely publicized interview with Nicholas D. Kristof, a *New York Times* correspondent, was reported in the August 2, issue of the *New York Times*. For this Woo was later charged with violation of the National Security Law and sentenced to a jail term.
39. "South Korea in 1987, The Politics of Democratization," *Asian Survey* (January 1988), p. 55.
40. Hwa Chu Kim, in his article, "No Taeu neun ireukke igyotta (This is how Roh Tae-woo)," *Wolgan Chosun* (January 1988): pp. 120-136, reports that the main strategy of Roh and his party was "stick (*kyonji*) to the simultaneous candidacy of both Kims to the very end."
41. *Sae Gae Ilbo*, December 30, 1987.
42. The real power contributing to the surprising success of the New Korea Democratic Party, which emerged victorious in all 35 urban districts, was large numbers of student activists who vigorously campaigned for the opposition candidates. In the 14 election districts in Seoul, the NKDP—and an older opposition party taken over right after the election—won 62.2 percent while the governing DJP received a humiliating 27 percent of the popular vote. See Dong, *op. cit.*, p. 242.
43. *Sae Gae Ilbo*, December 30, 1987.
44. *Ibid.*
45. Shin Haeng-lee, "Saechongch'i ui hwallo (The Road to Survival of the New Politics," *Shindong-a* (March 1988), pp. 174-213.
46. Professor Lee suggests that one realistic way to overcome the problem of incongruence between the event-creating students and the "establishment politicians" in the opposition camp is to encourage the intermediate generation of the 40s to assume a more active political role as a bridge between the generation of the 20s and 30s and that of the 50s and above in South Korea. *Ibid.*
47. One of the justifications for the military take-over of governmental power offered by General Chun and his fellow coup plotters, including General Roh Tae-woo, in 1980 was the reported squabbling among the three civilian politicians—Kim Young-sam, Kim Dae-jung, and Kim Jong-pil—the same threesome who ran for the presidency.

9

The Economic Problems of the Korean Political Economy

HANG YUL RHEE

Introduction

For more than two decades Korea has experienced remarkable economic growth. From 1962 to 1987, the Korean economy grew at an average annual rate of 8.4 percent. As a result of this rapid growth, Korea today is recognized as one of the outstanding newly industrializing countries (NICs).

However, the growth process during this period was neither smooth nor uniform. From 1962 to 1971, the country enjoyed both high growth and relative price stability. Between 1971 and 1979 this high growth continued, but it was accompanied by a high level of inflation. Korea experienced a severe setback in 1980. The economy then recovered and inflation dropped sharply, but for the next two years the growth rate was noticeably lower than it had been. In July 1985, the economy growth rate was below 6 percent and the overall economy was in recession.

Now (1987) Korea's economy is booming again. This is welcome news for South Koreans, who weathered a year of economic downturn and months of political turmoil in 1985. Recovery has been led by what people call the "three blessings"—lower oil prices, lower inflation, and a currency that has depreciated with the dollar. These three things have also made South Korean goods more competitive abroad, so that exports and economic growth are soaring. The annual economic growth rate for 1986 was 11.4 percent, according to the Asian Development Bank Report (see Korean Gross National Product Chart).

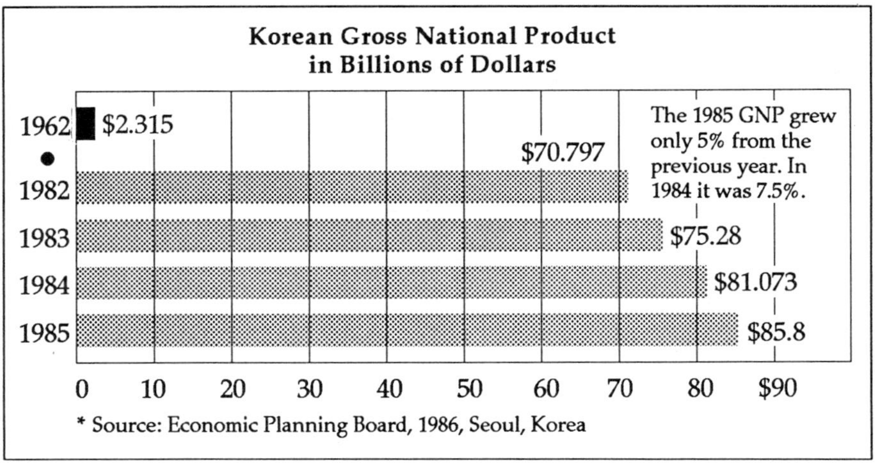

Having already increased its estimate of growth in the gross national product, the government now predicts that in 1987 the economy will expand between 9 percent and 10 percent in real terms, a forecast seconded by outside agencies such as the International Monetary Fund. For the first time since the Korean War, officials expect a current account surplus, which they predict will be between $6 billion and $8 billion.[1]

Overall Korean exports to the United States have increased dramatically: up 32 percent in the first quarter of 1986, according to U.S. custom statistics. With Japan's strong yen pushing up the prices of Japanese goods abroad, Korean goods attract more buyers. The Korean Economic Planning Board estimates that lower prices will add 1 percent to the Korean GNP growth this year and shave $1.8 billion off the cost of imported oil, which accounts for more than one-fifth of the country's total imports. With a total foreign debt of $46.7 billion (The third highest among the world's developing nations), Korea has gained from lower interest rates that are helping to reduce interest payments.[2]

The Economic Issues

Despite the spectacular economic development in Korea, there remain several outstanding economic issues that should preoccupy the nation's economic and political decisionmakers and that might hinder political development in the late 1980s.

Income Inequality

The first was the question of income inequality. The effects of rapid industrialization in Korea have been more equitable than in other developing countries. The income of the poorest 40 percent of the population had grown as fast as that of the wealthier classes, at least until the 1970s. Yet the gap between the rich and poor seemed to be growing wider in the late 1970s, and many Koreans tended to believe that they were being denied the benefits of Korea's economic success. There is presently an emerging segment of the population that feels very deprived and isolated. They believe they have not gotten their "fair share of the pie." Average Koreans are protesting bitterly about the gap between the rich and the poor, unlike average Americans who do not vigorously complain about the income inequality in the United States. Generally Koreans question the legitimacy of the wealth acquired by the few chaebols—big business groups owned and run by a single family. In the statistical sense, the Korean income inequality between the rich and the poor is far smaller than that in the United States.[3] Moreover, Korea's income distribution is far more equitable than that of other developing countries such as Thailand and the Philippines. Yet critical gaps between rich and poor remain, particularly in the perception of many Koreans. Public resentment against the rich runs very deep.

Generally, economic inequality is measured in terms of wages and income. However, information about individual annual income distribution in Korea is difficult to obtain. Here it must be assumed that the social structure of inequality results from the distribution of wealth. Also, it should be understood that this method is a crude one, since there is no way of identifying accurately the amount of household income in Korea. While this is also true in the United States, measurement is more difficult in Korea since subsistence salary scales force salaried workers to explore all possible means of additional income. Income reported for taxation is most likely far less than the actual amount of income. In this respect, measurement of income by the amount reported could be inaccurate and thereby distort the actual picture. Thus there must be reservations about making inferences in relating political behavior to economic inequality when measurement of the latter is based upon income figures. This is especially true in the Korean case.

Actually, economic inequality, including income inequality, is the by-product of the concentration of economic power. And the concentration of economic power issue in Korea is essentially the issue of "chaebol." The concentration of economic power is a paradox in that it is a product of free capitalism itself. The principles of the free competition and free enterprise system constituted the foundation of the modern bourgeois economic society in Western Europe, and its underlying legal principles were the guarantees of human rights, property rights, and the freedom of contract. Free competition was upheld on the ground that it achieves optimal resource allocation and thereby the maximal materialistic growth and contributes to the preservation of the democratic political and social system. But as the size of the firms became larger, due to the economies of scale embodied in mass-production technology, the discrepancy of the size between firms became more visible. There, the economic principle of natural discrimination or the survival of the fittest worked so that a few big firms preempted scarce resources and market opportunities, which resulted in the concentration of economic power.

However, capitalism in Western Europe has evolved in line with political democracy on the basis of rational choice by individuals as well as free and fair competition among individuals, both of which were secured through the struggle for civil rights. The public power of the government has been adequately exercised to deal with many problems—including the concentration of economic power under the harmony of the political, economic, and social systems—and this has contributed toward the preservation of fundamental vitality and the value system of capitalism.

This, however, has not been the case in Korea. Western capitalism and democracy were introduced to Korea upon her independence, where paternalistic bureaucracy and collective conservatism ruled for centuries. Moreover, the interaction of capitalism and democracy could not be effectively achieved as the country underwent the Korean War and later set the national goal of economic development under the direct intervention of the government. Economic activities in the private sector were led more by the national will than by individual choices. Consequently, government intervention in the private sector became ubiquitous, and with the exception of private ownership of firms, Korean firms were not capitalistic in the true sense of the word. The concentration of economic power which occurred, therefore, was not necessarily the product of the market system.

This may lead us to characterize the issue of the concentration of economic power as the concentration of wealth, the inequality of economic opportunities and benefits, as well as the government-business relations. It cannot be denied that Korea made economic development its primary national goal and tended to justify all economic consequences under the pretext of efficiency. Presently, however, the desire of the general public toward more equity can no longer be disregarded, and equity is, after all, a prerequisite for attaining efficiency in the long run. The concentration of economic power and the economic inequality should be viewed from this angle, for this will be a prerequisite to setting the direction of the evolution of Korean capitalism and to building the national consensus regarding this issue.

One cause of income inequality in Korea is the high level of inflation that has accompanied Korea's economic growth. Economic growth by itself may not solve or alleviate the problem of poverty within a reasonable period of time.[4] Actually, "higher growth rate generates greater inequality" and "—in the great majority of developing countries the benefits of economic development accrue chiefly to the upper groups—the highest 20 percent to 40 percent of the population, and—in some countries the poorest 20 percent or even a large percentile do not participate in the process of economic development at all."[5]

Korea, as evidenced in Seoul, is a typical case in point. High economic growth along with high inflation has bred income inequality among Koreans. This income inequality can be measured by comparing the inequality in the distribution of wealth. (see Table 1)

Table 1
Gini Coefficient of Income Concentration

	National	Wages & Salaries	Business Income	Farm Income	Urban Income
'58 (I.D.C.)	.359				
'58 (Chae)	.464	.446	.551	.371	
'60 (Chae)	.448	.450	.548	.387	
'61 (Chae)	.438	.429	.553	.393	
'58-'61 (Chae)	.450	.442	.550	.384	
'66 (Chung-Ang)	.335	.296	.278	.299	.315
'68 (E.P.B.)	.363	.241	.523	.310	.367
'70 (Chae)	.375	.380	.625	.309	
'70 (Renaud)		.250			
'71 (E.P.B.)	.339				
'76 (K.D.I.)	.390				
'84 (K.D.I.)	.356				

1958 (I.D.C. Survey) is based on an urban sample of 2,822 households.
1958 (Chae) is based on National Income Tax Returns, also '60 and '61.
1966 (Chung-Ang) is based on 799 urban and 971 rural households.
1968 (E.P.B.) is based on 10,000 urban and 10,000 rural households.
1970 (Chae) is based on National Income Tax data.
1970 (Renaud) is based on 1970 Census data and wage survey.
1971 (E.P.B.) 1976 (K.D.I.), 1984 (K.D.I.) are based on census data.

Chae, Mun-Kyou, "Income Size Distribution for Korea" in 1972.
E.P.B. Urban Surveys, E.P.B. Seoul, Korea, 1968.
Chung-Ang University, "Income Distribution and Consumption Structure in Korea," 1966.
Renaud, Bertrand, "Economic Growth and Income Inequality in Korea," Banking Staff Working Paper #240, World Bank, 1976.
K.D.I. 1986 Report on Korean Income, Seoul, Korea. 1986.

Income inequality, as stated previously, is the most difficult variable to operationalize since there is no consensus among economists on its definition. The "fair" distribution of income has been debated by professional economists for many years. No general definition has yet emerged. Still valid is the statement by Simon S. Kuznets that this "subject has been plagued by looseness in definitions, unusual scarcity of data, and pressures of strongly held opinion."[6] Despite this difficulty, since most developing areas have a large gap between rich and poor, income inequality must be treated as an important economic issue.[7]

Empirical studies on income distribution in Korea are usually based on two household surveys, namely the urban household income and expenditure survey by the Bureau of Statistics, and the farm households survey by the Ministry of Agriculture and Fisheries. Although these two household surveys are undertaken annually and their results are reasonably reliable, the major difficulty in estimating income distribution in Korea arises from the fact that some types of households are not covered in these surveys. For example, the urban households survey does not include the incomes of self-employed households, and the non-farm households in rural areas are excluded from both survey samples. Therefore, estimates of income distribution in Korea are inevitably based on patchwork from various data sources. Typically, the incomes of self-employed households are estimated from their consumption expenditures, and the income level and distribution of rural non-farm households are indirectly inferred from those of urban households. In view of these shortcomings in the data available on income distribution, the Bureau of Statistics undertook a comprehensive survey of income distribution in early 1981. As a result, the income distribution estimates for the year 1980 are based on one data source instead of a patchwork of different sources.

As shown in Table 2, income distribution deteriorated somewhat during the 1965-80 period of rapid economic growth, although the extent of deterioration was relatively small in comparison with other countries' experiences. The income share of the lowest 40 percent of all households declined from 22.6 percent in 1965 to 17.5 percent in 1980, while that of the highest 20 percent increased from 41.8 percent to 45.4 percent in this period. This observation perhaps bears out the famous Kuznets hypothesis that the distribution of income tends to worsen during the early phase of economic development.[8]

In examining the trend in different sub-periods of 1965-80, one finds that the distribution of income improved between 1965 and 1970, but deteriorated since 1970. The marked improvement in income distribution among urban households during 1965-70 was the major factor improving the overall distribution of income. The income share of the lowest 40 percent of urban households in-

Table 2
Trends in Income Distribution, 1965-1980

	1965	1970	1976	1980
Gini Ratio				
All Households	0.344	0.332	0.381	0.389
Rural Households	0.285	0.295	0.327	0.405
Urban Households	0.417	0.346	0.412	0.405
Income Shares of Lowest 40% (%)				
All Households	19.3	19.6	16.9	16.1
Rural Households	22.6	21.2	19.5	17.5
Urban Households	14.1	18.9	15.4	15.3
Income Shares of Highest 20% (%)				
All Households	41.8	31.6	45.3	45.4
Rural Households	38.0	38.6	40.6	42.2
Urban Households	47.0	43.0	48.7	46.9

* Sources: KDI estimates.

creased from 14.1 percent in 1965 to 18.9 percent in 1970, while that of the highest 20 percent declined from 47 percent to 43 percent in this period. These improvements notwithstanding, the distribution of income among both rural and urban households since 1970 has obviously deteriorated in Korea.

Although the degree of income inequality is relatively greater among urban households, it was the rural sector that showed a relatively greater deterioration in the distribution of income during 1965-70. This fact is contrary to the general expectation that the urban sector would be the major cause for income inequality in the process of rapid economic growth.[9]

As shown in Table 3 the income differential between farm households and non-farm households played a relatively small role in explaining the trend in overall income distribution. For example, the income differential between the farm and non-farm sectors widened between 1965 and 1970; nonetheless the overall distribution of income actually improved during this period. During the 1970-1980 period of widening inequalities in income distribution, the income differential between the farm and non-farm sectors actually became smaller. This is also an important point that merits study in the future.

Available sources show that during the last 22 years absolute poverty has declined significantly. This observation parallels the rapid expansion in employment opportunities that came as a result of high economic growth. The incidence of absolute poverty declined from 40.9 percent in 1965 to 9.8 percent in 1980. This drop clearly suggests that a high-growth strategy that creates many employment opportunities is a very effective way of reducing poverty in a developing economy such as Korea was in the early 1960s. However, the 1960s showed a higher rate of decline in the incidence of absolute poverty than the 1970s. This fact perhaps implies that the effectiveness of the high-growth strategy tends to diminish as the hard-core poor, who do not benefit directly from economic growth, come to constitute a relatively larger proportion of the poor.[10]

Table 3

Ratio Trends of Urban Household Income to Rural Household Income (Monthly Income: Won)

	Urban Wage Earning Households (A)	Farm Households (B)	B/A (%)
1965	9,380	9,350	99.7%
1970	31,770	21,317	67.1
1976	95,980	96,355	100.4
1980	267,096	224,425	84.0

* Source: Bureau of Statistics, Urban Household Surveys Ministry of Agriculture and Fisheries, Farm Household Surveys.

As shown in Table 5, the regional composition of poverty in Korea showed a marked change during the 1965-80 period.[11] In 1965 only 36.1 percent of the poor were in urban areas. As urbanization accelerated, this ratio increased to 61.7 percent in 1980. As a result, poverty is increasingly becoming an essentially urban problem. Several implications arise. First, as the price of land is much higher in urban areas, physical living conditions are likely to be worse for the urban poor than for the rural poor. Second, as there are far more frequent contacts among different socio-economic groups in urban areas, the urban poor are more likely to be aware of their relative economic position in society. For some people, this realization can act as a psychological motivation to work harder, but for others it may become a source of deep frustration.

Table 4
Trends in the Incidence of Poverty
(As a Percent of Total Population)

	1965	1970	1976	1980
Absolute Poverty [a]				
All Households	40.9	23.4	14.8	9.8
Rural Households	35.8	27.9	11.7	9.0
Urban Households	54.9	16.2	18.1	10.4
Relative Poverty [b]				
All Households	12.1	4.8	12.4	13.3
Rural Households	10.0	3.4	9.2	11.2
Urban Households	17.9	7.0	16.0	15.1

[a] Absolute poverty line defined as 121,000 won in 1981 prices per month for a five member household.

[b] Relative poverty line defined as one-third for the average household income in a given year.

Table 5
Regional Distribution of the Poor

	Urban	Rural	Total
1965	36.1	63.9	100.0
1976	59.1	40.9	100.0
1980	61.7	38.3	100.0

* Source: KDI estimates.

A result of empirical study shows that during the 1970s the distribution of income deteriorated in both the urban and the rural sectors. Identifying the major factors that gave rise to this widening of income inequality is important not only for understanding the past relationship between growth and equity, but also for formulating policy measures towards spreading the benefits of growth more equitably in the future.

Two factors can be singled out as the major causes of the growing income inequality in the urban sector. One factor is that wage and salary differentials by education level and job category widened in the 1970s. The coefficient for variation of wage and salary differentials by job category increased sharply from 0.398 in 1971 to 0.516 in 1976, but thereafter declined slowly to 0.487 in 1980. Furthermore, the ratio of the average earnings of a college graduate over those of a middle school graduate increased from 3.02 in 1970 to 3.60 in 1976. After 1976 this ratio declined to 3.32 in 1980. Thus, the trend in wage and salary differentials coincides very closely with the income distribution trend in the urban sector, i.e., a worsening of inequality in the 1970s with a peak around 1976.[12]

The deterioration in the distribution of wages and salaries during 1970-76 can be attributed to a temporary disequilibrium in the labor market. While the demand for highly skilled and educated manpower increased rapidly, due to a shift in Korea's comparative advantage position in export markets from less skill-intensive industries to more skill-intensive industries, the supply of this type of manpower lagged behind the demand. The slight improvement in wage and salary differentials since 1976 reflects the fact that the supply of highly skilled and educated manpower increased partly as a result of the natural market reaction to the increase in wages and partly as a result of the deliberate policy of the government to increase the supply of this type of manpower.

The other factor causing an income disparity in the urban sector can be attributed to the concentration of business that took place in the 1970s. A recent KDI study shows that the share of the 20 largest chaebol groups in the country's gross domestic product increased from 7.1 percent in 1973 to 17.1 percent in 1978. Such a concentration of business ownership gave rise not only to growing inequality in business incomes but also to a widening in wage and salary differentials between large and small firms.[13]

It is more difficult to identify the main factor that adversely affected the distribution of income in the rural sector. One factor could be the introduction of a vigorous price support program in 1968. As shown in Table 3, the price support policy improved the terms of trade in favor of agriculture, thus helping to narrow the income gap between farm and non-farm households. However, since large farms benefitted relatively more from the high price of rice, the price support program led to a deterioration in the income distribution among farm households. Further, various attempts to modernize agriculture, such as the introduction of high-yield varieties of rice and the cultivation of cash crops, may have contributed to further widening of income disparities among farm households, as the incomes of relatively more innovative farmers, who are likely to have already belonged to an upper income group, increased faster than the incomes of other farmers.

As stated previously, the Korean economy experienced tremendous growth, particularly during the 1960s. However, this economic growth was accompanied by high social mobilization. As defined by Deutsch, social mobilization is a "process in which major clusters of old social, economic, and psychological commitments are eroded or broken down and people become available for new patterns of socialization and behavior." [14] In addition, the rapid social mobilization in Korean urban areas brought high "rising expectations." [15] The government, with only a limited capability, could not provide enough to satisfy the high demand. Thus, the nation's high economic growth rate alone could not provide an adequate measure of satisfaction and support for the government and its party. As Ahluwalia and Adler state, it is likely that a "higher growth rate generates greater inequality."[16] In addition, Korea's economic growth has been offset by its inflation rate (see Table 6). From 1954 to 1957, this rate was 36.3 percent per year. The periods from 1958 to 1959, and that from 1983 to 1985 saw relatively little inflation, although there was an economic recession in Korea during this time. Examination of the level of urbanization and occupation mobility shows that the rate of mobilization has been rapid enough to be damaging to economic equality in Korea.

In addition to the national inflation, the consumer price index went up almost 120 percent between 1965 and 1971.[17] Most Koreans have been economically burdened since their income has not kept up with the inflation rate. The index of wages in real terms indi-

Table 6
Index of Inflation
Annual Change in Prices as Reflected by the Implicit GNP Deflator

Year	% Change
1954	32.8
1955	63.6
1956	29.6
1957	19.3
1958	1.7
1959	2.1
1960	9.1
1961	15.5
1962	13.4
1963	28.2
1964	31.8
1965	7.6
1966	12.9
1967	10.5
1968	11.9
1969	12.1
1970	15.2
1971	10.3
1979	29.0
1980	69.6
1981	22.0
1982	7.5
1983	4.0
1984	2.7
1985	3.0

* Source: Bank of Korea, *Economic Statistics Year Book, 1972*. From 1965, the annual rate of price increase has been close to 10%, World Bank Report, 1985.

cates that there was no substantial change in worker's real wages between 1954 and 1966.

The K.D.I.'s information on distribution of income in urban areas in 1985 indicates that the income of the top 10 percent is 8.6 times more than the income of the lowest 10 percent. This is an increase of 0.2 percent more than in 1984 (see Table 7).

Table 7
Comparison of Size Distributions of Monthly Earnings of Manufacturing Workers

% of Income Bracket	Income (Won)	Spending (Won)	Engel Ratio	% of Total Income
1	125,271	156,103	42.7	2.9
2	208,213	189,236	42.2	4.8
3	257,175	208,366	42.0	6.0
4	296,803	226,193	41.8	6.9
5	335,857	253,578	40.0	7.8
6	384,501	281,926	39.4	8.9
7	442,989	309,926	38.4	10.3
8	524,718	365,421	36.6	12.2
9	656,704	443,586	34.6	15.2
10	1,080,466	66,527	29.0	25.1

* Source: KDI Income Report, 1986, Seoul, Korea.

According to this table, the lowest 10 percent income bracket in cities earn 125,271 won while the top 10 percent receive an income of 1,080,466 won. This top income bracket represents 25.1 percent of the total income. Compared to the United States and other developing nations, Korea ranks well in terms of economic equality and income distribution, yet most Koreans greatly resent the rich and are particularly against chaebols.

More complex problems must be admitted in considering the issue of economic inequality. Streeten, in "Some Problems in the Use of Transfer of an Intellectual Technology," has pointed out the following:

> Inequality of income distribution touches only a small portion of the vast multidimensional problem of inequality. There is inequality of assets, of access to earning opportunities, of satisfaction from work, of recognition, of ability to enjoy consumption, of power, of participation in decision-making. The call for greater equality, for a genuine community of equals cannot be answered simply by measures that reduce the Gini coefficient or any other simple measure of inequality. It is possible to envisage a technocratic society, where decisions are

> highly centralized and in which a few enjoy the satisfaction from power and creativity while the many carry out boring and disagreeable tasks in a hierarchic structure and in which the Gini coefficient was zero.[18]

The Problem of Chaebols

Second, in conjunction with economic inequality, the problem of chaebols should be mentioned since the major portion of Korean wealth is concentrated in these industrial conglomerates.

When South Korea began its economic takeoff in the early 1960s, the government turned to a handful of entrepreneurs to make its plans work. Backed by massive amounts of low-cost funds, the businessmen built a series of industrial conglomerates or chaebols. These now account for the bulk of the country's manufacturing output; their huge backlog of debt, plus the inefficiencies found in many of these internally disparate empires has become a drag on the whole economy. Moreover, the concentration of wealth in a few hands is a simmering political issue.

The increasing shrillness of the attack against the chaebols has been symptomatic of the times. After a generation of free-wheeling growth and fantastic expansion, the chaebols in recent years have come to symbolize almost everything that has gone wrong with the country's economy. Up to fifty top privately owned groups are classified as chaebols, which were created in the 1960s and 1970s by the late President Park Chung-hee as executors of his ambitious policy of rapid growth through industrialization in export areas. Some of these big business groups have grown into economic behemoths scarcely capable of supporting their own weight.

While their overall sales dominate the country's economy, their size hides their lack of operating efficiency, which in most industries reflects an absence of specialization. They struggle under the load of an astronomically high amount of underpaid, and perhaps unpayable, debts. They have huge investments locked in areas such as construction, shipbuilding, and heavy machinery: sectors that were once synonymous with the country's phenomenal success, but which are now unprofitable because of accumulated debts and weakening markets. This has raised wider doubts about their future in the face of the worldwide economic slowdown, as shown in the tragic episode of the corruption and tax evasion of the Pan Ocean Company, which was one of the chaebols.[19]

Many chaebols have expanded by using the controversial technique of cross investment, which involves member companies of a group investing in stocks to acquire a new company without inputting any fresh capital input. Using the nominal increase in group capital resulting from the manuever, the group can then borrow more money from it's bankers. Some experts have estimated that up to 40 percent of capitalization in a newly acquired company would typically come from other group companies, with the rest funded by bank loans. This system weakens the financial strength of most members of the chaebol. With an average debt-equity ratio running to 4.5:1 in 1983 (compared with 3.6:1 for the whole manufacturing sector), the chaebols are said to be among the worst financially structured corporate bodies in the world.

Part of the public alarm over their growing power and influence stems from their dominant role in the economy. The combined net sales of the country's top thirty chaebols—those with a minimum capitalization of 30 billion Won (U.S. $33.7 million)—totalled some 36 trillion Won in 1983. This equalled about three-quarters of South Korea's output of goods and services in that year, according to a press survey. Using a somewhat defensive set of statistics, the Federation of Korean Industries (F.K.I. —the lobby group for the chaebols) estimated their total—added in economic output the cost of raw materials used) at 17.4 trillion Won or 39.2 percent of that year's gross domestic product.[20] In an economy so overshadowed by giant players, the small and medium scale industries, parched of funds and squeezed from the market, have had almost no room to grow (see Table 8). Indeed, the typical fate of a small subcontractor for a big group is to be paid with a nine-month promissory note for his supply, or be gobbled up by the giant if he cannot endure the financial pinch. In neighboring Japan, small businesses have not only survived, but prospered through specialization as suppliers of quality components, and in Taiwan they provide the sinews of the nation's whole economic strength. On the other hand, South Korea's business environment has evolved as a jungle where the big beasts prey on the smaller animals.

The thirty largest chaebols owned an average of 4.2 subsidiaries each in 1970, but the number jumped to 14.3 in 1979 due to the rapid growth of the Korean economy. During the same period, the total number of manufacturing firms increased 1.3 times, whereas the number of subsidiaries of chaebols increased 2.4 times. The seed of the so-called chaebol issue can be found in this unbalanced growth of business groups. Due to the recession at the end of the 1970s and the consequent rationalization of chaebols, however, the exit of subsidiaries surpassed the new entry in the early 1980s, and chaebols owned 13.4 subsidiaries in 1982. In other words, the 1970s was the expansion period of chaebols, whereas the 1980s is their consolidation period. The industrial composition of 402 subsidiaries of the 30 largest chaebols in terms of 2-digit industrial classification is: manufacturing 222, trade 18, construction 30, services 33, real estate and finance 29, transportation and warehousing 34, restaurant and hotel 11, wholesale and retail 15, and others 9.[21]

Table 8
The Integration of 30 Largest Business Groups

Year	New Establishment	Acquistion	Internal Merger	Divesture	New Increase	No. of Subsidiaries
1970						126
1971-79	202	135	27	7	303	429
1980	30	25	31	51	-27	402

Source: KDI working paper.

The relative size of chaebols is shown in Table 9. The share of chaebols in manufacturing reaches 39.9 percent in shipment and 17.9 percent in employment. Though not shown in the table, their shares in value-added and assets are 31.6 percent and 37.1 percent respectively. The striking difference between their shares in shipment and employment may be caused by their capital-intensive method of production and market power at the commodity level. We can also notice that recently the share of shipment has tended to increase while that of employment has generally decreased and that the share of shipment of the top five chaebols has substantially risen.

The concentration of economic power in Korea has yet another

Table 9
The Shares of Business Groups in Manufacturing

Business Groups	Shipment '77	'80	'81	'82	'83
top 5	15.7	16.9	21.5	22.6	22.3
top 15	21.2	23.8	28.4	30.2	29.3
top 20	29.3	31.4	35.3	36.0	36.0
top 30	34.1	36.0	39.7	40.7	39.9

Business Groups	Employment '77	'80	'81	'82	'83	No. of Subsidiaries
top 5	9.1	9.1	8.9	8.4	8.5	89
top 15	12.5	12.8	12.8	12.2	11.9	144
top 20	17.4	17.9	17.0	16.0	15.3	217
top 30	20.5	22.4	20.8	18.6	17.9	264

Source: KDI Report, 1984.

characteristic, the concentration of ownership. Taking a typical chaebol from the top 10, 49.0 percent of its total equity is owned by its subsidiaries and 11.7 percent directly by an individual shareholder who also controls those subsidiaries. In effect, the particular individual owns, on the average, directly and indirectly, 60.7 percent of a chaebol. Such a concentration of ownership of chaebols can also be demonstrated by the fact that only 91 out of 402 subsidiaries of the top 30 chaebols are listed in the stock exchange.[22]

Another of the controversial issues surrounding the chaebols is their heavy borrowing. The top 30 chaebols owe a total of 14.8 trillion Won in various payment guarantees covering overseas borrowings, deferred payment exports, and Middle East construction projects. The combined share of these two categories are equal to 48 percent of the country's total bank credits, from development institutions as well as commercial banks.[23]

A combination of factors, including the economic slowdown, has frustrated government measures aimed at forcing the chaebols to settle part of these debts by liquidating their vast property holdings (land and buildings), estimated by one opposition legislator to be worth 3.4 trillion Won, or by floating some of their companies on the local stockmarket. Many fear that cutting back on the weight and size of the chaebol, "shaping up" their corporate body, at the time of sluggish overall performance could worsen unemployment and depress investment.

Seven percent annual economic growth has been calculated as the minimum needed to generate the additional jobs required for those who leave school and college each year. Since slow growth means political problems for President Chun Doo-hwan, he must implement his chaebol curbs carefully.

In 1983, 64 percent of Korea's GNP and 70 percent of its exports were generated by the top 10 companies (chaebol), the most prominent of which are Hyundai, Samsung, Daewoo, and Lucky Goldstar.[24] The owners of these companies have come to wealth in a generation, and seem to increase both their wealth and their influence on Korean politics. Certainly, by encouraging the plutocracy, the concentration of wealth in so few hands would seem to be detrimental to the development of democracy. Time is running out for the government's effort to reform the chaebol situation. There is increasing pressure for change from radical students and opposition groups. Their ranks are now reinforced by labor's demand for a more equitable distribution of wealth. The radicals have become too strong to ignore. Indeed, public resentment against inequitable income distribution runs very deep. Nevertheless, Koreans are allowed few outlets for their anger. In recent months the government has clamped down on political dissidents and labor leaders, proposing "re-orientation" centers for student dissidents, arresting some opposition politicians, and roughing up newspaper editors.

Resentments have driven some workers to violate anti-strike laws, notably in the spring of 1985 at the Daewoo Apparel Company. Strike leaders were arrested, hundreds of workers were fired, and there were reports that several of the female strikers were hospitalized after being beaten with streetpipes. Government officials and business leaders charge that union activists are communist infiltrators. Unless the government alleviates the widespread belief among many Koreans that the benefits of Korea's success are being denied to them, continuous political instability seems inevitable.

Now, as the authoritarian government that has kept wages low through force and coercion loosens its control, workers are demanding a greater piece of the "economic miracle" in an explosion of rank-and-file strikes, sit-ins and other job actions. Spontaneous, leaderless and apparently beyond any institution's control, the labor stirrings have injected a new uncertainty into South Korea's fragile progress toward Democracy. Since government Party Chairman Roh's announcement of accepting free elections and other reforms on June 29, 1987, there have been more job actions than in all of 1986, involving tens of thousands of workers. The nation's five major automakers, including Hyundai plants, were shut down either by strikes or parts shortages caused by strikes at supplier firms. Shipbuilders, miners, bus drivers, even pop singers have staged protests or walked out, and small companies have been hit as hard as large.

So far, the cost of labor unrest to Korea's economy has been relatively modest. The Korean government estimated in August that $55 million in exports were lost during a 15 day stretch in late July and early August, hardly a dent in the nation's original total export projection of $44.5 billion for 1987.[25] However, the Korea Development Institute, a government think tank, predicted that the current account surplus would decrease by up to $2.6 billion, to $1.7 billion, and the unemployment rate could rise by as much as 1.5 percentage points to 4.9 percent. The K.D.I. also projects that a 5-6 percent increase in wages from current strikes will reduce this country's economic growth rate in the second half of 1987 by as much as 3.7 percentage points, to 5.8 percent.[26]

The negative image of business groups in Korea is generally attributed to the inequality of economic opportunities among firms as well as the general perception about the concentration of their ownership and their process of growth. Granting that an unequal distribution of ownership is inevitable in every economy, the reason that it is raised as a critical issue in Korea is that the capitalistic value system has not sufficiently harmonized with the traditional one and the process of capital accumulation itself is not yet fully justified in the eyes of the general public. It cannot be denied that the general public believes that most business groups have accumulated monopoly profits at the expense of consumers and other smaller firms with the help of loans, both domestic and foreign, in addition to government protection. They are also understood to have invested their profits in unproductive sectors such as real estate, and to have influenced government policies to further their private interests. These negative perceptions may—putting aside their justification—foment social tension, raise distrust to doubts about the economic system, and further distort economic morality among some segments of the general public. To summarize, the concentration of economic power in Korea has become an issue with political and social dimensions transcending the simple economic sphere; as a result, the value judgments of individuals are intertwined with objective facts, which renders solving the whole issue all the more difficult.

From the preceding analysis of chaebols in Korea today, the following suggestions can be made for the formulation of relevant policies.

First, the phenomenon called the concentration of economic power must be correctly understood in order to establish a true market system and to encourage economic and political democracy, which are the foundations of capitalism. Government intervention into the market, however, may fail as a result of irrational policy lines and means.

Second, in setting the basic direction of policy to regulate the concentration of economic power, we have to distinguish and harmonize the issue of efficiency and equity. Equity should be achieved within the limits of not hampering efficiency, and should not be valued for its own sake. It must be pointed out, however, that overall efficiency of an economy cannot be maintained for long unless there is enough equity to give an achievement motive to every agent and to cultivate a cooperative atmosphere in the society. Since the concentration of economic power is partly a result of the law of natural discrimination under given market conditions, it may be desirable to eliminate its negative effects while preserving the competitive spirit and efficiency. The issue of social equity should first be approached by guaranteeing equal economic opportunities to all agents, with other policy measures mobilized to supplement this goal.

Third, unless the concentration of ownership of business groups is levelled down, the seed of discontent will still remain. General policies of income or wealth redistribution can have only a limited effect on this score because they are not specifically designed against majority shareholders of business groups. For example, because the property tax, income tax, or death tax is levied on all taxpayers, the upward calibration of these tax rates cannot be considered a proper measure for preventing the concentration of economic power. Consequently, we must come up with a policy aimed specifically at dissipating the ownership of business groups. Such a policy must entail making subsidiaries of business groups go public with the issuance of stock and concurrently by inducing the general public to participate more in the stock market. This step must be preceded, however, by improvement in the general income level and distribution, upgrading of the corporation financial structure, enhancement of managerial professionalism, a reduction in opportunities for other speculative investments, and bettering the overall environment of the stock market. Consequently, we cannot jump beyond the factual constraints to reach the final goal, and we must instead make consistent, long-term efforts on a wide front. One effort in this direction is the recent proposal of the government to add a provision to the Monopoly Regulation Act forbidding the direct intercompany shareholding between subsidiaries of business groups and limiting their total investment.

Fourth, although its effects are not limited to the question of economic power, the disclosure of information cannot be overemphasized in Korea. If the real picture of business groups and related policies is sufficiently disclosed, then purely emotional biases and prejudices against the government and business groups will be eliminated. Through the analyses and evaluation of objective data, general doubts and distrusts will die down to the extent that they are ungrounded, and lessons will be learned from past mistakes.

Finally, whatever the policy may be, its intended effects will not be fully realized unless business groups are determined to observe the economic morality expected from them. This is true of all policies and laws, but is all the more so of economic power because of its origins and potential, as shown in the case of the Pan Ocean Company scandal. Chaebols should be strongly urged, even more than other firms, to follow economic morality, for much of the root of the issue of economic power lies in such extra-efficiency areas as distribution, equity, social justice, and the sense of community.[27]

The Public Debt and the Trade Issues

The third problem facing economic decision makers in Korea concerns the external public debt and the trade issues.

Of the four Asian NICs, South Korea is the highest stakes gambler. It has financed fifteen years average real annual growth in GNP of 7.75 percent since 1970 by a dramatic build-up of foreign debt. It is now the world's fourth largest debtor nation. This $44 billion or so debt of external borrowing, of which some 35 percent is short term, limits South Korea's freedom of maneuver compared with relatively unindebted Taiwan. The Seoul government cannot allow its current policy of steady depreciation of the won (to retain export competitiveness) to go too far without risking an increase in the debt-service burden (already very high if the short-term component of debt is included), as well as a rise in inflation. Yet exports must be boosted if the current account deficits, and thus future deficit-financing borrowing, are to be held in check.

In July 1986, the Ministry of Finance reported that Korea's external debt totaled $46.81 billion at the end of April. This represented an increase of $50 million since the end of 1985. In a report to the National Assembly, the Ministry also said that the short-term foreign debt that should be paid in a year had reached $9.8 billion or 20.9 percent of the total.[28]

The reason for the accumulation of so much debt in Korea is that Korean industrial growth has been financed primarily by external debt. In fact, much of Korea's industrial growth can be traced to the interaction of foreign capital inflows and government intervention, both direct and indirect. Foreign direct investment was insignificant before 1965. By the end of 1978, as corporations took advantage of cheap labor government incentives, and free-export zones, it was up to $940 million. Between 1970 and 1975 they accounted for 17 percent of all manufacturing investment.

Foreign corporate investments are primarily of Japanese origin and are concentrated in chemicals, electronics, and textiles. By 1974, some 31 percent of manufactured exports were produced by subsidiaries of foreign firms.[29] Still, foreign loans are a much more important source of investment capital: while foreign direct investment between 1970 and 1975 was $700 million, net borrowing was $3.7 billion. Foreign loans have been concentrated in some of the same export-oriented manufacturing sectors as foreign direct investment, as well as in non-metallic minerals, steel, transport equipment, and petroleum.[30] All in all, according to South Korea's Minister of Finance, foreign capital financed 40 percent of investment between 1962 and 1972.[31]

In order to expand production rapidly, the state also actively encouraged private businesses to borrow heavily both domestically and abroad. Indeed, Korea is unusual in that a good half of its external debt is owed by private firms, with the public sector providing only a guarantee to the lender.[32] As a result, Korean companies are among the most highly leveraged in the world, with debt-to-equity ratios of 5:1 and 6:1 not uncommon.

At the end of March 1987, South Korea's total external debt was about U.S. $44 billion,[33] some $16.6 billion more than at the end of 1980 (see Table 10).

Table 10
Korean Debt Profile (U.S. $ Billion, %)

	1979	1980	1981	1982	1983	1984
External Debt Outstanding	20.5	27.4	32.5	37.2	40.4	43.1
(Annual Increase)	(5.6)	(6.9)	(5.1)	(4.7)		
Long-Term	13.9	16.8	20.8	23.2	28.3	31.7
	(67.8)	(61.2)	(63.9)	(62.2)		
Short-Term	4.7	7.6	8.5	10.2	12.1	11.4
	(22.7)	(27.7)	(26.1)	(27.3)		
Foreign Bank "A" Account	2.0	3.0	3.3	3.9		
	(9.5)	(11.1)	(10.0)	(10.5)		

Note: Figures in parentheses indicate the composition ratios.
Source: EPB, Korea's external debt, Feb., 1985, Seoul, Korea, p. 1.

This apparently staggering sum was not so awesome as it seemed, since the ratio of payments on principal and interest to total export earnings was 20.7 percent. By comparison, Brazil's debt service ratio has been well over 70 percent for a number of years. Still, Korean foreign debts totalling $44 billion represent a clear warning to both the government and some creditors. Thus, economic policy-makers should plan to increase the growing trade surplus during the five-year plan period. Until 1985, Korea had suffered a chronic trade deficit around $1-5 billion (except for 1965 and 1977).[34] For the first time in 1986 (Jan.-June), the Korean trade registered $600 million surplus in trade balance because of rising merchandise exports, primarily to the United States.[35]

The central bank credited the significantly improved current account to increased commodity exports, spurred by the strengthening Japanese yen, lowered crude oil prices, and dropped international interest rates.

Overall exports, during the first five months in 1986 rose by 19.9 percent to $12,143 million, while total imports jumped by 10.6 percent to $11,935 million over the same period in 1985. As a result the total trade balance during the January-May period in 1986 saw a $208 million surplus compared with a $666 million deficit in the same period in 1985. Despite its trade surplus in 1986, Korea has been running up a growing deficit in its trade with Japan, undercutting its efforts to shore up its balance-of-payments position. In the first five months of 1986, the deficit reached $2.19 billion, up 68.3 percent from the corresponding period of last year, the Ministry of Trade and Industry reported. During the January-March period in 1986, the deficit rose 66.7 percent from the same period of 1985, to $1.1 billion; during the April-May period in 1986, the deficit figure totaled about $1 billion.[36] Contributing to the growing deficit are increased import prices of Japanese-made machinery, parts and raw materials, coupled with Korea's increasing demand for the importation of other Japanese capital goods. In its trade with the United States, however, Korea chalked up a surplus of $7.6 billion in 1986, up $2.6 billion from the $5 billion surplus of 1985.[37] This year's surplus is expected to reach about $9 billion, compared with $4.27 billion recorded in 1984. The growing surplus is likely to fuel protectionist sentiment in the United States against Korean-made goods and to prompt Washington to put more pressure on Korea to open its market.

Therefore, the Korean government should not expect to continue a trade surplus with the United States, which buys 35 percent of the nation's exports. American protectionists' resentment against Korea is already forming. In fact, the United States has already ruled that Korean color television manufacturers were guilty of dumping; several other cases are still pending. In 1984, Koreans were forced to accept "voluntary" restraints on steel exports to America. Moreover, some quotas on Korean textiles, which accounted for 23.5 percent of all exports in the first half of 1985, seem inevitable in the election year of 1988.

Basically, the over-dependence on exports (exports constitute almost 40 percent of the total GNP) has made the Korean economy highly vulnerable to the external trade environment. For example, in the first half of 1985, Korea's exports on a custom clearance basis totalled U.S. $12.44 billion; this is 4 percent less than during the same period of 1984.[38] The decline can be attributed to the slowdown of world economic growth, especially in North America, combined with the prevailing levels of protectionism. However, one of the most important factors of the export situation may prove to be the vulnerability of the internal industrial structure, which is characterized by both a lack of R&D investment and hampered by the overemphasis on heavy as well as chemical industry.

Trade conflicts with the United States may cause economic issues to become more political in the near future, as they did in 1985. Students demonstrated against U.S. protectionism and debated on the justice of the economic system, which is geared so highly to maintaining the external balance, while sacrificing internal harmony. In the future, students will use more of this trade issue in their political propaganda, in order to generate anti-American sentiment in Korea. Also trade protectionism from the U.S. and foreign debt will continue to trouble policy-makers. Still, the Korean government's major emphasis is on increases in production and export, which have placed almost all industries under the government's protection and support. Whether its role has been to encourage foreign borrowing by private firms, to borrow abroad itself for relending at home, or to have public corporations borrow for capital investment, the Korean state is in deep foreign debt.

The protectionist pressure from abroad and the need for increased trade for Korea will remain as a basic conflict that will continue to hamper efforts to stabilize the Korean economy. For the stability of the economy, the debt problem needs to be solved in a rational manner. Government and corporations should reduce the demand for foreign capital somewhat. For that purpose, they should strengthen the foundation for economic stability as well as further economic efficiency.

To lower the demand for foreign capital, it is necessary for Korea to sustain economic growth at an appropriate rate. To this end, Korea must continue to increase domestic savings, promote exports, and limit import demand to an appropriate level. The top policy priority should be given to technical innovations and technological development. Efforts should be made to see to it that imports and other transactions requiring payments in foreign exchange are made efficiently, taking full account of both the debt ratio and economic growth. Such efforts to save foreign exchange, however, should not be strenuous enough to adversely affect the national economy; still, non-essential imports and other foreign exchange spending should be curtailed. In addition, the efficient allocation of Korea's limited resources should be pursued, and the government should opt for non-inflationary monetary and fiscal policies with a view toward spurring domestic savings.

Unfortunately, Korea's national savings rate is considerably lower than the Republic of China's 34.3 percent, registered in 1984; Singapore's 40.2 percent in 1983; and Japan's 31.6 percent in 1984. Korea's savings rates were 20.9 percent in 1982, 25.3 percent in 1983, 27.9 percent in 1984, and 28.4 percent in 1985.[39] In particular, the nation's household savings rate stood at a significantly lower level than that of the high-saving countries, casting a gloomy picture for the nation's international competitiveness. Korea's household savings rate represented a mere 9.9 percent in 1984, as compared with 13.8 percent for Taiwan and 13 percent for Japan (both recorded in 1982). In terms of amount, Korea's average savings per household in 1985 came to 4.1 million won, compared with Japan's some 34 million won. On the other hand, the amount a Korean household borrowed during 1985 averaged 2.1 million won, accounting for 53.1 percent of its total savings, compared with Japan's 12 million won, which secured 36.2 percent of its total savings.

Likewise, the rate of savings by domestic private enterprise remained at a low level. The rate stood at just 11 percent in 1984 compared with 11.5 percent for ROC and 14.6 percent for Japan (both registered in 1982).[40]

Thus, measures to restrict foreign debt and to increase savings rates should be emphasized more in the Korean government's present economic plan. Because of its high debt and low savings rate, Korea is unlikely to become another Japan. In addition, South Korea's military needs to drain a far larger proportion of its economy than Japan's military spending. As stated, exports account for more than one-third of Korea's GNP while Japan, with its huge domestic consumption, depends on exports for only 17 percent of its GNP. Japan has a large balance of payment surplus, while Korea is still running current account deficits based on the burden of paying foreign debts. As has been pointed out, Korea still faces the fundamental economic problems of heavy foreign debt and the low savings rate. Thus, measures to restrict foreign debt should be considered seriously for the sixth plan, including greater increases in the level of domestic savings and improvements in the balance-of-payments position.

Conclusion

The concentration of economic power and economic inequality have been the critical economic and political issues for some time in Korea. Even great democratic philosophers like John Locke and J.J. Rousseau warned against economic inequality a long time before Karl Marx. Rousseau in particular espoused the ideal of economic equality, though the concept of equality should not be taken in a literal sense. "No citizen shall ever be wealthy enough to buy another, and none poor enough to be forced to sell himself," [41] Rousseau wrote in his *Social Contract*. Rousseau also saw more clearly than the conventional liberal doctrinaires that the end of government is not confined to the protection of individual liberty but also includes equality because "liberty cannot exist without it." Rousseau realized that in practice it is difficult to maintain the ideal of equitable distribution of property, but it is "precisely because the force of circumstances tends continually to destroy equality that the force of legislation should always tend to its maintenance." [42]

Whereas Locke failed to see economic power as a relation of domination over man, Rousseau clearly recognized property as a form of private domination that had to be kept under control by the General Will[43]—the public interest of the community. Rousseau's theory of equitable distribution of property was, however, hardly socialist in the modern sense of the term, because he was not thinking of industrial society. Yet, his concept of economic equality has aided the utopian socialism and the development of socialist sentiment by sharpening the awareness that political liberty and economic inequality are ultimately incompatible if democracy is to survive and expand. And in the long run, Rousseau foresees that from extreme inequality springs division and dissension that undermines the fabric of society and government. Despotism arises out of these disorders, but despotism is the "last term of inequality." [44] The phenomenon called the concentration of economic power must be correctly understood in order to establish a true market system and to encourage economic and political democracy, which are foundations of capitalism.

In the economic field, the openness of the Korean economy to the movements and trends of international markets mitigates the accuracy of a longterm view. The relatively high degree of dependence on foreign trade, as a characteristic of the economy, was a favorable attribute in the years of free trade in the 1960s and the early 1970s. However, the existing levels of protectionism in the advanced economies and the threat of new rising barriers cannot be said to benefit the Korean economy. Although most economic indicators point to an upswing in 1987's economic activities, the economic situation could be easily aggravated by political and social conditions. The variable political and social factors mean a measure of uncertainty created by disturbances, which in turn are created by student demonstrations, labor unrest, and a segment of the citizenry who are under the impression that freedom, itself, along with the elimination of the United State's economic influence in Korea would bring economic growth to the land. There are more demands for political freedom from many college students, even at the expense of economic progress. So far the government has managed to beat the odds, but it now faces growing political dissent and labor unrest. The successful and peaceful direct presidential election in December 1987 is essential for future economic and political development in South Korea.

The population of Korea is egalitarian minded, perhaps reflecting, among other things, their pride in the unique homogeneity of the Korean people - *danilminjok*. South Koreans therefore expect to be treated like members of a large Confucian family. Due to these special circumstances, Korea needs an uncommonly low income inequality. This has been demonstrated by the rise of homegrown communistic sentiment in the ranks of radical groups, as manifested in campus and street violence in 1986-87.

Although tensions about income distribution persist, more and more South Koreans think they belong to the middle class—53 percent at last count in an Economic Planning Board survey. These people have aspirations to match—hopes of spending more time together as a family, even to participate more in their government. Generally, these people do not want to risk their middle class life, unlike some radical students and some radical labor groups. Thus if the South Korean government and society respond positively to the aspirations of the middle class, the moderate working class and students, then South Korean politics and economics would be peaceful and stabilized. Again, the most immediate and imperative task for South Korea is to have a peaceful transition to democratic government through free elections.

As pressure for greater political freedom increases, so do calls for changes in the economic policy, which is under attack for over-dependence on foreign trade, failure to mandate fairer distribution of wealth, and neglect of Korea's domestic market. Ironically, Korean economic policies have been very successful with economists, but not with the people. Thus, the government should devote increasing attention to the demands of ordinary Korean people in their policy, instead of being obsessed with economic growth. What they should concern themselves with is political instability, which could disrupt the sound growth of the economy. Economic progress without political development is, as in the expression of the old Korean proverb, like building a sandcastle on the beach.

NOTES

1. *The Korea Herald*, May 2, 1987 p. 1.
2. *The Statistical Year Book-1986*, The Economic Planning Board, Seoul, Korea. For a detailed discussion of economic inequality, foreign debt, and other economic problems in Korea, see Hang Yul Rhee, "Urbanization, Communication, Economic Inequality, and Political Behavior: A Study of Seoul Citizens, 1952-1971," *Korean Political Science Review*, Spring, 1980, Seoul, Korea. Hang Yul Rhee, "Third World Debt and Third World Industrialization: The Case Study of Korea, Mexico, and Brazil," *Korea and World Affairs*, Vol. 7, No. 3, Fall, 1983. Hang Yul Rhee, "The New Protectionism and the Korean Trade in the World Political Economy," *Korea and World Affairs*, Vol. 9, No. 3, Fall, 1985.
3. *The Washington Post*, July 26, 1986, p. D1.
4. Montek S. Ahluwalia, "Income Inequality: Some Dimensions of the Problem," *Finance and Development*, Vol. II, No. 3, September, 1974.
5. John H. Adler, "Development and Income Distribution," *Weltwirtschaftlisches Archiv*, Band 108 (1972), Heft 3.
6. Simon S. Kuznets, "Economic Growth and Income Inequality," *American Economic Review*, 5:1, March, 1955.

7. L.B. Pearson, *Partners in Development*, (Praeger: New York, 1969).
8. Kuznets, *op. cit.*
9. Sang-Mok Suh, *Economic Growth and Change in Income Distribution: The Korean Case*, (KDI: Seoul, 1985), pp. 10-11.
10. Source, KDI estimates, 1985.
11. Source, KDI estimates, 1985.
12. Suh, *op. cit.*, pp. 14-15.
13. See Kyu-Uck Lee article "The Concentration of Economic Power in Korea: Causes, Consequences, and Policy" *Industrial Development Policies and Issues*, (KDI: Seoul, 1985).
14. Karl W. Deutsch, "Social Mobilization and Political Development," *American Political Science Review*, (Sept., 1961), p. 494.
15. David Riseman coined this term in *The Lonely Crowd*. (Glencoe, Ill.: *The Free Press*, 1958), p. 412.
16. Ahluwalia, *op. cit.*, Adler, *op. cit.*, Huntington also agrees on this point. Samuel P. Huntington, *Political Order in Changing Societies*, (New Haven, Conn.: Yale Univ. Press, 1966), pp. 58-59.
17. See Bank of Korea, Consumer Price Index, *Economic Statistical Yearbook, 1972.*
18. Paul Streeten, "Some Problems in the Use and Transfer of an Intellectual Technology," Paper presented at a conference in Bellario, Italy, on the financing of social science research development, February 12-16, 1974.
19. *The Korea Herald*, May 1, Friday, 1987, p. 8.
20. *Far Eastern Economic Review*, December 12, 1985, p. 71-75.
21. Lee, *op. cit.*, p. 239.
22. *Ibid*, p. 242.
23. *Far Eastern Economic Review*, December 12, 1985, pp. 71-75.
24. *New York Times*, October 6, 1986, business section, p. 2.
25. *The Washington Post*, Sunday, Aug. 16, 1987, p. A19.
26. *The Hanguk Ilbo*, Aug. 22, 1987, p. 6.
27. For excellent discussions on the problems of chaebols in Korea: Sakong, I., "Economic Development and the Concentration of Economic Power," *Korea Development Review*, Spring, 1980.
    Lee, K.U. and S.S. Lee, *Mergers and the Concentration of Economic Power*, Korea Development Institute, 1985.
28. *The Hanguk Ilbo*, June 20, 1986, p. 2.
29. Larry Westphal, "Korean Opportunities: Prospects for Direct Investment," *Business Asia*, February 9, 1979, pp. 47-48.
30. Anne O. Krueger, *Studies in the Modernization of the Republic of Korea: 1945-1975. The Development Role of the Foreign Sector and Aid*, (Cambridge, Mass.: Harvard Univ. Press, 1979), p. 145.
31. Duck-Woo Nam, "Mobilization of Domestic Resources," in *International Conference on Korean Future*, (Seoul: Asiatic Research

Center, Korea University, 1975), p. 263.

32. Krueger, *op. cit.*, p. 144.
33. *New York Times*, Sunday, April 5, 1987, p. 13.
34. *Chosun Ilbo*, July 21, 1986, p. 2.
35. *The Korea Herald*, June 22, 1986, p. 4.
36. *Ibid.*
37. *Wall Street Journal*, April 7, 1987, p. 30.
38. *The Korean Economy, Review and Prospects*, 7th edition, 1985, Korea Exchange Bank, September, 1985, Seoul, Korea, p. 23.
39. *The Korea Herald*, July 1, 1986, p. 4.
40. *Ibid.*
41. Jean Jacques Rousseau, *Social Contract*.
42. *Ibid.*
43. For the discussion of General Will, see Rousseau, "Discourse on Political Economy" in *Diderot's Encyclopedie*.
44. Rousseau, *Discourse*.

10

The 1987 Political Crisis and its Implication for U.S.-Korean Relations

HONG NACK KIM

No other country has played as important a role as the United States in shaping the political, economic and socio-cultural development of the Republic of Korea (ROK) since the establishment of the republic in 1948. Not only did the United States play the role of "midwife" at the birth of the republic, direct American involvement in the Korean War (1950-1953) was a decisive factor in defending South Korea from the North Korean invasion. In 1953, South Korea and the United States became allies by signing a mutual defense pact, and since then the United States has been the ultimate guarantor of South Korean security. Presently, some 40,000 U.S. troops are stationed in South Korea with a primary mission of deterring the military threat from North Korea.

The United States has also played a major role in fostering the economic reconstruction and development of South Korea in the post-Korean War period. Along with Vietnam and Israel, South Korea has been one of the largest recipients of U.S. economic and military assistance in the postwar world. From 1945 to 1976, the U.S. provided over $12.5 billion in economic and military aid to South Korea (i.e., $5.7 billion in economic aid and $6.8 billion in military aid).[1]

It is also a well-known fact that the United States has influenced political developments in South Korea. The United States has been entangled in South Korea's domestic politics initially as a protector and provider of massive aid, and more recently as an ally concerned with the development of a representative government and political stability in Korea. For example, the Eisenhower Administration supported the forces which overthrew the Syngman Rhee regime in 1960. The Kennedy Administration pressured the military junta headed by General Park Chung-hee to hold elections for the establishment of a legitimate political system in 1963. More recently, the Carter Administration not only was sharply critical of the Park regime's repressive policies, but attempted to pressure Seoul to adopt more enlightened policies.

The most recent political crisis in South Korea in 1987 posed a serious challenge to the Reagan Administration which had followed a policy of staunch support for President Chun Doo-hwan from 1981. As the crisis threatened political stability in South Korea, starting in the spring of 1987 the Reagan Administration adopted a more interventionist policy by advocating the creation of a more legitimate and democratic political system through free elections. Undoubtedly, such a policy change had a beneficial effect on the peaceful settlement of the political crisis and helped the process of the democratization of the South Korean political system which had been advocated by Chun's opponents. Their struggle for political democratization brought about sweeping reforms in South Korea by the summer of 1987 and a popularly elected new president of the republic by December 1987. What effects will the political change have on South Korea's conduct of foreign relations? What are implications of the political change for U.S.-South Korean relations? These are important questions for anyone interested in the future of the U.S.-Korean alliance.

It is the purpose of this paper to examine the nature of the recent political changes in South Korea and their implications for U.S.-Korean relations in general and security relations in particular. A major contention of this paper is that the democratization of the South Korean political system will improve U.S.-Korean relations, for it will strengthen the political and moral fiber of the alliance. For the first time since 1960, the United States and South Korea can say unequivocally that the U.S.-South Korean alliance is based on common values of liberal democracy in defense of South Korea against communist aggression.

An important political consequence of South Korea's rapid modernization since 1960 has been the rise of nationalism. As a result of South Korea's phenomenal economic success (e.g., the increase in per capita income from $86 in 1960 to over $2,800 in 1987),[27] the strides in education, and international recognition of South Korea's right to host the 1988 Summer Olympics in Seoul, nationalism and national pride are becoming stronger among South Koreans in the 1980s. To be sure, nationalism was a potent force even under the Japanese colonial rule (1910-1945). However, it was somewhat muted due to the division of Korea and the Korean War. As a consequence of rapid modernization, nationalism is reasserting itself. Not only radical students but also Koreans as a whole are increasingly more nationalistic; and they have become even more sensitive to unfriendly gestures or behavior by foreign powers, be it the distortion of history by Japanese textbook authors or economic pressures emanating from the United States.

Another important political consequence of rapid modernization in South Korea is the growing desire and demand for political liberalization and democracy among South Koreans. South Korea's economic development has raised popular expectations and demand for greater liberalization. The growing number of well-educated Koreans began to argue that the level of economic achievements required a more liberal, pluralistic and democratic political system commensurate to Korea's economic achievements.[3] They believe the political system has failed to keep abreast of economic developments;[4] and they refuse to accept the notion that political liberalization should await further economic development. The demand for political liberalization has been particularly strong among a new generation of Koreans who do not have first-hand experience of either the Korean War or Korea's poverty in the 1950s and 1960s.

To the degree government leaders have not accommodated popular demands for democratization and liberalization of the political system, South Korea's economic success and cultural development have bred political tensions and unrest which became quite serious by 1987. It is against the backdrop of rapid modernization fermenting acute political tensions and unrest in the South Korean political system that we should analyze recent U.S.-Korean relations in general and the rise of anti-Americanism in South Korea in particular.

Following the assassination of President Park Chung-hee in October 1979, there were great expectations among South Koreans that the much-awaited democratization of the political system would take place. However, their hopes were dashed after a brief interlude of political liberalization in the spring of 1980, when General Chun Doo-hwan seized power by staging a coup d'état.

Although Chun was able to govern effectively until the spring of 1985, he was not popular among the urban middle and working classes, religious groups, and the rapidly growing university population, which questioned the legitimacy of the new regime from the very beginning. Reflecting growing discontent among the students, anti-government demonstrations on the campuses began to intensify after 1983.

Unlike his immediate predecessor, Jimmy Carter, who was highly critical of the Park government's repressive domestic policies, Ronald Reagan was supportive of the Chun government from the very beginning, despite the regime's weak legitimacy and growing unpopularity. President Chun was invited to visit Washington in February 1981 as one of the first foreign dignitaries after the inauguration of the Reagan Administration. Reagan assured Chun that the U.S. had no plans to withdraw its combat troops from Korea, and that the security of South Korea was vital to the U.S.[5] In April 1981, at the annual Korea-U.S. security consultative meeting in San Francisco, Secretary of Defense Casper Weinberger reaffirmed the U.S. pledge to defend Korea. In addition, the U.S. also promised to support the South Korean Force Improvement Plan, which included the procurement of 36 F-16 jet fighters, a "stinger" air defense system, 1,000 M55-1 light tanks, and other military hardware at an estimated cost of $729 million over five years.[6] Thus, Chun received not only U.S. approval of his takeover of governmental power in South Korea but also U.S. reassurances for the security of South Korea.

Disenchanted with the Reagan Administration's staunch support for what they considered an anti-democratic and illegitimate military regime, students began to question the role of the American presence and influence in Korea. As an expression of their anti-American sentiment, students set fire to the American Cultural Center in Pusan in 1982. Both government spokesmen and American diplomats in Seoul quickly dismissed the incident as an aberration by a group of extremists.[7] However, this was not the first such incident. A fire had been set earlier in the office of the American Cultural Center in Kwangju in December 1980. In addition, there were anti-American student demonstrations when Vice President George Bush visited Seoul in 1982, and some students were arrested for burning an American flag.[8]

Radical students were not the only ones who were unhappy about the United States policy toward South Korea. In the spring of 1982, forty-two leaders of the Korean Christian Action Organization issued a statement requesting the Reagan Administration to recall both the commander-in-chief of the U.S. forces in Korea, General John A. Wickham, and the U.S. Ambassador, Richard L. Walker.[9] General Wickham was reported to have made a disparaging remark to the effect that the Korean people are like lemmings that follow anyone who becomes their leader and are not ready for democracy. Wickham made the remark in the summer of 1980 when such comments aided General Chun's takeover of governmental power.[10] No less serious was the case involving Ambassador Walker's undiplomatic statement. A staunch supporter of Chun, Walker had nothing but praise for the Chun government, while chastising dissidents, student demonstrators, and critics of the regime. After calling attention to the fact that most of the criticism of President Chun came from students, intellectuals, and westernized Koreans living in the U.S., he said in an interview with a reporter in South Carolina that the suspension of individual freedom was readily accepted by the Korean workers who had no sympathy for those "spoiled brats."[11] Walker's remarks angered many Koreans who demanded a public apology from him. Although the ambassador tried to skirt the criticism by insisting that he had been misquoted, he eventually had to acknowledge that: "I frankly admit that the term 'spoiled brats' was a major mistake."[12]

In the summer of 1983, while Ambassador Walker told a visiting Korean-American political scientist that the Seoul-Washington relationship was better than ever before and that America's "quiet diplomacy" was helping to improve the conditions of human rights in South Korea,[13] anti-Americanism was spreading rather than receding. In September 1983, a bomb exploded in front of the American cultural Center in Taegu. It resembled similar attacks at Kwangju (December 1980) and at Pusan (March 1982).

Against this background, President Reagan undertook a three-day visit to Seoul in November 1983. Just as he had done during his first summit meeting with President Chun in Washington in February 1981, Reagan expressed his unequivocal support for the Korean host and assured him that the Korean Air Lines tragedy (September 1983) and the Rangoon bombing incident (October 1983) did not diminish U.S. security commitments to South Korea. In the joint communique issued on November 14, 1983, Reagan and Chun agreed to affirm the "importance of defending and strengthening freedom and the institutions that serve freedom, openness and political stability."[14] The Reagan visit not only bolstered President Chun's political standing, but also reassured South Koreans who were uneasy about the U.S. guarantee of South Korea's defense.

By the spring of 1984, there were signs of growing anti-Americanism among a new generation of South Koreans, particularly young students. They were critical of the United States for not helping the cause of democracy in South Korea, because Washington had failed to prevent the coup of December 12, 1979, which eventually paved the way for General Chun Doo-hwan's ascendancy to power in 1980; it failed to prevent the use of South Korean troops under its command for the suppression of the Kwangju uprising in May 1980, resulting in the deaths of nearly 200 and numerous injuries and arrests.[15] Furthermore, they have criticized the U.S. not only for supporting the Chun Government but for going out of its way to legitimize the government through summit meetings. They tended to view the United States as propping up the authoritarian regime in South Korea, instead of supporting the cause of democracy.[16]

In a protest against the U.S. support of the Chun Government, in May 1985, 73 students occupied the USIS library in downtown Seoul for three days, protesting the alleged U.S. role in the Kwangju massacre and demanding apologies from the U.S. and withdrawal of U.S. support for the Chun Government, which they contended was the chief plotter of the Kwangju massacre. They were persuaded by the U.S. Embassy officials to leave peacefully.[17] In May 1986, radical students staged a violent anti-government and anti-American rally in Inchon. A similar demonstration was held on the Konkuk University campus near Seoul in October 1986, which was put down by over 8,000 combat police. Under the leadership of radical students, it became fashionable for the anti-government demonstrators to shout anti-American slogans on and off the campus.

To be sure, the growing trade friction between the United States and South Korea in the 1980s, particularly U.S. pressure on Seoul to lower trade barriers and to appreciate the value of Korean currency vis-a-vis U.S. dollars, tended to fuel nascent anti-Americanism not only among radical students but also nationalistic Koreans, including some government officials.[18]

Meanwhile, political confrontation between the Chun Government and its opposition was intensifying in South Korea following the parliamentary elections of February 12, 1985. [19] Both during and after the election, the New Korea Democratic Party (NKDP), the major opposition party, pressed for political liberalization, demanding among other things constitutional amendments to bring about direct popular election of the next President, instead of indirectly by the electoral college system. However, the Chun government refused to entertain the opposition's demand for constitutional revision, insisting that the constitutional revision question should be shelved until 1989 and that a successor be chosen under the existing electoral system.

As the opposition stepped up its petition campaign for constitutional revision by the end of May 1986, the ruling Democratic Justice Party (DJP) accepted the opposition's demand for the creation of the basic law revision committee in the National Assembly. However, there was no meaningful progress toward the constitutional revision until the summer of 1987, since neither side was willing to give in on the substantive issues of constitutional change. The government party wanted a parliamentary cabinet system of government, while the opposition advocated a presidential system of government based on the direct popular election of the chief executive.

Against the backdrop of escalating political crisis in South Korea, the Reagan Administration followed a policy of staunch support for the Chun government until 1987 by making good relations with the Chun government a primary objective, while failing to cultivate a good working relationship with the opposition. Such a policy inevitably irritated politically articulate groups, such as students, intellectuals, church leaders, and opposition parties. Even though the U.S. State Department did criticize certain individual acts of repression by the Chun Government,[20] the U.S. Embassy in Seoul had few contacts with opposition leaders until 1987.

Starting in early spring of 1987, the Reagan Administration began to show greater sensitivity and concern for the rapidly deteriorating political situation in South Korea. The deepening political crisis in Korea put the Reagan Administration in a dilemma of reconciling its desire for a more representative South Korean government and its concern for maintaining security and stability on the peninsula. Clearly, the United States became quite uneasy about the prospects of an intensifying political crisis, repression, violence and growing anti-American sentiments among Koreans.

The first clear indication was given by Assistant Secretary of State for East Asian and Pacific Affairs, Gaston Sigur, in a major policy speech delivered before the U.S.-Korea Society in New York on February 6, 1987. In the speech, Sigur declared that it "is essential for the future of the Republic of Korea and for the future of our bilateral relations, that any new constitution, and the laws which support representative government, create a more open and legitimate political system."[21] In addition, he emphasized the importance of "civilianizing" the government in South Korea, urging the military to concentrate on its "primary mission" of national defense.[22] He also stressed the importance of free elections for the establishment of a democratic government in Korea. The Sigur statement indicated, in a sense, the Reagan Administration's intention to adopt a new approach toward the political crisis in Korea. In a related move, the new U.S. Ambassador, James Liley, began to contact opposition leaders starting from February 1987.

When a serious political crisis was triggered by President Chun's announcement of his decision, on April 13, 1987, to suspend further discussion on constitutional revision until after the 1988 Seoul Olympics and to choose his successor through the existing electoral college system, Washington tried to restrain Chun from the use of force and to persuade him that the continuation of government dialogue with the opposition on constitutional revision was desirable.[23]

The political crisis was aggravated further when the ruling DJP went ahead with the nomination of Roh Tae-woo as its official candidate for President on June 10, 1987, despite the vehement protests of opposition parties demanding the rescinding of Chun's April 13 decision. As tensions mounted and protesters poured into the streets to demonstrate their opposition to the Chun Government's plan to elect the next President through the existing electoral college system, the U.S. government stepped up its pressure on President Chun. A U.S. State Department spokesman cautioned against using military force to quell what the U.S. considered essentially a political problem.[24] On June 18, President Reagan sent a letter to President Chun, urging him not to use excessive force against his opponents, to resume negotiations with the opposition parties, and to take steps toward establishing full democracy.[25] Reagan also dispatched Assistant Secretary Sigur to Seoul on June 22 to assess the situation and to find a solution to the deepening crisis.

Meanwhile, the U.S. House of Representatives adopted a resolution (H. Con. Res. 141), expressing regret over Chun's decision to suspend talks with the opposition and calling for resumption of serious negotiations to facilitate democratization of the Korean political system. It was endorsed by the Reagan Administration.[26] A similar bill (S. Res. 241) was approved unanimously by the U.S. Senate on June 27, 1987.[27] In a related move, several senators introduced a bill (S. 1392) that would impose economic sanctions on South Korea until there was progress toward democracy. The proposed sanctions included the termination of general system of preference (GSP) trade privileges for South Korean products and the suspension of U.S. government insurance for American firms investing in Korea.

The peaceful settlement of the political crisis through the June 29 announcement made by Roh Tae-woo was, therefore, a welcome development for the United States.[28] By accommodating almost all the major demands of the opposition parties for sweeping reforms, it not only defused the political crisis, but also enabled South Korea to embark on the path of democratization. Such a development was gratifying to the U.S. policymakers who had urged the Chun government and its opposition to avoid bloodshed and to work out a peaceful solution to the conflict.

In a speech delivered in New York on July 21, 1987, Assistant Secretary of State Sigur praised the important steps taken by the South Koreans: "We applaud those accomplishments and encourage both government and opposition parties to promptly complete the process which has been started."[29] At the same time, he declared his government's intentions to maintain neutrality in the Korean presidential election, promising U.S. willingness to work with whichever candidate South Koreans would choose to be their next president. Sigur's assurances notwithstanding, the warm receptions that Roh Tae-woo received during his pre-election visit to the United States in September 1987 indicated that Washington was favorably inclined toward the DJP standard bearer.

Through a series of negotiations, the government party and the opposition Reunification and Democracy Party (RDP) were able to work out constitutional amendments by October 1987. On the basis of the revised constitution, the presidential election by direct popular vote was held on December 16, 1987. In addition to Roh Tae-woo, Kim Young-sam (the RDP president), Kim Jong-pil (the New Democratic Republican Party leader), and Kim Dae-jung (the Peace and Democracy Party leader) ran for the presidency. When the votes were tallied, Roh Tae-woo was elected by receiving over 8 million votes (or 36.6 percent of the vote cast) out of over 23 million votes cast in the election. Kim Young-sam was second with 6.1 million votes (or 28 percent) and Kim Dae-jung finished third with over 5.8 million votes (or 26.9 percent). The election results stunned many South Koreans who had expected much closer margins between the winner and losers.

On December 17, the U.S. government congratulated Roh Tae-woo for his victory in the presidential election. At the same time, it urged reconciliation between the government and the opposition parties. Although the U.S. State Department spokesman, Charles Redman, acknowledged that the U.S. government was aware of charges by defeated opposition leaders that the vote was fraudulent, he hastened to add that the U.S. would not issue an independent judgment on the charges.[31] The Reagan Administration was aware of sporadic demonstrations staged by the opposition elements in protest against the alleged election fraud but doubted such demonstrations would threaten South Korea's stability unless the opposition could prove its charge of massive, flagrant election fraud. Many in the U.S. maintained that opposition candidates, Kim Young-sam and Kim Dae-jung, had only themselves to blame for the loss to the government party's candidate by splitting the opposition vote.

Although the two Kims refused to accept Roh's victory at the beginning, by the end of December 1987 they announced their willingness to participate in the forthcoming parliamentary elections in the spring of 1988, while not abandoning their intentions to take legal actions against election irregularities. Furthermore, by mid-January 1988, Kim Young-sam held talks with President-elect Roh to discuss outstanding political issues, while Kim Dae-jung accepted President Chun's invitation to discuss issues of mutual concern.

Insofar as the future of South Korea's relations with the United States under the incoming Roh government is concerned, one can be reasonably sure that the bilateral political relationship will be quite cordial and harmonious. Being elected through direct popular vote, the new South Korean President will be spared the controversy over his regime's legitimacy that plagued the Chun government. Moreover, in view of various democratic reforms already introduced, not to mention those planned in the future, the Roh government will project a much better image both within and outside of South Korea.

To be sure, there are certain bilateral issues which may not necessarily become easier to tackle because of South Korea's ongoing democratization. Rather, they may become even more difficult to manage. A case in point is U.S.-Korean economic relations.[32] In view of rising economic nationalism both in South Korea and in the United States, bilateral trade relations are likely to become more difficult to manage in the future. Unlike the Chun government, which could make its domestic and foreign policies without worrying about pressures from powerful interest groups, the Roh government will have to accommodate demands of various interest groups which can exert pressures more freely and effectively on the policy-making process due to political liberalization in South Korea.

The emergence of U.S.-South Korean trade friction should be attributed partly to the phenomenal economic development of South Korea and partly to the ever deteriorating trade deficit of the United States with its major trade partners in recent years. As a result of its rapid economic growth, South Korea is now the seventh largest trading partner of the United States, with the two-way trade totalling over $19.9 billion in 1986. While U.S. exports to South Korea have slowed considerably in the 1980s as compared to the 1970s, South Korea has succeeded in increasing its exports to the U.S. in the 1980s. As a result, the U.S. has incurred an increasingly higher trade deficit in its trade with South Korea: $4.3 billion in 1985, $7.3 billion in 1986, and approximately $9.5 billion in 1987.[33]

To cope with the trade deficit, the Reagan Administration has exerted heavy pressure on the Chun Government to open the Korean market further to U.S. products, to allow market access to U.S. service industries, and to lower tariffs and other trade barriers. In response to the U.S. pressure, in October 1985, the South Korean government adopted an import-liberalization package designed to lift restrictions on some 600 new items over a three-year period. As a result, by July 1986, 91 percent of commodities traded were imported without restrictions and the number of such commodities was to surpass 95 percent within a few years.[34] South Korea also made a number of other concessions to the United States in the areas of market access, intellectual property rights, and operations of U.S. banks and insurance firms in Korea. In the spring of 1987, Seoul announced new measures to increase the importation of U.S. products by $2.6 billion.[35]

While praising these actions taken by the Chun government, the Reagan Administration continued to pressure Seoul for more concessions. Among other things, the U.S. wants South Korea to import beef from the United States, to lower the price of American cigarettes sold in Korea, and to allow greater market access for U.S. insurance, banking, and advertising firms in Korea. It was reported that Washington informed Seoul of its intention to take retaliatory actions against South Korea by invoking section 301 of the Trade Act early in 1988 if Seoul did not comply with U.S. demands for widening its market for U.S. cigarettes, insurance, and beef.[36] The United States is also threatening to remove South Korean products from its general system of preference (GSP) privileges if Seoul fails to meet the U.S. demands.

These bilateral economic and trade issues are likely to create serious problems for the new President when he assumes office in February 1988. Already the President-elect has urged Deputy Premier Chung In-yong, who was scheduled to visit Washington for trade negotiations in early January 1988, not to yield to Washington's demand on the importation of American beef.[37] Apparently, Roh wanted to postpone such a decision until after the general elections scheduled in the spring of 1988. The question of beef imports is a sensitive political issue in Korea. The "mere mention of resuming beef imports causes an outcry from politicians and the general public, particularly farmers."[38] The Korean position is that allowing beef imports at this time may cause panic among the farmers.

Although the United States agreed to wait for Seoul's reply on the question of U.S. beef—after the forthcoming parliamentary elections in South Korea in April 1988—it was reported that the U.S. demanded that South Korea import more U.S. beef for more use not only in tourist hotels but in quality restaurants. When the news reached Seoul, some 5,000 farmers and cattle producers staged a violent demonstration in protest against beef imports in front of the Korean government building complex in Kwachon.[39]

What is fairly obvious is that U.S.-South Korean trade issues are not likely to be wished away even after the inauguration of the Roh government. Rather, they will continue to plague the bilateral relationship, because the U.S. trade deficit with South Korea will increase before it stabilizes or decreases.[40] While appreciating the American sentiments on bilateral trade issues, South Koreans argue that the United States should not expect too many concessions from South Korea, because it is a small developing country with heavy foreign debts ($39 billion) and a per capita income of only $2,800. They also argue that a too-rapid opening of the Korean market would adversely affect consumer-goods and financial sectors. They also believe that a hasty revaluation of the Korean currency against the U.S. dollar would only hurt the South Korean economy without substantially redressing the American trade deficit problem. The U.S. trade deficit with South Korea accounted for approximately 5 percent of the total U.S. trade deficit in 1986.[41] However, the Americans are dissatisfied with what has actually been done so far, arguing that unless "the gap is bridged soon, it will grow wider."[42] It is generally agreed, nevertheless, that hurting the Korean economy is not going to serve the interests of either the United States or South Korea.[43]

Another aspect of the bilateral relationship which will require the close attention of both Seoul and Washington after the inauguration of the Roh government is the security relationship. Washington will have to adjust its military ties with Seoul not only to accommodate the changing requirements of both powers but also the new nationalism in Korea. The problem of realizing greater equity in command relationships within the Combined Forces Command (CFC) is likely to become an issue in Seoul-Washington relations.

At present, a senior U.S. general is commander-in-chief (CIC) of the Combined Forces Command, which includes in wartime all U.S. and Korean forces. In addition to command of the combined forces, the U.S. general has command of the United Nations Command to fulfill U.S. responsibilities in enforcing the armistice agreement in Korea.

The present command structure is being questioned for several reasons. First, the growing capability of the ROK forces, including their increased professionalism, has led to dissatisfaction with the Korean role in the CFC command structure. Second, there is a growing feeling among Koreans that giving the U.S. commander of the CFC complete control over all U.S. and Korean forces, largely a legacy of the Korean War, is not only anachronistic but an affront to South Korean nationalism. Third, there is also a widely held perception that the existing command structure creates unnecessary confusion and misunderstanding about the nature of the U.S. commander's control over South Korean forces in peacetime.[44]

Under the 1978 agreement between the U.S. and Korea, the U.S. commander has operational control of all forces assigned to him by the U.S. and ROK. However, neither the U.S. nor South Korea assigns all its forces in Korea to the CFC in peacetime. And even for those that are assigned, both nations reserve the right to withdraw units from the command when either partner's national interests demand such action. Thus, if the ROK wants to use units assigned to the CFC for domestic purposes, and make proper notification, the CIC CFC cannot prevent the ROK from using the forces for such actions.

A lack of understanding of existing command arrangements has caused many Koreans, especially students, to accuse the U.S. of complicity in suppressing violent protests in the past in South Korea, including the Kwangju incident of May 1980. In that incident, heavy civilian casualties were inflicted by the Korean forces initially dispatched by Seoul. They were not under the CFC command and the U.S. was not aware of their deployment.[45] Different ROK units withdrawn later from the CFC after serving notification to the CFC were dispatched to Kwangju to restore order with minimal bloodshed. Nonetheless, the charges of U.S. complicity have never been successfully cleared. This incident has been used by radical elements in South Korea in their opposition to the Chun government and to the pro-Chun policy of the U.S. It is believed to have widely influenced Korean students' negative attitudes toward the United States.

The question of recovering operational control of South Korean armed forces placed under the CFC was raised as a campaign issue in September 1987, when the opposition RDP pledged that, if its candidate were elected as the next President, he would begin negotiations aimed at eliminating U.S. control over Korean military forces in the CFC.[46] Roh Tae-woo, however, maintained that "a change cannot be made at this moment," and that it "is too serious for a campaign issue."[47] Nevertheless, during his visit to Washington in September 1987, Roh endorsed a future change in U.S.-South Korean military command arrangements that would give South Korea more control over its own armed forces by saying: "It is natural for any sovereign country to exercise operational control over its military forces."[48] However, he indicated his willingness to wait until the 1990s to recover the operational control from the United States, because South Korea's military capability is only 62 percent that of North Korea. Roh maintained that when that capability reaches about 80 percent or more of the North's it would be possible to discuss such a change. Thus, insofar as the Roh government is concerned, the issue is not a pressing one, at least for the time being.

Since the U.S. is responsible for the maintenance of the armistice agreement by filling the post of the U.S. commander in Korea, and since the security of South Korea still depends heavily on U.S. air and naval power, it may not be possible to change the existing command structure of the CFC in the near future. Nevertheless, in view of the fact that South Korea provides more than 90 percent of the combined ground forces, it seems logical that a Korean officer should command the combined ground forces. Such a change would improve Seoul's position in the CFC joint command structure in time of peace. As pointed out by a group of U.S. experts, such a move would have "the political benefit of giving due recognition to Korean national pride and encouragement to its professionalism."[49] It would also help reduce confusion and misunderstanding concerning the relationship between the CIC of the CFC and the South Korean forces under his operational control.[50]

Another potential issue likely to draw the attention of the United States in the future is the question of the optimum size and composition of the U.S. troops stationed in South Korea. South Korea's growing defense capability will eventually make it possible for the United States to modify the number and composition of its troops stationed in Korea.[51] Already, some U.S. experts have advanced their views on possible changes that can or should be made to the existing U.S. troop strengths in Korea. Insofar as South Korea is concerned, however, both the government and opposition parties do not want any reduction in the present level of U.S. troop deployment in Korea. Until such time as a real breakthrough occurs in Seoul-Pyongyang relations, no one in South Korea, except some radical elements, wants any drastic change in the existing U.S. troop strength in Korea. Any indication of the weakening U.S. security commitment to South Korea will have a destabilizing effect on South Korea, as happened during the Carter Administration's abortive troop withdrawal plan in South Korea in the 1970s. Furthermore, revival of such a plan could complicate the task of democratization under the Roh government.

From the foregoing analysis, several basic conclusions can be drawn with regard to the effects and implications for U.S.-South Korean relations of the political changes in South Korea:

First, it will strengthen the ideological and moral fiber of the U.S.-South Korean alliance. Although anti-communism has been a common denominator of the alliance, it is insufficient to serve as the moral and ideological foundation. Only through the establishment of a genuine democratic system can the ideological affinity between the two nations be strengthened. Such a development can also make South Korea politically more compatible with the United States. These developments in turn will strengthen the U.S. commitment to defend South Korea in the future, since there is a strong correlation between the American public's willingness to defend an ally and the ideological affinity and political compatibility of the ally to the United States (e.g. the NATO member nations, Japan, etc.).

Second, political democratization of South Korea will also drastically improve its image abroad, especially in the United States. It is a well-known fact that South Korea has experienced a serious "image problem" in the United States. Writing in 1981, William Watts pointed out that the U.S. public in general "looks upon Korea as a continuing problem, beset with internal political process, and generally bearing an unsavory image."[52] Among other things, South Korea has been criticized for the repression of human rights. The democratization of the South Korean political system will undoubtedly help improve its image in the United States, which should have salutary effects on the future U.S.-South Korean relations.

Third, the establishment of a democratic government in Seoul will also help alleviate anti-American sentiments in South Korea. The root cause of that anti-Americanism can be traced to the resentment of a new generation of Koreans, particularly college students, against Washington's unabashed support of the Chun government, instead of maintaining a more even-handed policy toward the government and its opposition. There has been a growing perception among radical elements in South Korea that the United States has been propping up Chun's authoritarian regime and thus hindering the cause of democracy in Korea. The establishment of a legitimate democratic government through free elections will alleviate much of the problem, because the U.S. support of such a new government should not pose any problem to democratically inclined South Koreans.

Fourth, in order to accommodate South Korea's new strength and national pride, Washington will have to adjust its military ties with Seoul. In this context, it is desirable to realize greater equity in command relationships and to lower the current high visibility of U.S. forces in Korea. While retaining control of the U.S.-Korean Combined Forces Command for the time being, the United States should accept a Korean as commander of the ground forces component to improve South Korea's position in the joint command structure.[53]

Fifth, a successful U.S.-South Korean relationship requires a reasonable degree of political compatibility between the two nations. The development of a mature, pluralistic, legitimate political system in South Korea is an important element in this equation. The U.S. should make it clear that it supports the democratization as well as civilianization of the South Korean political system, lest its intentions in this matter are misunderstood. It should also make it known that the United States will not support any takeover attempt by a self-designated group employing violent means.

Sixth, the United States should maintain its armed forces in South Korea during the period of the democratization in Seoul. Any indication of a U.S. troop withdrawal in the next several years will adversely affect the delicate process of democratization. It will not only weaken the position of the newly-established Roh government, but divert the primary attention of the new government to the troop withdrawal issue, instead of concentrating on the task of constructing a democratic political system. Such a development could be detrimental to the cause of democracy in South Korea.

Lastly, the United States and South Korea should exercise caution in dealing with bilateral economic and trade issues.[54] In view of the rising tide of South Korean nationalism, utmost caution should be exercised lest the United States unnecessarily irritate South Korean sensibilities or pride. In return, South Korea should reciprocate by adopting necessary measures to help alleviate trade friction with the United States. In view of growing protectionist sentiments among Americans, who are increasingly frustrated and angry with a rising trade deficit, it is important for South Korea to take necessary measures, such as lowering trade barriers and diversifying its export markets to reduce trade friction with the United States. It is important to bear in mind that prolonged trade friction will not only sap the vitality of the alliance system but also undermine the foundation of the alliance system itself.

NOTES

1. Edward S. Mason et al., *The Economic and Social Modernization of the Republic of Korea* (Cambridge, Mass.: Harvard University Press, 1980), p. 182.
2. South Korea's per capita GNP was $2,813 in 1987. See *Hankook Ilbo*, December 29, 1987.
3. Young Bok Ko et al., "Hankuk Chungkanchong kwa Chongchi Palchon," *Minchok Chisong*, October 1987, pp. 138-140. See also, Shim Jae Hoon, "Emerging Middle Class Wants Greater Say," *Far Eastern Economic Review* (cited hereafter *FEER*), May 1, 1986, p. 27; Shim Jae Hoon, "Growing Rich at the Cost of Democracy," *FEER*, June 6, 1985, pp. 26-27; Daryl Plunk, "Chun and Critics on a Collision Course,"

FEER, February 13, 1986, pp. 36-37; and Christopher Madison, "Korea: A New Interest," *National Journal*, April 5, 1986, p. 809.
4. Shim, "Emerging Middle Class Wants Greater Say," p. 27.
5. *Korea Newsreview*, February 7, 1981.
6. Dae-Sook Suh, "South Korea in 1981: The First Year of the Fifth Republic," *Asian Survey*, January 1982, p. 111.
7. Dae-Sook Suh, "South Korea in 1982: A Centennial Year," *Asian Survey*, January 1983, p. 95.
8. *New York Times*, April 25, 1982.
9. *Ibid.*
10. *Los Angeles Times*, August 8, 1980.
11. *The State*, February 14, 1982.
12. Suh, "South Korea in 1982: A Centennial Year," p. 97.
13. Chae-Jin Lee, "South Korea in 1983," *Asian Survey*, January 1984, p. 120.
14. *New York Times*, November 14, 1983.
15. Wonmo Dong, "University Students in South Korean Politics: Patterns of Radicalization in the 1980s," *Journal of International Affairs*, Winter/Spring 1987, vol. 40, no. 2, pp. 236-237.
16. *Ibid.*, p. 246.
17. Gaston J. Sigur, Jr., "Prospects for Continuing Democratization in South Korea," *Department of State Bulletin* (Washington, D.C.: U.S. Department of State), July 1986, p. 48. See also, Dong, *op. cit.*, pp. 238 & 244-246; and Shim Jae Hoon, "Guarded Friendship," *FEER*, December 26, 1985, pp. 12-15.
18. Larry A. Niksch, *South Korea and the United States: The Changing Relationship*, Congressional Research Report 87-522 F (Washington, D.C.: Congressional Research Service, June 11, 1987), pp. 37-38; Edward A. Olsen, "Korean Politics and U.S. Policy," Asian Survey, August 1987, pp. 850-851.
19. For a detailed analysis of the 1985 election, see B.C. Koh, "The 1985 Parliamentary Election in South Korea," *Asian Survey*, September 1985, pp. 883-897. See also, Eugene C.I. Kim, "Korea in 1985: An Eventful Year amidst Uncertainty," *Asian Survey*, January 1986, p. 69.
20. Niksch, *op. cit.*, pp. 22-23. The Reagan Administration played a decisive role in saving the life of Kim Dae-jung, an opposition leader, who was sentenced to death by the Chun government on charges of sedition in 1980. Largely due to the pressure exerted by the United States, his death sentence was commuted to a 20 year imprisonment in 1981 and subsequently he was allowed to go to the United States for medical treatment. Again, it was the United States which made it possible for Kim to return safely to Seoul in February 1985 from exile in the United States. In addition, it is also a well known fact that U..S. Ambassador Walker played an important role in persuading the

Chun government to scrap the plan to enact a tough "Campus Stabilization Bill."

21. For the text of the speech, see Gaston J. Sigur, Jr., "Korean Politics in Transition," *Department of State Bulletin*, April 1987, pp. 23-25.
22. *Ibid.*, p. 24.
23. Larry A. Niksch, *Korea's Political Crisis: Policy Alert*, Congressional Research Service Report 87-523 F (Washington, D.C.: Congressional Research Service, June 22, 1987), p. 7.
24. Nayan Chanda, "Cause for U.S. Concern," *FEER*, July 2, 1987, p. 10.
25. *Washington Post*, June 19, 1987. See also, Niksch, *Korea's Political Crisis: Policy Alert*, p. 8; and Robert G. Sutter, *Korean Political Tensions: Implications for the United States*, Issue Brief 186071 (Washington, D.C.: Congressional Research Service, October 14, 1987), p. 12.
26. *Ibid.*, p. 12. See also, Niksch, *South Korea and the United States: The Changing Relationship*, pp. 16-17.
27. Sutter, *op. cit.*, p. 12.
28. *New York Times*, June 29, 1987. See also, *Wall Street Journal*, June 30, 1987.
29. Gaston J. Sigur, Jr., "Korea: New Beginnings," *Department of State Bulletin*, September 1987, p. 32.
30. *Korea Herald*, December 18, 1987.
31. *Korea Herald*, December 19, 1987. See also, *Washington Post*, December 18 & 19, 1987.
32. For a detailed analysis of recent U.S.-South Korean trade relations, see William H. Cooper, *South Korea and Taiwan: Expanding Trade with the United States*, Issue Brief (Washington, D.C.: Congressional Research Service, 1986). See also, U.S. Congress, Joint Economic Committee, *The Korean Economy in Congressional Perspective*, 99th Congress, 2nd Session (Washington, D.C.: Government Printing Office, 1986); and Bruce Stokes, "Korea: Relations Worsen," *National Journal*, April 5, 1986, pp. 814-819; and Council on Foreign Relations and the Asia Society, *Korea at the Crossroads: Implications for American Policy* (New York: Council on Foreign Relations and the Asia Society, 1987), pp. 23-34.
33. *Ibid.*, p. 31. See also, *Korea Herald*, December 30, 1987; and *New York Times*, April 7, 1987.
34. *Washington Post*, August 20, 1986.
35. Niksch, *South Korea and the United States: The Changing Relationship*, p. 35.
36. *Korea Herald*, December 30, 1987.
37. *Korea Herald*, December 31, 1987.
38. *Korea Herald*, December 27, 1987.
39. *Hankook Ilbo*, January 9, 1988.
40. U.S. Congress, Joint Economic Committee, *op. cit.*, p. 7. See also,

Niksch, *loc. cit.*

41. Council on Foreign Relations and the Asia Society, *op. cit.*, p. 31.
42. *Ibid.*, p. 34.
43. *Ibid.*, p. 51.
44. *Ibid.*, pp. 47-48.
45. *Ibid.*, p. 48.
46. *Korea Herald*, September 16, 1987.
47. *Ibid.*
48. *Ibid.* See also, *Korea Herald*, October 7, 1987.
49. Council on Foreign Relations and the Asia Society, *op. cit.*, p. 54.
50. *Ibid.*, p. 55. See also, Selig S. Harrison, *The South Korean Political Crisis and American Policy Options* (Washington, D.C.: Washington Institute Press, 1987), p. 19.
51. For example, the CATO Institute, a public policy research organization located in Washington, D.C., issued a policy paper advocating a phased withdrawal of the U.S. troops from South Korea in the next five years. For details, see Doug Bandow, *Korea: A Case for Disengagement* (Washington, D.C.: CATO Institute, December 1987). In May 1987, 64 members in the House of Representatives supported a resolution calling for a five-year phaseout of U.S. troops in Korea by 1992. See Harrison, op. cit., p. 17.
52. William Watts, "The United States and Korea: Perception versus Reality," in Gerald L. Curtis and Sung-Ju Han (eds.), *The U.S. - South Korean Alliance* (Lexington, Mass.: D.C. Heath Co., 1983), p. 65.
53. William H. Greysteen, Jr. and Alan D. Romberg, "Korea: Asian Paradox," *Foreign Affairs*, Summer 1987, pp. 1047-1048. See also, Olsen, *op. cit.*, pp. 854-861; and Council on Foreign Relations and the Asia Society, op. cit., p. 4.
54. Richard Holbrooke, "East Asia: The Next Challenge," *Foreign Affairs*, Spring 1986, pp. 750-751. See also, Council on Foreign Relations and the Asia Society, *op. cit.*, p. 51.

11

The Sixth Republic: Problems, Prospects, and the 1988 Olympiad

YOUNG WHAN KIHL AND ILPYONG J. KIM

The movement toward political change and democratization has been occurring over the past several years but the direct election of the president on December 16, 1987 and the subsequent inauguration of President Roh Tae-woo have enhanced greatly the possibility of further political change and democratization of South Korea. The demand for political change and democratization captured momentum when the parliamentary election was held on February 12, 1985 and the opposition parties received more than 57.9 percent of the popular votes while the ruling Democratic Justice Party (DJP) received only a little over a third of the popular votes (35.3 percent). Thus, the movement for political change and democratization in the 1980s culminated in constitutional change and the direct election of the president on December 16, 1987.

The Birth of the Sixth Republic

Analysis of the December, 1987 presidential election returns (See Table 1-b, Chapter 1) shows that the DJP candidate Roh Tae-woo won the presidential elections with only a plurality vote of 36.6 percent and that the combined total of 55 percent by the two opposition candidates of Kim Young-sam (of the RDP) and Kim Dae-jung (of the PPD) was more than sufficient to defeat the ruling party candidate. The split in the opposition rank between Kim Young-sam and Kim Dae-jung was primarily responsible for the failure of the opposition to capture the presidency in the 1987 election and was thus instrumental for the election of the ruling party candidate Roh Tae-woo.

If the opposition rank was united behind either one of the two Kims however, the support base and level of Roh Tae-woo would have been different, possibly raising Roh's overall support level. The exact percentage of Roh's support would have varied depending upon which one of the two Kims was the standard bearer of the opposition party. For instance, in a hypothetical Roh versus Kim Dae-jung matchup, many of Kim Young-sam's supporters, especially in South Kyongsang Province, would have gone to Roh, instead of to Kim Dae-jung. Likewise, in a Roh versus Kim Young-sam election, many of Kim Dae-jung's supporters in the Cholla provinces would have sided with Roh Tae-woo.

On Febuary 25, 1988, history was made in the constitutional annals of South Korea. On this day the first peaceful and orderly transition of power took place, from Chun Doo-hwan to Roh Tae-woo, and a new Sixth Republic was officially born without blood shed. The leadership style of Roh Tae-woo's administration seems to be reform-minded and one of distancing itself as much as possible from an identification with the old regime under Chun Doo-hwan. The new administration, since its inauguration, seems thus far to be low-keyed and firm, yet conciliatory.

The Sixth Republic, under the leadership of Roh Tae-woo, will face similar problems to those that Chun Doo-hwan encountered during the period of the Fifth Republic (1981-88)—issues of further democratization of the political process by instituting local self-government, amnesty for all political prisoners, the full restoration of government control to civilians by curtailing military intervention, and the equitable distribution of wealth, all of which Roh Tae-woo pledged to resolve during his presidential campaign. These problems will have to be dealt with during the honeymoon period. Otherwise the students and discontented opposition groups will again unite to demand political change and further democratization.

Now that Roh Tae-woo has been inaugurated as the thirteenth

president of the Republic of Korea the students and the opposition groups are waiting to see how the new leadership will implement its campaign pledges. Therefore, the achievements of the new president should be evaluated in the context of continuity and change in government policies. There are forces of political change as well as forces for maintaining the status quo, which means to continue the same policies of the Chun government. Those who are loyal to former president Chun are pushing for the continuity of policies instituted by the Fifth Republic. These loyalists are entrenched in the military establishment, the bureaucracy and the business community.

The new cabinet that President Roh appointed after his inauguration seemed to indicate that the forces for maintaining the status quo had the upper hand as half (eight) of the 17-member cabinet was reappointed to serve the new president. The most important cabinet posts—such as the ministers of internal affairs who are in charge of the police force, general affairs which is in control of the bureaucracy, finance, and the director of intelligence—were all appointed by the former president and will continue to carry on the same policies. Moreover, the three important military posts—the commander of the defense security forces, the commander of the capital defense forces, and the commander of the third army—were appointed by former president Chun before he stepped down from office, thus forcing the new president to live with the continuity of the Chun loyalists.

Analysis of the 13th National Assembly Election

A major political event in South Korea's Sixth Republic was the holding of the new National Assembly election on April 26, 1988. A new election law was passed through the National Assembly by the Roh government on March 8, 1988. On the eve of the election, on March 30, Chun Kyung-hwan, ex-president Chun's younger brother, was arrested on charges of embezzlement and influence peddling. On April 13, the former president Chun Doo-hwan apologized for wrongdoings by his younger brother and resigned from all official posts.

A general election on April 26, 1988 was held to choose 224 of 299 National Assembly seats, the remaining 75 to be chosen at large.

The 13th National Assembly Election held on April 26, 1988 was a defeat to the ruling Democratic Justice Party as it deprived the

Roh Tae-woo government a majority in the legislature. The ruling DJP failed to win the majority of seats in the election, capturing only 87 of the 224 seats. The remaining 137 seats went to the opposition: The Party for Peace and Democracy, led by Kim Dae-jung, emerged as the first opposition, with 54 seats, while the Reunification and Democracy Party, under Kim Young-sam, received 46 seats, and the New Democratic Republican Party, under Kim-jong Pil, received 27 seats. The remaining 10 seats went to the camp of Independents. With the 75 at-large seats distributed proportionally according to the new election law provisions, the new legislature had the following overall distribution of the seats:

Table 1
The April 1988 National Assembly Election Returns by Region
(# of Seats Won)

Region	% voter turnout	DJP	PPD	RDP	NDRP	Others	Total
Metropolis							
Seoul	69.3	10	17	10	3	2	42
Pusan	77.7	1	-	14	-	-	15
Taegu	76.9	8	-	-	-	-	8
Inchon	70.1	6	-	1	-	-	7
Kwangju	78.0	-	5	-	-	-	5
Provinces							
Kyonggi	71.3	16	1	4	6	1	28
Kangwon	82.0	8	-	3	1	2	14
Ch'ungbuk	83.1	7	-	-	2	-	9
Ch'ungnam	78.8	2	-	2	13	1	18
Chonbuk	80.1	-	14	-	-	-	14
Chonnam	80.3	-	17	-	-	1	18
Kyongbuk	83.1	17	-	2	2	-	21
Kyongnam	79.9	12	-	9	-	1	22
Cheju	82.6	-	-	1	-	2	3
Subtotal		87	54	46	27	10*	224
PR seats		38	16	13	8	-	75
Total	75.8	125	70	59	35	10*	299

*Subsequently, two of these ten independents switched their position by rejoining each of the two opposition parties, one belonging to PPD and the other to RDP.
Source: NEWSREVIEW; April 30, 1988, pp 6, 7.

This is the first time in the forty-year constitutional history of the Republic of Korea that the ruling party lost the majority in the National Assembly. Prior to this election the ruling DJP was rumored to win the general election easily, following a bandwagon effect of Roh Tae-woo's victory in the December 1987 election and the split in the opposition ranks. The honeymoon period of the newly elected president seems to have been short-lived.

The rather unexpected result of the defeat of the ruling party deprived the new president Roh the luxury of a compliant National Assembly and an automatic majority in the legislature. This will also increase the opportunity for a legislative-executive branch confrontation, thereby undermining political stability.

The less than majority position of the ruling party in the national Assembly may be a "blessing in disguise" however, because the ruling party and other oppositions will henceforth be forced to learn to play the game of political compromise and cooperation. If successful, this will improve the chances for democracy and accelerate the pace for democratization of politics in South Korea.

Challenges Confronting the Roh Government

Roh Tae-woo's government has inherited the authoritarian system of the previous regime with its heavy handed influence on the military and intelligence bureaucracy that always sought to preserve its own continuity and to somewhat impede the process toward democratization. However, the new president outlined his program of democratization in his inaugural address and said he will eliminate authoritarianism from all aspects of the government. Some astute observers of Korean politics suggested that if the Roh government does not move quickly to release all the political prisoners and to bring about fundamental changes in the authoritarian system of government, the students, discontented intellectuals, and the opposition groups will not stand idly by and will continue to oppose the new government since they will perceive the new regime to be nothing but a duplicate of the old regime. Therefore, the immediate task of the new administration is to eliminate authoritarian rule, introduce a free press, and to support freedom of speech and pluralism in the society by lifting the governmental control that the police and military intelligence have over the academic community and over religious groups.

This authoritarian system of rule has been entrenched for a quarter of a century, ever since the military coup of 1961, and it will not be easy to remove its influence.

Some observers have even speculated that it would be easier for Roh to eradicate the authoritarian rule of government-he is a former army general and knows how to control the military industrial complex—than it would be for a civilian leader who would have to accommodate military pressure in order to avoid a coup. Thus Roh's government may take its time in bringing about fundamental changes in the state apparatus, the military establishment, and the ruling party by slowly introducing democratic reforms. However, the students, intellectuals, and the opposition groups will be quite impatient with any slow or gradual process of political change that might be introduced under the leadership of Roh.

The Roh Tae-woo government underwent severe tests both at home and abroad in the summer of 1988. One of the most pressing challenges and tasks confronting the Roh government was the successful hosting of the 24th Summer Olympiad held in Seoul from September 17 to October 2, 1988. With the Seoul government's honor and prestige at stake, the successful outcome of the hosting of the 1988 Olympic games would have stabilized the Roh government's political strength. Because this book went to press in July, 1988 the outcome of these events was unknown.

An outbreak of the radical student demonstrations in early summer, 1988, taking an anti-Roh and anti-American stance, was the first of a series of crises to confront the newly elected government of President Roh. The radical students planned a march to Panmunjom on June 10, 1988. They were demanding a meeting with student delegates from North Korea to conduct deliberation on the issue of Korean reunification. The march was forcefully broken up and suppressed by the Roh government. Several students were able to reach Im Jinkak in South Korea, a place on the southern side of the Im Jin River, a few miles from the Demilitarized Zone. There, they staged a rally in support of Korean reunification.

On July 7, 1988, the Roh government announced a six point policy on the new initiative toward North Korea. The new policy of the Seoul government was widely hailed as bold and positive as it included the announced measures of, among others opening trade with the north, exchange of dispersed family members and students' visits, removal of the travel ban to North Korea by overseas Koreans and encouraging Seoul's allies to establish cross contacts with North Korea. However the new policy was also interpreted as a measure to detract the students' attention away from the planned resumption of the march to Panmunjon on August 15, 1988. Clearly the students were motivated in their political moves and in their anti-Roh and anti-American rhetoric. It was commonly believed their motivation was to steal the show by enticing the world press attention to focus on their political grievances, thereby diverting attention away from the scheduled opening of the Seoul Olympic games.

The government party suffered its first defeat in the regular session of the National Assembly in July, 1988. The government party nominee for the Supreme Court Chief Justice failed to obtain the necessary simple majority of votes in unicameral legislature. The alternate nominee, however, was acceptable to the opposition, and so were all the Supreme Court associate justices who were subsequently voted in by the legislature.

President Roh Tae-woo also used his veto power for the first time in July to reject the new legislation enacted by the coalition of opposition parties in the National Assembly. A power to subpena ex-President Chun Doo-hwan was to be given to a special investigatory panel of the National Assembly to investigate past alleged wrongdoings of the Fifth Republic. To counter the executive veto, the opposition forces in the legislature could easily resort to the vote of no-confidence of the prime minister and his cabinet, although such an option has not as yet been invoked by the legislature. If the executive versus legislative conflict and impasse continues in the future, however, the stability and viability of the Roh government in the Sixth Republic will suffer as a result.

Hopefully, in the post-Seoul Olympic era South Korea's march toward democracy will continue and succeed in reaching the destination. The spirit of inter-party dialogue and negotiation in the legislature, as well as the resumption of the inter-Korean dialogue and negotiation in Panmunjon, will restore civility to South Korea's scarred political landscape. A series of bold and imaginative policy measures taken by the Roh government, such as the July 7, 1988 initiative toward North Korea, will hopefully enliven

South Korea's domestic politics and will also provide a new modus vivendi to resume the inter-Korean dialogue on Korean reunification, so that not only tension can be reduced but also the prospect for peace can be improved on the Korean peninsula in the post-Olympic era.

Prospects

What, then, has changed since the inauguration of the new president? Control over the press has been lifted, thus many more newspapers and broadcasting stations are appearing and freedom of expression is being restored. Government control over educational institutions has been eased and the faculties and the student bodies have been given increased autonomy by being allowed to elect their own deans and presidents. Also employees of institutions are being allowed to organize professional organizations or trade unions to bargain with their employers for better wages and benefits. Thus, negotiations between management and the labor unions to settle their disputes are being encouraged in order to eliminate the government control or intervention that had been characteristic of the Fifth Republic under Chun.

The new leadership of the Sixth Republic is moving in the direction of pluralism and democratization by creating a new style of leadership and a new image of the president as a "common man" who is accessible to the ordinary citizens on the street. In addressing the new president, the subordinates in the Blue House, the presidential palace, no longer use "His Excellency" and he is encouraging the presidential staff to open the presidential palace to the public so that the public may have access to him. In recent cabinet meetings in the Blue House President Roh has not given an address to the cabinet members as was the style of previous regimes, but instead he conducted roundtable dialogues with them.

The style of leadership has changed following the inauguration of the new president. However, the substance of leadership has not changed due largely to the authoritarian political culture and many other constraints placed on the institution of the presidency. The surprisingly weak showing of the ruling DJP in the Thirteenth National Assembly Election of April 26, 1988 may serve as a reminder to the Roh Tae-woo Government. An automatic majority in the legislature is not guaranteed as it has been in the past. The ruling and opposition parties must now learn to play the political game of compromise and bargaining in order to push various legislative bills through the National Assembly. Future local self-government elections will test the degree of political change to which the new leadership is committed. The democratization process will largely depend on whether the new president can effectively carry out his campaign pledges. South Korea's democracy will also depend on how well the legislative and executive branches can cooperate in conducting the day-to-day business of the government, especially at the time when the ruling party has lost control of the majority seats in the legislature.

The future prospect, seen from the perspective of the summer of 1988, is one of guarded optimism for South Korea's making continuous moves and progress toward democracy. The hosting of the 1988 Olympiad in Seoul, regarded by many as South Korea's rising to the occasion of claiming international prominence, kept the government and opposition parties in the legislature on a temporary truce, pursuing the strategy of compromise and bargaining rather confrontation and conflict. A modicum of civility and cooperation has been restored in South Korea's domestic partisan politics. Whether such trends born of political expediency will continue, and if the politics of dialogue will replace that of confrontation in the post-Seoul Olympic era, will remain to be seen. South Korea's traditional political culture of authoritarianism is deep-rooted, and it will take time before a genuine civic and democratic culture takes hold on the politically embattled Korean soil.

About The Editors

Ilpyong J. Kim

Dr. Ilpyong J. Kim is Professor of Political Science at the University of Connecticut. He specializes in comparative and international politics of East Asia (China, Japan, and Korea). He received a Ph. D. from Columbia University. Dr. Kim has taught at Columbia, Indiana, and Tokyo Universities and lectured at Brown, Smith, and Wesleyan Universities as well as at the World Affairs Councils and International Relations Clubs. Professor Kim is a past president of the New England Conference of Asian Studies and Chairman of the Columbia University Seminar on Korean Studies. He has chaired numerous professional and academic conferences in the United States and abroad. He recently taught a course at Columbia University entitled, "The Politics of North and South Korea in International Perspective."

Dr. Kim has written and edited six books and published more than three dozen articles in professional and academic journals. He is the author of *The Politics of Chinese Communism* and, more recently, the editor of *The Strategic Triangle: China, The Soviet Union and the United States,* as well as this book, *Political Change In South Korea*. For further information please contact Dr. Kim at (203) 486-2533 (office) or (203) 429-2428 (home). His home address is 61 Hillyndale Road, Storrs, Connecticut 06268, U.S.A.

Young Wahn Kihl

Dr. Young Whan Kihl is a Professor of Political Science at Iowa State University, Ames. He specializes in International Relations and Comparative Asian Politics (China, Japan and Korea). He received his B.A. from Grinnell College, M.A. and Ph.D. from New York University. Dr. Kihl was a visiting scholar at various institutions including Columbia University (1966), George Washington University Institute for Sino Soviet Studies (1978), and the University of California at Berkeley, Institute of East Asian Studies (1985). A recipient of numerous awards and grants, including the Social Science Research Council Award (1966) the Fulbright Award (1972), and the Joint Committee of the Social Science Research Council and American Council of Learned Societies (1973, 1977). He served as president of the Association for Korean Studies in North America (1979-1981) and member of the Committee on Korean Studies, the Association for Asian Studies (1982-85; 88-89).

Dr. Kihl has been active as a research scholar on wide-ranging topics including International Civil Aviation, U.S.-Japanese Agricultural Trade Relations, Asian-Pacific Security Issues, and World Trade Issues. He has authored and co-edited eight books and more than one hundred articles and monographs. Included in the list of most recent publications are: *Politics And Policies In Divided Korea* (1984), *World Trade Issues* (1985, co-author), *Asian-Pacific Security* (1986, co-editor), *East Asian Conflict Zones* (1987, co-editor), and *Security, Strategy And Policy Responses In The Pacific Rim* (1989, co-editor, forthcoming).

Contributors

Sunki Choe

Sunki Choe is an Assistant Professor of Political Science at Pennsylvania State University, York Campus. He has collaborated with professor Hong Nack Kim on the chapter dealing with South Korean election and voting behavior studies.

Wonmo Dong

Wonmo Dong is Associate Professor of Political Science and Director of the Asian Studies Program at Southern Methodist University. An authority on Japanese colonialism in Korea and opposition politics in South Korea, Dong has received three postdoctoral research fellowships from the Joint Committee on Korean Studies of the Social Science Research Council and the American Council of Learned Societies. He is a former National Fellow at the Hoover Institution and a research associate at the Institute of East Asian Studies of the University of California at Berkeley. His most recent publication on Korean politics is "University Students in South Korean Politics: Patterns of Radicalization in the 1980s," *Journal of International Affairs*.

Gregory Henderson

Gregory Henderson (MA in Far Eastern Studies, Harvard and MBA from Harvard Business School) is a Research Associate at Harvard University's Fairbank Center for East Asian Studies. He served as a Foreign Service Officer from 1947 to 1963 in locations that include Korea, Germany and Japan. He is the author of the book *Korea: The Politics of the Vortex*. He has also served as the Project Director and Associate Professor of Diplomacy at the Fletcher School of Law and Diplomacy and as a Senior Research Officer at the UN Institute for Training and Research.

C. I. Eugene Kim

C. I. Eugene Kim (Ph.D., Stanford) is Professor of Political Science and Chairman of the Asian Studies Program at Western Michigan University and a member of the Governing Board of Inter-Varsity Seminar on Armed Forces and Society and U.S.-Korea Security Studies. He is also one of the founding members of The Research Council on Korean Reunification. Author of many books and articles on Korea and Northeast Asia, his recent works include: *An Introduction to Asian Politics* (co-author), *The Asian Political Dictionary* (co-editor), *Korea and the Politics of Imperialism* (co-*author), Journey to North Korea* (co-author) and *Party Politics and Elections in Korea* (co-author).

Chong Lim Kim

Chong Lim Kim (Ph.D., University of Oregon) is professor of political science at the University of Iowa and the Director of the University's Comparative Legislative Research Center. He is the author of many books including *Legislative Connection: The Politics of Representation in Kenya, Korea and Turkey* (1984). *Patterns of Recruitment* (1974, co-author), *Legislative Process in Korea* (1980, co-author), and *Political Participation in Korea* (1981, editor). His numerous research monographs have appeared in "American Political Science Review," "American Journal of Political Science," "Legislative Studies Quarterly," and "Asian Survey."

Hong Nack Kim

Hong Nack Kim (Ph.D., Georgetown University) is professor of political science at West Virginia University. He is also the past President of the Association of Korean Political Scientists in North America. He is a co-editor of several books including *Perspectives on Inter-Korean Relations* (1987), *Korean Reunification: New Perspectives and Approaches* (1984), and *Scholars Guide to Asian Studies* (1979). He has served as editor of *Political Studies Review* and contributed more than 50 articles to various publications. He also contributed a chapter to the U.S. Congress Joint Economic Committee Report *China Looks Toward the Year 2000.*

Sung Moon Pae

Sung Moon Pae (Ph.D., the University of Kansas) is professor of political science and Chair, Division of Behavioral and Social Sciences, Bellevue College, Bellevue, Nebraska. He was a recipient of grants from the National Science Foundation in Summer 1980 and Summer 1981. He is the author of *Testing Democratic Theories in Korea* (1986) and many articles. He is currently engaged in research on U.S. Foreign Policies for Democratization.

Hang Yul Rhee

Hang Yul Rhee (Ph.D., American University) is professor of International Law and Relations at Shepherd College in West Virginia. He is the author of *Political Behavior of the Citizenry of Seoul* and has published many articles in the *Journal of Korea and World Affairs* that include "The Need for Democratization of the Korean Political Economy," and "Third World Debt and Third World Industrialization."

South Korean Politics
A Selected Bibliography

Bridges, Brian. *Korea and the West.* Chatham House Papers: 39. London: The Royal Institute of International Affairs, 1986.

Choe, Sang-yong et. al., *Hyondae Han'guk Chongch'iwa Kukka* (Modern Korean Politics and the State). Seoul: Korean Political Science Association, 1986.

Clough, Ralph N. *Balancing Act: The Republic of Korea Approaches 1988*. FPI Policy Briefs. Washington, D.C.: Foreign Policy Institute of the Johns Hopkins University School of Advanced International Studies, 1987.

________________. *Embattled Korea: The Rivalry for International Support.* Boulder, Co.: Westview Press, 1987.

Gleysteen, William H., Jr. and Alan D. Romberg, "Korea: Asian Paradox," *Foreign Affairs* Volume 65, No. 5 (Summer 1987): 1047-1054.

Harrison, Selig S., "Dateline South Korea: A Divided Seoul," *FOREIGN POLICY* Number 67 (Summer 1987): 154-175.

Jacobs, Norman, *The Korean Road to Modernization and Development.* Urbana and Chicago: University of Illinois Press, 1985.

Kim, Dae Jung. *Mass-Participatory Economy: A Democratic Alternative for Korea.* Cambridge: Harvard University Center for International Affairs/Washington, D.C.: University Press of America, 1985.

______________. *Prison Writings.* Translated by Sung-il Choi and David McCann. Berkeley: University of California Press, 1987.

Kim, Kyong-Dong, ed. *Dependency Issues in Korean Development: Comparative Perspectives.* Seoul: Seoul National University Press, 1987.

Koo, Youngnok and Sung-jee Han, eds. *The Foreign Policy of the Republic of Korea.* New York: Columbia University Press, 1985.

Korea: A Teacher's Guide. New York: The Asia Society, 1986.

Korea At The Crossroads: Implications for American Policy. New York: Council on Foreign Relations and The Asia Society, 1987.

Nam, Joo-Hong. *America's Commitment to South Korea: The First Decade of the Nixon Doctrine.* New York: Cambridge University Press, 1986.

Olsen, Edward A. *U.S. Policy and the Two Koreas*. Boulder, Co.: Westview Press, 1987.

Pae, Sung M. *Testing Democratic Theories In Korea*. Lanham, N.Y.: University Press of America, 1986.

Polomka, Peter. *The Two Koreas: Catalyst for Conflict in East Asia?* Adelphi Papers No. 208. London: International Institute of Strategic Studies, 1986.

Pye, Lucian W. *Asian Power and Politics: The Cultural Dimensions of Authority*. Cambridge: Harvard University Press, 1985, especially chapters 3 and 8.

Scalapino, Robert A. and Sung-joo Han, eds. *United States - Korea Relations*. Research papers and Policy Studies No. 19. Berkeley, Ca.: University of California Institute of East Asian Studies, 1986.

Sneider, Richard L. *The Political and Social Capabilities of North and South Korea for the Long-term Military Competition*. Santa Monica, Ca.: Rand, 1985.

Sullivan, John and Roberta Foss, eds. *Two Koreas--one Future?* Lanham, Md.: University Press of America, 1987. Co-published by arrangement with the American Friends Service Committee.

Wolf, Jr., Charles, Donald P. Henry, K.C. Yeh, James H. Hayes, John Schank, and Richard Sneider. *The Changing Balance: South and North Korean Capabilities for Long-term Military Competition*. Santa Monica, Ca.: Rand, 1985.

Index

C

D

E

G

H

I

J

K

M

O

P